THE
HOAX
OF ROMANCE

JO LOUDIN, Ph.D.

A SPECTRUM BOOK

PRENTICE-HALL, INC., Englewood Cliffs, New Jersey 07632

Library of Congress Cataloging in Publication Data

Loudin, Jo.
  The hoax of romance.

  Bibliography: p.
  Includes index.
  1. Marriage.   2.   Sex role.   3.   Fantasy.
  4. Interpersonal relations.   I.   Title.
  HQ734.L755   306.7   80-21986
  ISBN 0-13-392456-4
  ISBN 0-13-392449-1 (pbk.)

To my mother and to the memory
of my father, romantics both.

© 1981 by Prentice-Hall, Inc., Englewood Cliffs, New Jersey 07632

A SPECTRUM BOOK

Printed in the United States of America

10   9   8   7   6   5   4   3   2   1

PRENTICE-HALL INTERNATIONAL, INC., *London*
PRENTICE-HALL OF AUSTRALIA, PTY. LIMITED, *Sydney*
PRENTICE-HALL OF CANADA, LTD., *Toronto*
PRENTICE-HALL OF INDIA PRIVATE LIMITED, *New Delhi*
PRENTICE-HALL OF JAPAN, INC., *Tokyo*
PRENTICE-HALL OF SOUTHEAST ASIA PTE LTD., *Singapore*
WHITEHALL BOOKS LIMITED, *Wellington, New Zealand*

CONTENTS

INTRODUCTION

While working on my master's degree over fifteen years ago, I studied a book that was to alter my thinking from then on. It was a slim, unpretentious volume called *The Art of Courtly Love*, written centuries ago by Andreas Capellanus, an author previously unknown to me. I was fascinated. The little book outlined the rules of the game of love we know as "romance." All the rules were there—rules of how one should act, think, and feel to be worthy of winning one's beloved. There were rules for every facet of the game: how to dress, speak, plead, glance, whisper, love sincerely, or dissemble. Everything was written out in detail on how to be the perfect lover.

I recognized almost all the rules. They were rules I had accepted unquestioningly as a part of my own value system, rules that people in our society commonly believe to be normal and natural ways of relating to lovers and spouses. But the thought that chilled me was that these rules—which I and my contemporaries have accepted so unequivocally, which described in detail the ways in which we should (and do) behave, upon which we have built our value systems, our relationships, our lives—were written out and codified *in the twelfth century.*

All the years between, all the giant steps we've taken in technology, science, industry, education, and medicine since then, have done little or nothing to alter the beliefs we hold about our relationships. We've sent men to walk on the surface of the moon, but our understanding of love and romance is still primeval!

In all the years that followed I couldn't put the contents of *The Art of Courtly Love* out of my mind. Someday, I knew, I would write my own book on a subject similar to that ancient work. Finally, my life experiences have provided me with enough material. I'm ready now to write my book, deferring to that other one long ago as the source and inspiration of my idea.

I feel compelled to write this book now because I know the time is right—not only because I have the words to express my ideas, but because others can use them to apply to their own lives. As a therapist I continually hear people telling me about their confusing and miserable relationships. They know they're unhappy, but they don't know how to change their situations. Most of them don't even realize that they *can* change; they don't know what they're doing to create their problems, so they have no idea of how to change what they're doing. When I've shared some of my insights with these people they've been able to change their beliefs, their attitudes, and, consequently, their lives. I want to share with you some of this information that my clients have found so helpful. If you choose to use it, you—like my clients—can make your relationships more enjoyable, creative, and fulfilling.

Many people are beginning to realize how destructive our beliefs are to any ongoing relationship. They say that romance destroys us. I've read recent articles and books describing some of the pitfalls of our unrealistic attitudes, but no author has yet explored the beginnings of romance in relation to our present-day relationships. No one has examined our beliefs of today and shown through case histories how we still follow our origins. This book is about the beginnings of our romantic concepts—because they had a definite beginning—and how we still use those outdated ideas to our, and our partners, detriment.

Now I, for one, am tired of seeing people's lives shattered by outmoded concepts. I have wasted years of my own life because of my antiquated beliefs. After experiencing my own broken marriages, and having worked as a therapist for ten years with confused and pain-filled survivors of broken relationships, I'm acutely aware that our

INTRODUCTION

archaic concepts routinely destroy our friendships, partnerships, and marriages. I have talked to hundreds of people who still adhere to standards formulated in the Middle Ages. These standards, created for the benefit of people then, have been turned into dogma in the centuries between; now, no longer beneficial, they drag us down into despair.

We grope through dense fogs of misunderstanding on interpersonal problems, blinded by our own beliefs. We cling to our beliefs in desperation because we know of no others, and no one has adequately challenged our ancient rules. Our beliefs, peculiar by now to our culture, shape themselves into substance only in the recesses of our minds. When everyone believes in these concepts, however, and agrees that people should behave in these ways, anyone who acts differently may be called wrong, strange, or even crazy. "Everyone" is a powerful arbiter of sanity. Yet who can say who is really wrong—the one who deviates according to what he or she feels is right, or all the rest of us who proceed along the path of established beliefs because we have been taught that we should do so?

We lack information about the concepts of romance—what they are, how they began, and how we still use them today. Not knowing about their origins, we've believed these concepts have always existed as they are now. We've believed romance is a natural part of love and that we must act in predetermined ways. Not so! We've created our concepts and the society in which we act them out by our own brain power. We have more ability than we even know—to alter our concepts, our behavior, perhaps the very structure of our brains. We *can* change. We can alter our concepts by feeding new information into the computers of our minds. By doing so we gain some new tools to use in confronting our outmoded belief systems. We can understand then what our problems are and how to solve them. We can see clearly, without our self-imposed fogs, that our archaic concepts about romance no longer apply to the realities of our love, live-in, or marital relationships. And we can change our lives with the clarity that comes from our new awareness.

Our greatest societal problem in

INTRODUCTION

relationships today is neither divorce nor the breakup of the family. In many instances, divorce may be a healthy solution to the problem of irreconcilable differences. People have legitimate reasons for getting divorced, as well as those hasty excuses of which we're all aware. As most people do, marital partners may change over the years, and if their changing takes them too far apart they may find little reason to stay together. They may find that the breakup of their marriage is a vital step in their continued growth as individuals. A breakup may also be healthy if family members have resorted to physical abuse or generated serious, ongoing emotional hostility toward each other. It is far better for spouses in such families to break out of their web of bitterness and start new relationships with partners to whom they can relate with affection and on whom the children can constructively model their behavior. No, I have little quarrel with our rising divorce rate. But I still ask *why*. Why, if we marry for sound and honest reasons, do we reach the point of divorce after two or seven or twenty years?

The answer has to do with the word *sound*. Most of us marry with honest intent, hoping for long and loving relationships. Most of us do *not* marry for sound reasons. We cannot! Our reasons are based on our beliefs and attitudes about love and romance, beliefs created so long ago that they have little validity for us today in our present society. Our main problem, as I see it, is not the growth that may carry two people who married for honest reasons far apart. Open differences between partners do not bother me. It is the deception inherent in relationships founded on our archaic beliefs that concerns me. We don't have a problem with divorce; we have a problem with marriage—those marriages that are based on our deceptive fantasies. We create stifling dead-end relationships by building impossible dreams in our own minds, fantasies totally unrelated to the reality of our feelings for each other and the business of living together under the same roof on a day-to-day basis. Our main problem, our main self-deception, is marrying for *romance*.

ACKNOWLEDGMENTS

Whom can I thank for this book but those who opened their doors to the past and those who enabled me to share their present experiences. I wish to thank Professor Ruggiers of the University of Oklahoma, who introduced me to medieval writings and Andreas Capellanus. A special note of gratitude goes to Markham Harris, known affectionately to me as Mark, who instructed me in the craft of writing at the University of Washington years ago and persists now in giving careful editorial attention to my manuscripts.

      I also thank my clients, men and women who've come to me for therapy; in seeking answers they have sometimes found pain exploring the workings of their minds, and occasionally reasons. Through knowing them along with the details of their lives, I have sorted out my own. Finally, I thank the people close to me—my mother, father, husband, daughter, relatives, and friends whom I've known intimately and through whom I've gained insight into their lives and mine. All of these people have added immeasurably to the contents of this book, which resulted from the spark of an idea long ago and which may continue to fire minds in the future.

J.L.

AUTHOR'S NOTE

The people cited in this book are composite characters; the dialogues are not exact quotations but are representative of the essence of various people and our conversations. All names and other identifying features have been changed to protect the privacy of the individuals involved.

1. OUR ROMANTIC NOTIONS

OUR BELIEFS, FOUNDED ON
TRADITIONAL NOTIONS,
DESTROY OUR RELATIONSHIPS.

Romance is a popular word in our culture. From childhood we are taught to see life through the rose-colored glasses of romance. If the realities of our own lives don't glow with the hint of romance, we believe fervently that somewhere, in some other kind of life, some other place, with some other person, we can find it. What "it" is, we're not quite sure, but everybody else seems to believe in it too, so why shouldn't we? Besides, others seem to have attained it: the couple holding hands affectionately after twenty years of marriage; the group with beaming faces around the dinner table, from grandparents down to the third generation; the vacationing family on the beach, complete with frolicking dog. They're all smiling, apparently happy. You don't know any people like that, you say? Of course you do! Look at any magazine ad—there they are, our models for romance!

How can we *not* believe when we're bombarded with the pervasive concepts of romance on every side—in the songs we hear on the radio; in the novels, magazines, and newspapers we read; in the television shows and movies we see. Ads and commercials are designed to titillate our romantic sensibilities on either an overt or a subliminal level, ensuring, or so the advertisers hope, popularity and therefore success of their particular product. As I was writing this book, in April of 1978, I noticed an ad in our local newspaper for dresses captioned, "Undercover Romance." The fine print told me, "A flirt of romance. A hint of nostalgia. Camisoles and petticoats, soft and pretty as a summer night . . . plunging necklines . . . the petticoat flounce peeks out."[1] Sex, darkness, flirtation—all are suggested as a part of romance. If *you* wear this dress, the ad implies, *you* will have all of these things—*your* life will be filled with the excitement and the seductiveness of Romance.

Of course, romance is not always intertwined with sex. In modern-day America the tentacles of

---

1. Ad for Lamonts, *Seattle Times* (April 25, 1978, sec. D), p. 3.

3

OUR ROMANTIC NOTIONS

romance creep in all directions. As children we're taught to become romantic idealists in our unceasing consumption of the great American product. The word disseminators of Madison Avenue and the cartoon distributors of Hollywood tell us, subtly or overtly, that those toys advertised on television will make us as happy as the kids in the commercial; that the sugar-coated cereal, prize enclosed, will make us grow big and strong; that the candy displayed next to the checkout counter will nourish our empty, grumbling bellies. We know holidays are coming weeks and even months before they arrive, and our expectations build as each decoration appears in the stores. We expect happy times, instant harmony, and loving families gathered together around laden feast tables. We fantasize being rewarded by a jolly, fat man, and if he doesn't leave us our heart's desire under the Christmas tree it's because we were bad. We expect happy bunnies toting colored eggs, sky-blazing firecrackers, ice cream picnics, turkeys and pumpkins, birthdays, cakes and presents, presents, presents—never realizing until we grow up ourselves that it was Mommy's and Daddy's pocketbooks providing all the goodies. By then, although we dread the work and fatigue that inevitably accompany holidays, although we resent the drain on our decreasing bank accounts, although we are aware that the hullabaloo is solely designed to whet our consumers' appetites, we still feel a hidden twinge for the happy, warm holiday celebrations we visualize from our own childhood—whether or not we experienced such happiness in the reality of our youth.

By the time we arrive at that so-called rational state of adulthood, we're sunk. We have been so propagandized, emotionally subverted, and instructed, both tongue-in-cheek and seriously, that we take our romantic notions for granted. If there is something wrong with our lives, we never think it's because our beliefs are fallacious and our consequent behavior destructive to a creative life or a healthy relationship. We cannot comprehend that we can change our feelings, thoughts, or actions; we feel too powerless for that. Someone, or something, must do it for us, for, of course, it's *romance* that's missing from our lives. So what do we do to find it? How do we go about seeking that elusive grail? Some seek it behind closed curtains, such as the lonely housewife who searches for vicarious thrills by reading novels about powerful heroes and wilting heroines or by watching soap operas on television. Some seek it in a bottle, hoping that just one more drink will bring the happiness that has thus far eluded them, but finding muddled minds and rotting livers instead. Some seek it on the street—the nameless pushers and takers seeking another mark, another hit, another thrill—anything to prevent them from feeling their own boredom, their sense of meaninglessness, their pain. Some seek it through buying—a fur coat, a new appliance, this year's car, a more expensive house—whatever, they reason, might bring happiness. Others seek it through selling themselves and others a fantasy—do this or buy that or go there and you (I, we) will be happy.

Whether the romantic promise of never-never land comes with the mind-glazing halo of alcohol, the upper, the downer, the travel brochure, the sales ad, the calorie-laden dessert, it helps us escape our daily life, our feelings, our partners, ourselves. It helps us keep up the struggle toward an unreachable paradise. We may find *something* as a result of our quest—a house full of things we never use, bankruptcy, addiction to booze or pills, an unrelenting obesity—but *it* still eludes us. It continues to beckon us on, for it is the romantic dream itself, the promise of happiness, and, like the leprechaun's gold, it is found only in fairy tales.

Originally the word, "romance" had to do with a language and its literature. A roman, or romantic tale, was one of knightly adventures and chivalric deeds undertaken for the sake of a lady.

After centuries of use and mis-

5

OUR ROMANTIC NOTIONS

use, romance has come to mean an ideal, whether it be of love, chocolate bunnies, or a fairy tale existence on the open road. Romance is an exaggeration, a fervent wish, a fabrication, a fantasy, an impossible dream at its best—or an expectation and an absolute demand at its worst. Romance, in terms of our relationships, is usually thought of as an inevitable preliminary step to a deeper form of love.

We accept our romantic notions as an invaluable part of our value system, believing they're valid. Unless we deliberately analyze our beliefs, we find it hard to separate our fallacies from reality. Our romantic ideals surround us. Granted, our movies have taken a turn toward realism and away from the cloying sentiment of the thirties and forties, but romanticism still pervades our lives. The romantic novel is very much alive, flourishing and making millions for authors of the genre. Television writers are restricted from most controversial subjects, so they endlessly romanticize the cowboy, the detective, even the comic strip hero. On the radio we're told, with accompaniment, how we should feel if we're in love or out of love or teetering on the brink. What else do we hear but songs about love in all its romantic aspects? (How often do we hear a song like "Is That All There Is?")

What would our lives be like without romance? Is it not far more appealing to visualize future adventure than drudgery and boredom? Isn't life more interesting with promises to lure us on: holidays, vacations, places to go, people to meet? As for romance in our relationships, it is much better, we believe, to fall in love with and marry the partner of our choice rather than having to wed someone because of convenience, political intrigue, or parental edict. The desire, the struggle, the chase adds excitement to our courtships. Romance provides a hidden promise for our otherwise hundrum lives—that someday, somewhere, we will get exactly who and what we want. Don't we need that promise to put some spice in our lives? My answer to all these questions is an emphatic *yes*, and an equally emphatic *no!*

6

OUR ROMANTIC NOTIONS

In dealing with emotional problems and marital conflicts daily in my work as a therapist, I've thought long and hard about romance. I have analyzed, dissected, and probed romantic beliefs and how they affect our relationships. I've had to think about romance because, quite frankly, I've been confused. I used to try to clarify my own muddled relationships by asking the question, "What is love?" After years of getting nowhere on that one, I began to realize that "love" has a myriad of different meanings, and just about everyone was as confused about it as I was. After I started practicing therapy, clients came to me for help in their troubled relationships, and we struggled together through the fog. If I helped them at all, I've thought, it has been because I shared my own confusion with them. I've heard many of the same complaints:

"If I love him so much—and I do love him—why am I so unhappy with him?" one woman asked.

A man phrased a similar question, "I love her so much I go nuts without her. But she's such a bitch I can't stand to live with her. What's wrong with me?"

Another woman said, "My husband left me three months ago without telling me why. When I ask him, he says he loves me but he won't come back. That's love?"

And then the classic, which I've heard over and over again, which I've even caught myself saying, "I've got everything a person could want—a husband (or wife) who loves me, beautiful kids, a lovely home. Why am I so unhappy?"

As I've listened to these and related questions I've become more and more aware of the ambiguity of the word "love." It's bad enough when the word is applied to feelings. People have all kinds of feelings behind the catch-all word love—need, guilt, anger, loneliness, hurt, resentment, sadness—none of which creates a climate for healthy, intimate love. But when the word love encompasses not only

7

OUR ROMANTIC NOTIONS

what we feel but what we believe, we swamp ourselves with confusion. So much of it is tied up with what we've been taught to believe about romance. Often we use "love" and "romance" interchangeably. Do we really know what we mean by either word? The more we mix them up, the more bogged down we get. Certainly there is a feeling called love. Certainly there is romance. But which is which, and how do we ever separate the two?

Through trying to clarify my own and my clients' muddled thinking, I began to see that our confusion about love and romance obscures the reality of our feelings about each other, even destroys the relationships we want most to preserve. I also realized that our misapprehensions often cause us to choose partners who are sheer poison for us. I understood that we divorce not only because our relationships crumble under the strain of living together in an increasingly stressful society but because we pick partners who are incompatible with us in the first place. And why? It is not because of our innate stupidity, aggressiveness, or killer instincts; not because of our inability to live together in constructive relationships; not because we are indiscriminate, promiscuous, or just plain crazy; none of these. The answer has to do with our beliefs about romance and our unquestioning use of these concepts in our daily lives.

I do not believe that *all* romantic concepts are destructive, nor do I mean to give you that impression. Providing we're aware, romance can be a barrel of fun. Romance can give us renewed interest in living through its very escapism. A romantic fling, whether it be a vacation, shopping spree, or night on the town can lift us out of the doldrums. We can give our relationships renewed zest through a romantic interlude. We can purposely interject a dash of romance, excitement, and adventure into our otherwise prosaic lifestyles. We can use romance in a positive sense, if we are aware.

If we are not aware, if we expect romance to solve all our problems, we may find the bitter dregs of disappointment instead. If we demand romance as an integral

8

OUR ROMANTIC NOTIONS

part of our relationships, we may find ourselves clinging to an empty dream instead of a live partner. We may live our lives according to our unrealistic expectations rather than our actual feelings. When each person feels miserable because those expectations remain unrealized, each will tend to blame the other. Then, stuck with disappointment in place of romance, with the miseries come to stay, what do most people turn to but separation or divorce? Yet the dream of romance persists—and if our present relationship doesn't provide it, we cling even tighter to the image. Merle Shain says:

> *The romantic myth is so strong that it survives the wear and tear of marriage by simply detaching from it and floating up on ahead, and women who are rather fond of the men they married as well as ones who are not, go through life with a bag packed for the day when the shining knight on a white charger arrives, just in case he does.* [2]

Women are not the only ones who cling to the romantic dream, although they may be more obvious; certainly, the cultural joke is about women and their romantic imaginings. Men are just as involved, although they may be unaware of their own fantasies and dreams. Because of our respective fantasies, men and women together create failure-prone relationships. So apparent is this trend today toward easy separation and divorce that we've begun to joke about monogamy in our society. Instead, we say, we practice serial polygamy—marriage and remarriage. Shain comments:

> *The dream of romantic love is taken more seriously in North America than it is anywhere*

2. Merle Shain, *Some Men Are More Perfect Than Others* (New York: Bantam Books, 1973), p. 43.

9

OUR ROMANTIC NOTIONS

else in the world, which is why we believe in fidelity and why we believe in infidelity as well. It is also, of course, what makes our divorce rate as high as it is. Falling in love at first sight and instant gratification are part of the world in which we live, so there are people who believe adamantly in fidelity. They just don't believe in it for long.[3]

If we want to give more than lip service to fidelity, we need to explore our fantasies and the origins of our romantic expectations. We need to examine how our belief system affects the ways in which we behave. We need to look at the genesis of our philosophy to understand how our beliefs continually cause us to conflict with each other in destructive patterns we repeat throughout our lives, our relationships, interminably.

Conflict within a relationship rarely has a simple explanation. It is not easy to decide whether the relationship itself is the problem, or the people in it. Some people carry so many repressed feelings within themselves, left-overs from unhappy childhood experiences, that no relationship could ever be satisfactory for them. These people may have sought out their partners for the misery they provide, not because misery is enjoyable, but because it is familiar on an internal level. Forever dragging their misery along, these people may leave their present partners only to find replacements that are twice as bad. No matter how many relationships these people establish, each will be filled with unhappiness because of their individual problems.

Others do not have that much repressed childhood pain. They have had enough nurturing dur-

3. Ibid., p. 89.

10

OUR ROMANTIC NOTIONS

ing their childhood years to enable them to grow into reasonably mature adults. They don't necessarily seek out other people for the mistreatment they'll get. Frequently they find not actual mistreatment but constant quarrels and resentment that persists on both sides. They may wonder, knowing that they have the ability to get along with other people, why they cannot seem to live harmoniously with their partners.

I know all too well that every partnership, composed of two highly individual people, has its own set of problems. No pat answer will solve all problems for all people. But I also believe that certain attitudes imposed on us by our cultural milieu affect our feelings about our partners to our mutual detriment. These beliefs haunt our relationships throughout our lives, preventing us from attaining intimacy with those closest to us, providing us with ongoing misery, alienation, and despair.

The origin of our system of romantic beliefs lies farther back in time than the Victorian age, or the Puritans, or even the Renaissance. To discover the origin of our beliefs we need to go back eight centuries, and beyond. In classical times, romance as we know it today was nonexistent. Marriage was regarded in a manner totally alien to our way of thinking. Woman were viewed as chattel property to be disposed of at the discretion, or the whim, of their husbands. Generally regarded on about the same level as that of slaves, they had few rights and low status. To these people long gone "love" was a word that held little mystery. Marriage was contracted for political, economic, and procreative purposes. People believed that husbands and wives did not need to be in love to marry. In fact, love had little to do with successful married life. If love was involved at all, a man directed it toward either another man or another man's wife. So although the ancient Greeks knew nothing of romantic love, their philosophy laid the cornerstones for our beliefs and for the kind of love we know today. Eventually (see Chapter III), we must take a brief look at Greek philosophy.

11

OUR ROMANTIC NOTIONS

The version of love we accept as a normal, even necessary part of our lives didn't come into existence until medieval times. It was born in southern France at the end of the eleventh century, an outgrowth of many factors pertinent to that time. It was fostered, enlarged upon, and disseminated to the rest of the world largely by the efforts of one woman, Queen Eleanor of England, Duchess of Aquitaine in France. Through her, aided by her daughter, Countess Marie of Champagne, and their relatives and friends, romance as we know it came to be.

Eleanor's reasons for creating a code of manners unheard of before her time were personal politically expedient, and entirely rational in the framework of her particular society. With the help of her daughter and the influential noblewomen around her, she developed a complex plan of behavior and an arbitrary set of rules to manipulate the young men and women of her court. These rules, debated within their "Court of Love," became the basis for a concept unknown before their time, a concept that spread rapidly throughout western civilization and became known as romance. Adding to the rapid acceptance of the new code was a book written by Andreas, the chaplain of Eleanor and Marie. *The Art of Courtly Love* (the book that so impressed me years ago) was written by Andreas Capellanus in about 1185. The book, codifying the rules of love developed by Eleanor, perhaps dictated in part by Marie, proved to be extremely popular not only at that time but throughout the centuries to follow. The rules he spelled out had tremendous influence on the philosophy of people of that time, as well as on ours.

The code of manners evolved at the court of Eleanor of Aquitaine and her daughter, Marie of Champagne, was not the capricious whim of man-hating women. Nor was it a purely fantastic creation pulled out of nowhere. The concepts these women developed tangibly expressed the movement of an entire people. Europeans of the twelfth century, due to a number of factors, were undergoing a kind of spiritual renais-

OUR ROMANTIC NOTIONS

sance. But it was primarily Eleanor's court, occurring at the right moment in history, which so greatly influenced the beliefs of people of that time that their behavior began to change as a result.

Perhaps romance as a concept would have evolved even without these noblewomen, but certainly it would have been different. Without Eleanor and Marie, history itself would have taken a different turn. They set their indelible stamp on the movement toward increased spirituality, emotionalism, expression of feeling—call it what you will. They were directly instrumental in changing the ways in which men thought about women and acted toward them. Through their code, they helped men change the way they felt about themselves. Above all, they helped elevate women to a higher position than they had ever before occupied.

The alteration of existing beliefs excited the imagination of their world, changing beliefs from that time on. After the twelfth century, the beliefs on which people had built their lives began to change. A woman was no longer regarded as she had been in ancient times, as just man's slave. Owing to the newly lighted flame of romance, woman was beginning to have some power and influence, if not over man's kingdom, then over his heart. After the twelfth century, woman had some control at last and could no longer be thought of as a mere household possession or only another one of man's servants. Her image had changed irrevocably. In romantic literature and in theory at least, she was the whip holder. Woman was finally on her pedestal.

We know that theories and real life are often light years apart, and the romantic novel does not really have anything to do with day-to-day living. Or does it? Our mental images alter our perceptions. The fact that woman was beginning to have a new image altered the way she thought of herself and the ways in which she was treated by men. In theory if not in broad actuality, woman's new image had some effect on her treatment by men of that time. The troubadours and the lyric

13

OUR ROMANTIC NOTIONS

poets of the time rhapsodized her new image, so much so that men began to see ordinary women in a new light. Men of later ages were far more affected. Few would dispute the control that woman's image exerts on our culture today. C. S. Lewis says:

> . . . *most of us have gone shopping in the twentieth with ladies who showed no sign of regarding the tradition as a dead letter*. . . .[4]

Not only women profited from the new belief system. Men, too, began to see themselves as individuals with the potential of acting for themselves. They began to realize that they could respond to situations with their feelings rather than relying on the previously unquestioned authority of their superiors. The new concepts of romance provided, in the words of one author, "a constructive response to the profound crisis in which society, the 'state' and the existing political and ecclesiastical regimes were all involved."[5]

The concepts of romance have lived on throughout the centuries, fueled by the Arthurian legends, German mysticism, the nineteenth-century English romantic poets, Victorian rules of conduct, and the never-ending supply of tales based on romantic legend. M.C. D'Arcy observes:

> *Once upon a time the education of children used to begin with the Bible, the fairy tales of Grimm and Hans Andersen and the Arthurian legend, and so deep was their influence that the ideals of truth and romance seemed to be identical. The image of the search for truth was the quest of the Holy Grail. . . . it is difficult for a younger generation*

4. C.S. Lewis, *The Allegory of Love, A Study in Medieval Tradition* (New York: Oxford University Press, 1958), p. 7.

5. Friedrich Heer, *The Medieval World* (New York: New American Library, 1961), pp. 185–86.

14
OUR ROMANTIC NOTIONS

PRENTICE-HALL, INC. PUBLISHERS ENGLEWOOD CLIFFS, N.J. 07632

89574 CR

Mrs. Betty Dietz Krebbs,
Book and Art Editor
THE DAYTON NEWS
Fourth and Ludlow Streets
Dayton, Ohio 45401

FREE COPY FOR REVIEW

SC	TITLE CODE	QTY.	TITLE - EDITION - AUTHOR	PRICE	TO BE PUBLISHED
0	392449	1	The Hoax Of Romance Jo Loudin Spectrum Paper 6.95	12.95(C)	12/15/80

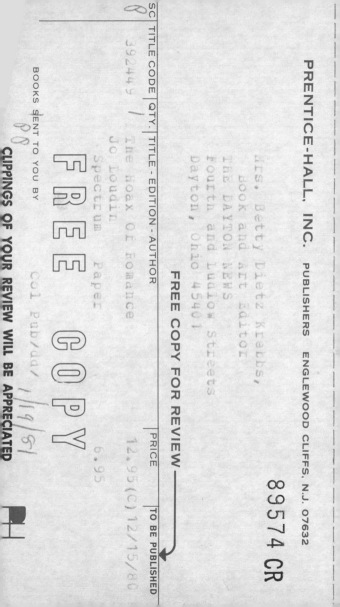

FREE COPY

BOOKS SENT TO YOU BY   Col Pub/day   1/19/81

CLIPPINGS OF YOUR REVIEW WILL BE APPRECIATED

PH

*to realize how closely woven into thought and
imagination was the romantic ideal of love.*[6]

Certain art forms have been dedicated to the concepts of romance: the opera, the ballet, much of the subject matter of painting and sculpture. Even today, with our cynical reliance on material things as the basis of the good life, we can still be inspired by a musical such as *Camelot,* based on the original Arthurian tale. Other tales modeled on the legend continue to proliferate, as they have throughout the years, from *A Connecticut Yankee in King Arthur's Court* to the latest passionate romance set in that place and time.

Although the code of manners based on romantic concepts has essentially remained the same throughout the years, as is evidenced by any contemporary book of etiquette, certain changes have taken place. One of the biggest changes in our own time is that romantic love has been applied to married couples. When woman was given her new image in accord with the original concepts of romance, wives were not included. Romantic love was a phrase that could be applied by a troubadour to his mistress but not to a man's marital partner. Today the code has almost reversed itself. Romantic love is expected as the marital norm by wedded lovers as well as those intending to marry, while adulterous love is regarded as shameful (although romantic love applied to live-in partners is increasingly acceptable today).

Originally, the concepts developed by the code of romance were beneficial to society. Women were gradually brought into a kind of partnership with men and were granted more equality than ever before. Men were given encouragement to express their tender feelings and to act toward women (and men, too) with greater courtesy. But as

6. M.C. D'Arcy, *The Mind and Heart of Love: Lion and Unicorn. A Study in Eros and Agape* (New York: World Pub. Co., 1962), p. 33.

15
OUR ROMANTIC NOTIONS

romance solidified into an unquestioned, unbending code, it became a destructive force. In contemporary American society romance has failed us; it has become detrimental, even devastating to our relationships. The price both men and women have paid for that failure has been enormous.

Through the centuries, women began to believe not only that they *should* be treated with more respect because of their sex, but also that they *must* be treated in privileged fashion. They insisted that they be worshipped as romantic objects, according to the vogue, in novels, poems, and songs—and, more importantly, in their relationships. If they were not treated as they demanded to be, they accused their men of being unfair. They earnestly tried to change their male counterparts into romantic, chivalrous lovers. When their men remained ordinary human beings, the women felt demeaned and victimized. They could not see that their acceptance of their own romantic image had caused them to become victims. By clinging to these beliefs they were, indeed, powerless to change. And by continuing to blame men for their problems, they ensured that they remained stuck in their victim positions.

Women have accepted the belief that to be feminine—and therefore desirable to men—they should be passive, submissive, and helpless. After years—centuries—of acting out these role traits, women actually *feel* helpless. Even if they want to change, their shackles of passivity weigh them down. Because they feel trapped by their image but sense that they can't entirely pin their inadequacies on men, women may be overwhelmed with a nameless rage. Far from being fulfilled by their "feminine" image, they find themselves feeling desperate and embittered, yet not knowing any way out. The solution, to many, has been to repeat, parrotlike, that they have everything they've ever wanted, therefore they shouldn't feel the way they do, and they *should* be happy. They may temporarily sweep their problems under the rug by repeatedly discounting their own feelings, but their discontent will reappear to taunt them when they let down their guard.

16

OUR ROMANTIC NOTIONS

Women have grown up waiting for Santa Claus, or Prince Charming, or some tall, dark stranger to carry them off to the good life. Believing they should be delicate and helpless "ladies," they have given themselves little permission to rely on themselves without the support of a man. Their rage at their self-imposed humility has been taken out on their children first, because it seems safer to get mad at small ones who can't fight back effectively—yet. Next they have taken it out on their husbands—if not directly, then in sneaky ways such as turning off their sexual feelings, with the result that their men get little pleasure from sex (if they get any sex at all), and the women themselves come to believe that they are frigid. Women have hidden their anger under smiles of acquiescence, letting it out only in disguise. But who is to say if a woman, smiling sweetly, is displaying amiability or bared fangs?

The children of angry women have felt that rage, whether or not their mothers tried to disguise it. The daughters have felt it as repression, hearing the wordless message, "Because you are like me—a woman—you must follow my example. Be a lady—and be angry!" (Of course, the two go together for it's humanly impossible to be sweet and ladylike all the time.) The sons have felt the anger as emasculation, some rebelling against it by trying to control women in turn, while others accept, even emulate, that control in homosexuality.

Men have accepted the romantic code too, believing they should be woman's protectors and providers. They have been ready to battle for their lady loves in the arena of war or the marketplace, whichever was necessary. They have offered to take care of their women and solve all their problems. But when the women complain that their strength and protection is suffocating, men have become confused. Many have just written off women as silly creatures who never know what they want, incomprehensible beings incapable of rational thought and subject to the whims of their hormonal ups and downs.

Many men have not liked the control anymore than women have. When the subject of control

17

OUR ROMANTIC NOTIONS

comes up, a good question is, "Who is controlling whom?" As George Bernard Shaw said in *Heartbreak House*, "The slavery of women is the tyranny of women." Many men, although they would not admit it, have resented being the strong, dedicated protectors of women. Their hearts have expressed their reluctance to go on in the traces, however, even if their lips have held back the inadmissible words. The high heart-attack rate in America bears mute witness to the stress men have felt in bearing the load of their womenfolk.

Men have raged too, some exploding outwardly in bursts of violence, some imploding inwardly in physical ailments like sick hearts, ulcers, or high blood pressure. Many have gritted their teeth nonetheless, willing themselves to become successes in their chosen fields. Anger can be a powerful fuel that provides the force to win. But at the peak of their success, when they should be able to rest and enjoy all their effort has brought, many have become acutely aware of the vague ache inside that reminds them of their unhappiness. And they wonder, if they give themselves a moment (most fear to take that moment), whether it has all been worth it or whether they would have been better off way back when just to hit the open road. Of course, there are those who do that! Some say they are going to the store for a pack of cigarettes and simply disappear, leaving their women at home to wonder for the rest of their lives: "What did I do? Where did I go wrong?" (Recent statistics show that wives are beginning to disappear more frequently today.) Neither the men who stay nor the men who go, the wives who acquiesce in sweetness or the ones who act out in rage, ever know that they have been caught—conned—by a system that not only predicts but guarantees alienation, repression, and the gradual embitterment of themselves as individuals and as marital couples.

I know that we no longer adhere strictly to the romantic code, as did our forefathers. We let go a few more of our romantic delusions every day. Certainly women are not the "ladies" they were earlier in our history, nor are they as powerless politically. In the nineteenth century women had so little power in the arenas of business and politics that they had no other choice but to apply their energies to the home. They dominated their homes, and sometimes their husbands, with all the finesse of a slave master. While the man was out working, the woman controlled the domain of the home and the behavior of the children. When servants became scarce, the ladies relied on their husbands to help around the house as well as hold down a job, an indication of what was to come later in modern suburbia. The man became, in the words of one writer, the woman's only servant, "a groundsman with sex privileges."[7] In their reliance on their image, American women developed a particular reputation for arrogance and rudeness. A tale has it that shortly after the advent of the "motorbus," a man riding on one rose and gave his place to a lady, ". . . and she fainted. When she came to, she thanked him—and he fainted."[8]

But even though women were granted the right to vote sixty years ago, though the ratification of the Equal Rights Amendment has been approved by a great number of the states, though new strides are being made daily toward liberation of women and the consequent easing of the burden on their men to support them, old values die hard. The women who live the image and the men who help them keep it are still controlled by their own thought processes. Those same concepts of romance which promised so much freedom in the beginning, and indeed granted a great deal, have placed women—and, through them, men—in bondage. And the bondage of a controlled relationship, a marriage founded on romantic illusions which gives way after (and sometimes during) the honeymoon to the business of living together, is exactly what we find hardest to bear.

7. Russell Lynes, *The Domesticated Americans* (New York: Harper & Row, Pub., 1963), p. 173.
8. Arthur M. Schlesinger, *Learning How To Behave: A Historical Study of American Etiquette Books* (New York: Macmillan Co., 1946), p. 67.

19

OUR ROMANTIC NOTIONS

The fact is that when we live our lives according to our romantic notions, we automatically cut ourselves off from knowing what our feelings really are. Men, even more than women, have suffered from being so cut off. Willard Gaylin says:

> The right, and therefore the capacity to display physical affection has been severely limited in men. By labelling emotion, tenderness, softness and sensuality as "feminine" traits, we have deprived our insecure male population of the easy pleasures of physical affection. . . . We have hardened our gender stereotypes to such a point where "being a man" seems to imply an immunity to all affection and emotion.[9]

Romantic values change somewhat according to each time and place, but the illusive quality persists. In the nineteenth century romantics were far more inhibited sexually than we are today but could display without censure sentiment, melancholy, or tears. Morton Hunt comments, ". . . where the rationalists had repressed their emotions and acted out their sexuality, the romantics restrained the sexuality and poured forth their emotions."[10]

The objects of their emotional outpouring were similar in idealistic qualities to their earlier medieval ancestors. Hunt says:

> . . . men sought an ideal woman rather than a real one, and pinned their ideal image on some girl of whom, because she had been so quiet and retiring, they knew very little.[11]

9. Willard Gaylin, M.D., *Feelings: Our Vital Signs* (New York: Harper & Row, Pub. 1979), pp. 180–82.

10. Morton M. Hunt, *The Natural History of Love* (New York: Minerva Press, 1959), p. 310.

11. Ibid., pp. 310–11.

20

OUR ROMANTIC NOTIONS

The frailty of the image of woman revered in the romantic era of the nineteenth century surpassed even that of medieval times. According to Hunt the "clinging-vine personality" developed then: "Along with modesty, virtue, sweetness, and similar qualities, she was supposed to be weak, fearful, and anxious to lean on, and be dominated by, a strong kind man."[12] The clinging vine has come down to us today as a part of our romantic heritage, but we've been taught to call her traits "feminine."

Men were not solely responsible for foisting the romantic stereotype of femininity on the opposite sex. Women were equally at fault for accepting and acting it out. Today we are changing that image; it's about time! Although we still cling tightly to some of our antiquated beliefs, we increasingly give ourselves permission to feel, to be individuals, not just stereotypic men and women. Men are finding out that they will not be ridiculed or rejected if they show their tender, even helpless, feelings. They're discovering that they can display their full range of changing emotions without always having to act the part of the strong, silent provider. Women are gradually permitting themselves to display more aggressive feelings. They are bringing their previously hidden anger out into the open, upsetting the equilibrium to be sure, but being straight about it. Women are asserting their innate right to be treated as thinking, as well as feeling, people. They're even entering fields long closed to them, and men are encouraging them to do so.

The overwhelming discontent of women today, and of some men, is a positive sign. Both are becoming aware that they have more possibilities available to them than traditional roles provide. Knowing that such freedom exists, however, may cause us more frustration than if we did not. Our grandmothers did not seem to be as dissatisfied, in retrospect, as the modern-day woman. In the late nineteenth and early twentieth centuries, there was no alternative to "woman's lot." Now we know that there is, and yet we still may not be able to throw off the shackles of our life situations quickly. Women may have to deal with problems such as lack of marketable skills

12. Ibid., p. 310.

21

OUR ROMANTIC NOTIONS

when they would like to enter a career field; they may have dependent children to care for and limited finances on which to do it. They may realistically be afraid to raise their children alone and may feel that they have to defer to their men more than if they were financially independent. Men might like to quit their jobs and enjoy freedom from their daily business grind but may stay on to support their families. They may continue to repress their feelings on the job, knowing that times are changing and all feelings are permissible, but also realizing their bosses might fire them if they were more expressive.

Even if the reality of our lives cannot change fast enough to suit us our role images are changing rapidly. We're discovering that despite our belief in the stereotype, women are not really too delicate or too helpless to work like men. We have believed that women were not as smart as men, or as capable; therefore they couldn't be corporate presidents, or go to war, or be leaders of their country. But women hold some of these positions elsewhere. India, Israel, and now Great Britain have believed a woman could be Prime Minister. In other countries women take military training and fight wars alongside men. Why not here? Who says women are so fragile that men have to spend, waste, ruin their lives taking care of them? Who says men can't keep house, or quit their careers to find occupations more satisfying, or cry when they hurt? Who says women have to be so protected that they lose any sense of themselves as competent, useful, participating members of society? Who says men have to be so strong that they lose awareness of themselves as feeling human beings? Why, romance, of course!

22

OUR ROMANTIC NOTIONS

2. MY OWN ROMANTIC NOTIONS

A PERSONAL CASE STUDY

I lived by my own romantic notions until a few years ago. An idealist, I dreamed that someday I would find a perfect love and all my problems would be solved. I was rarely in touch with the here and now, hoping that the future would be different than whatever reality I was experiencing—all happy and wonderful. I envisioned a fantastic someone with whom to share that improbable future. I agonized through the present, however, filled with apprehensions. I was depressed, insecure, self-critical, and generally unhappy. I hurt with unexplained but all too constant pains.

My convictions were ambivalent. I believed that I had nothing to offer anyone, and no man would ever want me. Yet I also fantasized that someone, someday, would marry me. Believing implicitly in marriage—that goal of all romantic dreamers—I automatically put "Mrs." in front of the name of every man I met, just to see how it would sound. Had I not learned that marriage was the be-all and end-all, the most important concern in life? Love, marriage, and that nebulous someone—was there anything else? Not to me—not work or play, career or avocation. Nothing was clear in my mind but the passive conviction that I would be married sometime in the future whether or not I had anything to do with it. I didn't think beyond that. Who did? All the plays and the movies ended with wedding bells. I never once thought that marriage might be the beginning rather than the end. I believed that marriage would be the panacea to all my problems. The trip to the altar would magically erase all the mental and physical pain I had known previously, and that perfect someone would forever after make me happy. Beyond that the future was an inconceivable blank.

Even if I had thought beyond my fantasized wedding date, I would have had little on which to base any realistic thinking. My own parents had separated when I was very small. They later divorced, and both had remarried several times. Marriage, to me, was a coming together and a splitting

25

MY OWN ROMANTIC NOTIONS

apart. All I knew of love was that one fell into it with ease, and out of it with equal abandon. I had seen the negative side of relationships—the arguments, bitterness, hurt, and anger—but I knew little of the positive side. I knew nothing of the joy that two people can find in each other. I had no idea of how relationships might work, since I had only known ones that did not.

Nor did I have a way to decide on that special someone once he came along. I had no faith whatsoever in my ability to make decisions or to form opinions. I remember my dad telling me once he thought it was a shame that a young person had to make the most important decision of life—whom to marry—at a time when he or she was least capable of making it. I agreed. I didn't know what I felt about anything. Since I blocked most of my feelings from my awareness, the idea that I could use my feelings to evaluate my relationship with another person was beyond my comprehension. I discounted my feelings in deference to other people because I believed that others were more important than I was. I felt wrong no matter what I said, did, or felt, believing that everybody else was automatically right. I realize now that I often did act on my feelings, but I was confused. I ordinarily castigated myself when I disregarded my beliefs and acted according to feelings. In my confusion I felt helpless to clarify my situation, let alone change it through decisive action. I had no tools for analyzing the behavior and mental processes of anyone, especially myself, other than the meager ones provided by my culture. Those beliefs—those romantic fantasies—I clung to fervently.

Someday, I believed, someone would come along and take me away from my unhappiness. I did not want someone who was rich or famous or terribly handsome. To be truthful, I don't think I really wanted *someone*. I just wanted to get away. I had a vague idea in my head that if I got away—wherever that was—things would be better. I had no idea that I could stay wherever I was and get what I wanted in this world by myself. I believed that I had to have a man get it for me. Whatever it was—position, money, security, even good

26

feelings—I had to have it given to me. I couldn't comprehend that I had any responsibility for my own feelings, thoughts, or actions. If I felt turned on or off, high or low, joyful or depressed, it was somebody else who had done that *to* me. I felt like a puppet, waiting for somebody else to pull my strings and make me dance. I fully believed the dance couldn't start until *he* came along. So I waited and hoped, and created a dream in my mind of the perfect man.

Of course, what I believed, I got. I've realized since that we have tremendous power to shape our world. I've seen it happen again and again. I, or someone else, may believe strongly in something, and, as if I actually had a hand in its creation, my mental image will come into existence. There it springs, in full relief, almost as if my mind has shaped the material essence of the real person or thing. There is some kind of reciprocity in imagining, a give and take with the real world that I find inexplicable, yet it occurs more often than I'm even aware. It happened when my image of the man who would take me away from it all became flesh. He appeared during my senior year in college—a foreign student, tall and dark, perfect for my romantic dream.

He was not so perfect in reality. My folks were dismayed, expecting problems in the relationship, not only because he planned eventually to return to his own country, but because he and I were so different. I wouldn't listen, determined as I was to hang onto my dream. I believed in the vision. Years later I realized that what I'd seen as charm on his part was really manipulation, but then I couldn't evaluate his behavior. I was fascinated—by his swarthy skin, his stories about his country, his heavily accented speech. He talked constantly, and I thought he was the most intelligent man on earth. I felt like a clod in comparison.

Prior to meeting him I'd necked and petted with my dates but beyond that my sexual education was sketchy. Mom had told me that men only wanted "one thing," but she wouldn't elaborate on what that was. Dad had told me

27

MY OWN ROMANTIC NOTIONS

that sex was "fun," but when I asked how, he'd only grin as if he'd been caught out behind the barn with a cigar in his mouth and repeat that it was fun. I had never tried to masturbate; I must have gotten the message very young that it was a no-no. My education to that point had consisted of guiltily reading *Anthony Adverse* one summer. I wondered if sex was as exciting as that book. I didn't find out until I was twenty-one years old with my foreign student. Then I discovered that I got more thrills from *Anthony* than I did from my impatient, inexperienced lover.

My feelings didn't matter that much anyway because he promised to take me away. I could see life in his country as a sybaritic paradise—being surrounded by servants, pampered and waited upon—my every demand instantly attended to. I did not think that I might get bored in such a setting, or that adapting to a culture so different from my own might present its own set of problems. All I could see was me, the center of importance, getting what I had never gotten enough of in my whole life, attention. I visualized being given everything I'd wanted as a child and of course had never had, womblike security and the guarantee that everything would be forever all right, happiness guaranteed ever after.

That's what the ads and the movies and the songs had promised me, happiness forevermore. And marriage was the key to that never-ending source of contentment—all I had to do was say "yes." In the end I couldn't say it. I felt wrong about the relationship even though I kept repeating the romantic creed, "I have everything I've ever wanted, and I should be happy." I wasn't, and I knew it. But, not wanting to make the final decision, I ran away to Mexico. I found it easier to avoid making decisions altogether. Running is a great way of avoidance, especially since I left no forwarding address. Eventually I ran out of money, so I came back. I told my lover "no," doubting my decision, yet feeling that I had made the right one and already, before he was gone, exalting his image out of all proportion to the real man.

28

MY OWN ROMANTIC NOTIONS

A few months later I decided to marry someone else, someone I knew my parents would accept. Mom made plans for the wedding. Dad said that he seemed like a fine young man. Only my yoga teacher, perceiving feelings I was unwilling to admit, sounded a sour note. "You're not going to be happy," she told me. I ignored her prediction, but I never forgot her words.

I had overwhelming doubts about getting married, but I set my teeth and decided to go through with the ceremony. Characteristically, I ignored my feelings and decided, intellectually, that this man would give me what I wanted. He planned to go to college in Australia, and we would sail immediately after the wedding. There it was again, "away." I didn't understand that my misery was inside me, that my unhappiness wouldn't leave just because I left my present environment. I was trying to escape from myself, but there was no leaving my feelings behind.

When we got to Australia, I realized that I'd not only dragged my problems with me; more were waiting for me there. The romance of traveling had nothing to do with the reality of living in a different culture. I tried to tell my husband how I felt but I couldn't. I felt guilty about complaining and told myself I was being a "bad" wife. He agreed with me, saying that there were such things as right and wrong and that I was not acting "right." Neither of us could express personal feelings to the other because we didn't know the words to use.

I did not cope with misery gracefully. Once I took a razor blade, thinking I should cut my wrists, but I threw it across the room. Another time, riding the elevated train, I thought I should jump out the open door. Instead, I gripped the pole I clung to even tighter. I went for a walk one day and waded a stream. Feeling something on my legs I looked down and saw fat black leeches ringing my boot tops. I ripped them off, leaving the heads to fester under my skin, and ran screaming, panicking through the bushes until I was too exhausted to run any more. For the first time I experienced the madness of total

29

panic. It may have saved my sanity. Realizing how close I was to losing my grip entirely, we scraped together enough money for me to take a freighter home.

My husband never forgave me. He refused to rejoin me. A year later, a lawyer told me I might as well get a divorce. It seemed easier to follow his advice than to think for myself. My husband made no comment on receiving the divorce papers, nor did I try to express my feelings. We were totally insulated from each other by our mutual inability to communicate.

Now I realize that I had few options to behave differently. Between my negative childhood feelings and the beliefs I had learned from my parents and society, I was stuck in my self-abnegating behavior patterns. Nor did I have the tools to confront my romantic illusions and find reality in my relationships. I clung to my illusions, suffering the most for the men I romanticized. Each time a romantic attachment ended, I was devastated. Hoping each time that a new man would be the one, expecting that he would live up to my fantasy, I was continually disappointed. No one ever fulfilled my expectations. No one person could have, but I didn't know that then. Every time my romantic bubble popped, I'd quickly create another much like the one that had just vanished. The fantasies were the same; only the people that I built the romantic dream around changed.

I decided to go to Europe because I had no romantic interest in the States. I had been dating a man, but I was not fascinated with him; I heard no poetry or ringing bells. I took a job with the military and cried all the way across the Atlantic. But I was still hoping for an "away" to solve all my miserable feelings. The promise of someone, somewhere, was still inside my head, pulling me on.

My European dream was only another illusion. I was no happier there than I'd been anywhere else. I stayed because I didn't have enough money to break my employment contract. A couple of years later I found an officer in the army on whom to focus my romantic fantasies. As usual I deprecated myself for not being as intelligent as he was.

30

MY OWN ROMANTIC NOTIONS

I was as fascinated by him as I'd been by my first lover. I had no way of knowing then that fascination amounts to nothing more than a head trip. I've realized since that when I'm fascinated with someone I numb my own feelings by putting all my attention on that other person. I criticize myself continually while I'm inflating his image. By creating a phony picture of him in my own mind, I set myself up for a fall. My image of him is bound to crack when I begin to realize he has as many rough edges as I do. And my own previously numbed feelings are bound to surface, heaping me with whatever I haven't let myself feel.

But then I was fascinated. I constantly put myself down. I remember leaving him at a party once because I felt ignored and rejected. But I scolded myself, saying, "Grow up. Don't be so petty. You shouldn't feel like that. He didn't mean it. Now you go right back to that party like a big girl and apologize." I did, and so we got married.

I don't suppose I would actually have married him except that I got pregnant. I didn't have the courage to have a child outside of marriage, and I still had my fantasies. He promised me a future that sounded great. So I ignored my rotten feelings in the present and our bitter, accusational, unresolved fights. I disregarded my unhappiness, and we went through with the ceremony. A month later, on my thirtieth birthday, I lost the baby. I remember the doctor bending over me after I'd miscarried, saying, "You didn't really want that baby, did you?" I felt relieved, even though I felt guilty for being relieved; he was right.

I stayed in the marriage because of my internal, commanding "shoulds." I told myself one *should not* get married, then divorce a month later; one *should* give it a try. I did try, whipping myself mentally for five years. I told myself that I was being ridiculous, that I *should* appreciate what I had, that I *should* try to be a good wife. I failed miserably. I could not communicate with my second husband anymore than I could with my first. No matter how much I'd try to figure out our relationship intellectually, I only got more confused. I said to my

31

MY OWN ROMANTIC NOTIONS

husband once, trying to tell him what I felt, "You box me in." He responded, "You knock my boxes down." That's where we had to leave it because we had no language to use in discussing our feelings.

Now I know why I could not communicate—because I could not recognize or express my feelings. I had no tools at all without that. Communication is based on having the internal permission to feel and share feelings verbally. Without that permission, all I could do was to state opinions and beliefs. When we tried to use our opinions as a basis for our communication, we got into arguments that generated more confusion and went on interminably, resolving nothing, escalating our anger, leaving us even farther apart.

My fantasies about travel in this marriage turned out to be factual. We lived in Europe, the United States, and Mexico, visiting exotic vacation spots and new cities. But despite the changing scene, I was bored and depressed. I don't remember one day without a fight. Sex was a teeth-gritting experience for me. I began to have a drink before so I wouldn't start screaming hysterically during. Although I'd had satisfying sexual experiences prior to my marriage, I began to believe I was frigid. The books I read corroborated my fears. If a woman didn't experience orgasm through intercourse, they told me, she was aggressive and masculine, incapable of being feminine. I believed those words, telling myself I was at fault even though I knew I harbored a mountain of resentment.

I remember those years as a kind of physical as well as mental craziness. My body was screaming, "I'm hurting, I'm aching, I'm not well." I haunted doctors' offices, only to be told, "There's nothing wrong with you; take two aspirin (or tranquilizers) and it'll all go away," or "Try a glass of wine before dinner and you might relax." Once I pleaded with my husband to go with me to a psychiatrist; we went. I poured out my frustrations. From the psychiatrist's wide-eyed reaction to my jumble of words, I felt crazy; from my husband's, I felt bad. He corroborated my feeling for me when we left. "Bend over and

32

let me kick you," he said. I understood then that one does not reveal such secrets to an army psychiatrist. Later I heard tales of men who'd had their careers ruined by revealing secrets to supposedly confidential sources, secrets that were later used against them. But what was I to do with my craziness? My body did it for me. I had two bouts with suspected cancer, neither confirmed nor lasting. My body was screaming out its madness in the only way it could, through symptoms. I understood my physical pain in those years, and perhaps my brush with an actual malignancy, when I read the words of a doctor recently:

We must consider emotion as a factor in all illness. I know of none in which emotion may not be a major causative factor. I'm not so sure but what emotions may even be at the basis of cancer. . . . Laugh if you will but let us remind ourselves what cancer is—it's a cell gone mad.[1]

The promise of my romantic dream had kept me in the marriage; my fear got me out. I began to think, in my craziness, that I might either kill myself or him. I couldn't hold down my rage any longer. I finally realized that the fantasies I had lived by could never take shape. If I could not be with my husband for one full day without a fight, how could we ever have the good life that I had envisioned in my romantic dream? I knew for my own sanity I would have to leave him.

Yet, I was afraid to do it. After living with criticism for so many years, both his and my own, I had very little confidence left. Though I had worked for years before my marriage, I doubted that I could support myself. My anger finally drove me out. I was too scared of my own rage *not* to leave him. I knew I'd destroy myself if I stayed—if not literally, then I'd kill off my initiative and creativity, my essence. So I got

1. Donald D. Fisher, *I Know You Hurt, But There's Nothing To Bandage* (Beaverton, Ore.: Touchstone Press, 1978), p. 145.

33
MY OWN ROMANTIC NOTIONS

out, before I acted out my rage on either of us. I got out of a relationship, a romantic fantasy, that I never should have gotten into in the first place.

Since then I've met people who have found themselves in similar bitter, stifling relationships, and who've stayed. They have lacked the confidence to make any move at all so they've remained, allowing themselves to be eroded away from within while they've screamed, and complained angrily about their partners. And, listening to these people, I have wondered if it was my anger alone that got me out of my destructive relationship, or if something else helped me make the actual decision to move.

I know now that I had something else—a certain amount of permission to act according to my feelings. Unlike the people who remain trapped in their misery because they may only moan about their situation, I had permission to change. When things are roughest for me, no matter how much I criticize myself, I still have a wee voice inside my mind, my father's voice, saying, "Your feelings are okay with me!" And that has made all the difference—one parent who allowed me to express my feelings without criticism!

Not that my mother didn't in her way, but she had little permission from her own parents to express her feelings. How could she give me permission to recognize my anger when she had been taught to bury her own pain? When I tried to express my unhappiness as a child she would tell me, "Smile, don't look so glum!" So I tried to act as I believed she wanted me to act, repeating the message to myself, "Smile!" In later years I smiled so much my jaws ached, but I still planted a big smile on my face—no matter how much I hurt!

I had other supporters when I was a kid—aunts, friends, my step-mother—people who gave me not only permission to express my feelings but corroboration. If I was angry at mom or dad they would not say as some people do, "You shouldn't feel that way about your parents!" My supporters would tell me in various ways, "You've got a right to feel the way

34

you do; she's (or he's) not treating you well." If I didn't end up feeling on top of the world, at least I didn't feel crazy. I had somebody to validate my unhappiness, to tell me my feelings were real and appropriate to what was going on around me.

Many people had no one there to give them that kind of corroboration. Their parents showed one side of themselves to friends and neighbors, another to their children. When such children felt hurt or angry at their parents, the message they got back from other adults showed disbelief: "Your mother and father are such fine people; they couldn't treat you as badly as you say they do!" The implication was, "You must be crazy to feel like that!" These people who stay in destructive relationships may do so because they still have no one to give their negative feelings corroboration. Like some of my clients, they inactivate themselves by doubting their own sanity and the validity of their feelings.

I believe that if I had no supportive figures in my childhood I would have spent years in therapy, instead of being a practicing therapist. But I've been able to act, despite my internal barrage of criticism, because I have had one saving grace. When it came to breaking out of my marriage I had enough permission to do it, even though I had to battle critical voices in my mind that said I shouldn't. The voices were wrong, as they usually are.

Two years after I left my officer husband I visited him to see if I still felt the same. I did. Feelings don't disappear that easily. I knew after being with him for one day that we could never get along. My rage took me by surprise with its immensity. I remember yelling angrily at a department store clerk and thinking, "Why am I screaming at her when it's him that I'm angry at?" I knew I did not need that kind of life again. I left him in relief. For once I didn't fantasize about the relationship to throw doubt on my decision.

Then I rediscovered a man I'd had an unromantic relationship with ten years before. We were able to be straight about our feelings because we both felt the

35
MY OWN ROMANTIC NOTIONS

other would survive if we expressed them. I know I had held back before because this man offered me no fantasy of the future. Our relationship had always been in the here and now. Nothing would be handed to me; nothing was promised. I knew that if I wanted anything in the future I'd have to work for it in the present. So, finally letting go of my romantic delusions, I married him. Then we had a little girl.

Having her also helped me to change. The reality of having a baby is far different from the romantic dream of wanting one. I was ignorant of the facts of child-raising. Mom had told me she found me in a cabbage patch; Dad had implied that babies dropped from heaven, but it was hell if one arrived before the wedding. I knew that conception was not the result of swallowing a watermelon seed, but it wasn't until I saw her in the delivery room that I knew I'd had a real baby growing inside me for nine months. She became more real as nights blurred into days through fatigue. My step-mom kept saying that my daughter would be a help to me when she got older. The physical help I question. When she helps by washing the mirrors with furniture polish or cleans her room by hiding everything under the bed, I wonder how much older she'll have to get. The mental help I don't doubt.

She has helped me to understand. That's a value I wouldn't ever dismiss, worth all the sleepless nights of her infancy and strain of the years since. She's helped me become aware not only of herself as a unique human being, but of myself. I understand many of my own feelings through hers, and I've brought to light many of my interior, sneaky messages by my interacting with her.

I remember saying one time, as she started out for school, "How about a kiss before you go?"

"No," she said, and opened the door.

I started to say, "Someday, when your mommy is gone, you'll be sorry you didn't kiss her." I stopped after "Someday."

36

MY OWN ROMANTIC NOTIONS

"What did you say, Mommy?" she asked.

"Nothing, dear," I said quickly. "Have a good day at school." She left while I marveled at that message I'd never before unearthed. But the implication corroborated some of my own guilt feelings: "Do what Mommy tells you; if you don't you'll feel guilty when she's gone." Maybe these aren't words that I've heard, but they're words that have risen from my feelings, that I've received nonverbally, telling me how to act—or else.

I learned, as other children do, to behave in ways my parents expected, even though they didn't always verbalize their expectations. I learned to think about what they might want me to say or do before I did it, and to feel only that which they approved of. The feelings that were unacceptable to them I refused to acknowledge. Anger, in particular, in any of its degrees from irritation to hate, was inadmissible, so I wouldn't admit its presence. When I got older and became more secure about separating myself from my parents, I became more convinced I could live without their approval. Eventually I was able to use the permission messages in my mind and allow myself to feel, to think, to be—even *not* to smile or *not* to do what they wanted me to. I began to feel the load of anger I carried around inside me, and I realized one day that all my craziness during my two marriages—my suicidal thoughts, my overwhelming and sometimes inappropriate rage, my fears that I might act out toward my husband—was not craziness at all, but anger. Since then I've wondered what would happen if all the depressed housewives, all the ulcerated workers, and all the drugged inmates of the psychiatric wards were helped to get in touch with their anger instead of calling it a particular kind of craziness.

While I was constantly seeking my parents' or other authority figures' approval, I stayed in my romantic future because I had no permission to exist in the present. I had no inner surety that whatever I felt in the here and now was all right and that I could use my feelings as indicators in

37

MY OWN ROMANTIC NOTIONS

making decisions and changing my life situations. I continually tried to be better because I never felt good enough. Now I don't have to try anymore; I figure I'm okay as I am. I don't have to rely on somebody else to tell me what to do; I can make up my mind on the basis of what I feel. And I can give others that right too—my child, my husband, people around me. If others display feelings, of whatever kind, I don't have to rush to make their feelings go away or to criticise them for having such feelings. I don't have to take responsibility for their feelings, so I can let others exist as feeling beings too.

I know that the beliefs I lived by and that caused me so much misery were taught to me by my parents, but I can't blame them. They were even more trapped than I was. When they were growing up such beliefs were inviolable. Our society and their parents taught them, as they taught me, to be romantics. All of us, parents and children alike, have had little choice but to live by what we've been taught; we haven't known any other way. We've been taught to be good, to do what we're told, and to be happy. For the rest of our lives we try to live by these teachings, to seek approval for what we do and be better than we are.

I, like my parents and other romantics had to cling to fantasies: the good life, the perfect love, an idealization of what people should be. I know the pain that their fantasies have caused my parents and others. Certainly those nebulous but fixed ideas of mine caused me to waste years on relationships that, had I followed my feelings, I would never have entered into.

I was a romantic in attitude if not in accomplishments. I achieved some very realistic goals. But, not content with what I had, I always sought something else, some rainbow, or, better yet, the pot of gold at the end of it. Anything was better than what I had in the here and now because I never really experienced it. Future-tripping continually, I slipped through the present without ever knowing sensually that I was there. I did not see those around me as people with bones

38

MY OWN ROMANTIC NOTIONS

and skin and feelings. I saw them as I wanted them to be, and they were shadows. Nor did I feel my world with its changing moods; I blocked out the present by imposing on it my romantic dreams of something better tomorrow.

There must be some escape hatch, I thought, and if only I looked hard enough I'd find it, or him. So I looked all over incessantly. Somebody, I believed, could make me happy. There must be someone I could keep on his pedestal without eventually realizing that he, too, had maddeningly human feet of clay. Maybe I was slower than most, perhaps faster than some. I was thirty-five before I started sloughing off my romantic notions. I began to understand that each day I lived was the only one I could hope for, that tomorrows are nonexistent until they arrive, and that nowhere would I find complete happiness. Worse still, I began to get fleeting notions that nowhere in the world would I find perfection, either of climate or of place, and that each moment I existed, wherever I lived, would have its drawbacks. I began to see the mosquitoes along with the sunsets, but, strangely, I began to appreciate their bite. Once I decided I could exist along with the imperfections and the insecurities of life, I began to see people as they were without trying to mold them into my ideal. I discovered that no one is perfect, that each person has his or her own composite of positive and negative traits, likeable and disagreeable chacteristics. Once I accepted people for what they were I no longer had to set myself up for disappointment. I began to come out of my dream world and into the real one with all its imbalances of good and bad, pleasurable and painful, enjoyable and irritating vargaries.

I discovered that *nothing* is forever, there is *no* total security; life is chancy and tenuous and full of pain. I began to see that no love, no marriage can be guaranteed forever, that feelings do not last, and that the only enduring relationship is one in which the partners continually express their changing feelings to each other. I saw that the harder one tries to hang onto a feeling, or a lover, the likelier one is to lose out entirely, and that one can't trap a feeling, just as, in Alan Watt's

39

MY OWN ROMANTIC NOTIONS

words, ". . . you cannot walk off with a river in a bucket."[2] The more I accepted change as an inevitable part of my life, the more I found that I could live with it.

So too with pain. The Mexicans have a saying that I used to scoff at, "Vivir es sufrir" (to live is to suffer). Now I believe even that. Pain is a part of my life, and if I accept it in my body and into my awareness, I get through it faster and let it go. When I try to avoid pain by ignoring it or tensing myself against it, I keep it around to taunt me. Pain insists that something is wrong and needs taking care of. So whether my pain is "real" and can be diagnosed in my body, or "imaginary" and hides away in my mind, my emotions, it speaks to me. When I accept it and pay attention to it, I heal myself. Now I believe that life means suffering—what else are negative feelings, headaches, sore muscles, sickness, and fatigue but suffering? But I can survive that, still believing that life is worthwhile despite, or perhaps because of, my pain.

I know too without a doubt that the only possible way of growing is by feeling my fear and my pain. Fighting my pain, running away from my fear, may seem like survival but it's the opposite—a sure death even though that death may take years. Paradoxically, once I give up fighting and accept the pain, I can then give up the pain and start to live. Fearing the pain is like fearing to die, but accepting death turns out to be the doorway of life. If that life isn't entirely free of pain, at least what pain there is leaves quickly because I have leaned into it, welcomed it, explored it, and then let go of it. Strange, isn't it? We are motivated to get out of pain because it hurts. What we need is motivation to get into it in order to let it go.

I needed motivation to get into my pain and I got it—life. My living patterns hurt too much, chronically and persistently, to hold onto. Either way I had pain—either the repetitive pain of future-tripping with my romantic attitudes or the sharp, relieving pain of being in touch

2. Alan Watts, *The Wisdom of Insecurity* (New York: Random House, Vintage Books, 1951), p. 24.

40

MY OWN ROMANTIC NOTIONS

with my feelings. I chose the latter. It hasn't been easy, and at first I didn't particularly like living in the here and now. The present didn't hold as much promise as my irrational journeys in search of rainbows and happiness. But when I began to accept my life as it is rather than as I thought it should be, I found I could continue to exist. Before that I had thought, consciously or otherwise, that I did not want to struggle through a tedious life. I believed I could not exist with only that. I found that I could, however, and that knowledge was most important. I realized that even unromantically, I could survive.

So I have. And I discovered that reality has its own special joy and meaning. It is certainly not always fun, and has its uncontrollable ups and downs, but ups nonetheless—and downs not forever. I found not happiness but moments, special moments that bring me an inner glow, a warmth that shows in a smile I don't have to paste on my face as I used to, but one that appears of its own accord. A few days ago I stood in my living room and watched a small seaplane skimming the water, its white wake scarring the surface of Puget Sound, and I smiled. I'm happy, I thought, and I had no idea why. Moments, that's all, just moments. But they're enough.

So I came to terms with the reality that I call the here and now, decided to quit looking for escape hatches, and live with what I've got. Not that I don't sometimes miss romance with a twinge of nostalgia. The dream of finding something better was so promising. But I know that "better" is impossible, not because I could never find it, oh no! Sometimes I did find it! At times I found my dream, but then came the catch. As soon as I held it in my hands, the dream faded, dribbled out between my fingertips, and faded out into the mist. While I watched it dribble away, in my romantic days, the thought would come creeping into my mind, "what next?"

I remember the day I got my M.G.A. I had wanted one for many years—a new sports car. Its shape had filled my thoughts along with an image of myself once I got it. I would become, I thought, what all the ads implied about

41

MY OWN ROMANTIC NOTIONS

the sports car—international, sophisticated, and seductive. This new me would be as irresistible as the sleek machine that dared the winding European roads, especially to that shadowy someone sitting beside me. I slid under the wheel, sinking into the red leather upholstery. As I eased the white sportscar onto the cobbled road, the thought popped into my head, "what next?"

The "next" came, right along the lines of my dream and just what I had asked for. My army officer was soon sitting beside me and we raced off through Europe together, fighting, every kilometer of the way. I didn't realize, in those romantic days, that when one asks for a dream and gets it, you get it whole. I had requested the outlines of the dream; reality filled in the details. Those finer points didn't feel so great. I didn't like being with my new partner in romance; I felt put-down, frustrated, and angry. But out of old habit, I disregarded the details of the present and concentrated even harder on that glorious but hazy future. I told myself my feelings didn't count anyway, just as I always had, and proceeded to fit him into the rest of my dream. When I divorced him five miserable years later I knew about the details of reality. So much for dreams.

I must admit, in all my talk about leaving romanticism behind, that at times I still ask myself, "what next?" Every time I finish a major project, such as a book, I ask myself that question. I admit to having a hopeless addiction to writing, and if I don't indulge myself in it I am impossible to live with. To stay straight I need to write and to communicate my feelings to others. Communication, being what it is, lets me share in the feelings of others. I know that touching others through feelings has grounded me to life; that my clients, no matter how much they believe I've helped them, have helped me more. I cannot continue whatever games I'm into when I'm practicing therapy. Sooner or later, usually sooner, someone will confront my kinkiness. Then I must admit: "Yes, I did that; I misunderstood; or I discounted you; or I laid my trip on you. You have a right to be angry with me, and I accept your anger. You are okay with me whatever you feel, as I am okay no matter what I feel. We each have a right to our feelings, whatever they may be."

42

MY OWN ROMANTIC NOTIONS

We do *not* have a right to our *shoulds*, our expectations of how others should feel and be. If you lay your should on me today, I'm usually sharp enough to reject it. (Usually, that is, unless I'm down with sickness or fatigue and I allow myself to be intimidated.) I could not reject shoulds in years past because my mind was filled with so many of my own. Mine would awaken and whip me into line at the least instigation. But today I reject your shoulds and my own as well. As I trust you to reject any expectation I might lay on you.

Shoulds are fantastic nonsense. Nevertheless, they are, as they have been from the beginning, an integral part of romance. Shoulds, on which romantic relationships are built, encourage partners to control one another. They ensure that the partners will first entrap each other by fantastic expectations, then constrict each other by manipulations such as jealousy and striving to please, and finally destroy the relationships altogether by the unattainable but pervasive concept of happiness. The shoulds, so inherent in romance, are the parts of our romantic heritage that I want us to root out and eradicate. Shoulds are the hoax of romance!

43
MY OWN ROMANTIC NOTIONS

3. OUR AUTHORIZATION FOR BELIEF SYSTEMS

CONCEPTS HANDED DOWN THROUGH
GENERATIONS GIVE US AUTHORIZATION.

That concepts developed during the Middle Ages still affect our society today seems incredible, yet I know of some that have been handed down from generation to generation. Although these beliefs have been accepted without question by the people concerned, they seem ridiculous to outsiders. When I've asked those people why, they have invariably replied, "It's always been done that way!"

I remember a friend of mine who kept her butter in the freezer. "Why?" I asked. "I don't know," she answered, "I've always done it that way. Doesn't everyone?" When she thought about it, she realized that her grandmother, who owned an icebox, had instructed her mother to keep the butter on the ice. Her mother had obeyed, and when refrigerators became available she and her daughter, continued to keep their butter on ice, in the freezer.

I've heard of many other concepts handed down from one generation to another, laughable but extremely frustrating to deal with. I remember joking about a maid in Germany, who used the floor polisher as a leaning post while she resolutely rubbed out marks with a rag under her foot—she had always done it that way. It was no joke, however, to teach her to clean the floor with the polisher.

I talked to a biologist once who had tried to convince some Alaskan villagers that their typhoid problem was due to polluted water. "They'd been using the same water hole for generations," he said, "and it was located downstream from their toilet area. They couldn't understand why they should change their path. They told me their ancestors had used the path before them and they used it too because that was the way it had always been done. Meantime they keep on getting sick."

One of the most ludicrous examples I know of was told to me by a shopkeeper in Oaxaca, Mexico—ludicrous to me, not to the shopkeeper. He had decided

47

AUTHORIZATION—BELIEF SYSTEMS

to go into farming, so he bought some land and hired some Indians to work it. One day he told a farm hand to plant peppers in a certain area. Awhile later he went out to check on the work and saw the man planting corn seeds, a naked old crone riding complacently on his shoulders.

"What are you doing?" he asked incredulously.

"I'm planting corn, Senor," said the worker.

"I told you to plant peppers," the owner said angrily.

"Oh, but, Senor, this land has always grown corn," the worker replied. "It would not know how to grow anything else."

The owner took another tack. "What is the old woman doing on your shoulders?" he asked.

"She blesses the corn so that it will be fertile," the worker said patiently. "It's always been done this way."

Soon afterwards the owner sold his acreage and reopened his shop in the city.

I used to scream in frustration whenever I heard the words, "It's always been done this way." Now I only sigh. I've realized how much my own unthinking acceptance of cultural beliefs and parent messages has affected my own life. I've colluded too, conspiring against myself out of ignorance. I've accepted my cultural beliefs until I asked that most valuable of questions, "Why?" A child asks, "Why does the rain fall?" or "Why do I have to wear shoes?" or "Why do I have to kiss grandpa?" If the answer is, "Because," any further questioning is squelched, that child is well on the way to accepting every other unchallenged pronouncement of what has gone before: "Because it's always been that way."

Concepts are not only handed down from one generation to another, but from one century to another. These building blocks of history cause us to create our

48

particular societies. We accumulate our concepts from centuries past, from people before us—not as cold facts or irrelevant dates in our minds, but as beliefs we live by. We are what we are because of the past and because of these beliefs handed to us by people long gone. These messages, communicated to us through the ages, however long ago, have not left us untouched. C. S. Lewis says, "Humanity . . . has the privilege of always moving yet never leaving anything behind. Whatever we have been in some sort we are still."[1]

We trace the foundations of our modern-day philosophy through medieval times, to classical Greek society almost three thousand years ago. From the resurgence of interest in the Greeks and Romans during the Renaissance come many of our present living patterns. We can find historical precedent in the buildings we live in, the education we receive, in science and medicine, in the arts, in language itself. We know of other civilizations as advanced as the Greeks, some of which preceded theirs. But it was the Greeks, and the Romans after them, who communicated their ideas to us most effectively down through the centuries through drama, epic, and treatise. It was the Greeks who provided western man with the opportunity to escalate his ascent to consciousness through the development of logic.

In cultures earlier than the Greek civilization, man used enough reason to function efficiently. We might not call him conscious, however, in the same sense that we are today. That he could even think logically about his existence is a moot point. Julian Jaynes points out in his discussion of the origins of consciousness, "Logic is the science of the justification of conclusions we have reached by natural reasoning. . . . The very reason we need logic at all is because most reasoning is not conscious at all."[2]

1. C. S. Lewis, p. 1.
2. Julian Jaynes, *The Origin of Consciousness in the Breakdown of the Bicameral Mind* (Boston: Houghton Mifflin Co., 1976), p. 41.

49

AUTHORIZATION—BELIEF SYSTEMS

The ascent to consciousness has taken place over the millenia, but we are not fully conscious today by any means. Just how much of our brainpower we use in our thinking processes is still hotly debated. But we have more ability today to use our consciousness, our powers of rationality and of choice, than did men in prehistory. It was through the development of language that man was able to change from a nonthinking, although functioning, human being, into one with a rudimentary ability to make decisions through the use of his rational powers. Language, Jaynes postulates, increases our perception of the world about us, creating new objects through the use of metaphor. He says, "Indeed, language is an organ of perception, not simply a means of communication."[3]

As man's language developed, the ability of his brain to use that language also expanded. He grew able to communicate with other men, and not only about the exigencies of daily life, the practicalities involved in living with a group of heterogeneous individuals in a common territory. He also began to formulate abstract concepts that had little to do with the realities of living. By the time of the classic Greeks, man's brain had developed enough to enable him to contemplate his place in the universe.

Prior to Plato, the goal of Greek aspiration was excellence, or *arete*, a harmony of the whole man in relation to the world about him. Of this time H. D. Kitto says, "The Greek hero tried to combine in himself the virtues which our own heroic age divided between the knight and the churchman."[4] Plato changed that, envisioning man as a disparate variety of parts. He went on a "quest of intelligibility,"[5] teaching that men should seek life's answers through intellectual understanding. Plato formulated the idea that European philosophical tradition (which one scholar has said consists in "a series of footnotes to

3. Ibid., p. 50.

4. H. D. Kitto, *The Greeks* (New York: Penguin Books, 1969), p. 172.

5. Arthur O. Lovejoy, *The Great Chain of Being: A Study of the History of an Idea* (New York: Harper & Row, Pub., 1936), p. 23.

50
AUTHORIZATION—BELIEF SYSTEMS

Plato"[6]) has followed with varying intensity ever since, that there is mind and matter, perfect and imperfect, infinite and finite. There is a perfection that man must strive for but because he is imperfect and finite, man may never truly attain it. He may conceptualize it (though imperfectly) in his mind, but that perfection may never be actualized in his earthly existence. With Plato, man began to divorce his mind from his body, his intellect from his emotions, his ideal from his actuality. The concept of body, mind, and soul, separate and apart from each other, became entrenched in man's thinking. By following Plato's philosophy, man became divided against himself.

Man also became divided against woman. In Plato's philosophy man was important, woman was not. Plato's influential student, Aristotle, continued the line of thought, listing man in his hierarchy first and woman second. Man, not woman, was believed to have the intellect to conceptualize the Perfect, the Good, and the Ideal. So it followed that man, the thinker, was superior to woman, who was not supposed to be able to think.

Woman was supposed to be the keeper of the emotions, whereas man alone was able through his intellect to quest after the highest good. The "chaos of emotion" and the "crude matter of life"[7] were left to woman, while man turned away from a sensory perception of the world in his quest for the Ideal. Not only were women divided against men; because of their differing approach to problems, men were divided against each other, as they still are. Those who use intellectual analysis find it hard to understand those who feel their way through problems emotionally. The opposite of the intellectual approach is used by those who view life through the sensibility of the romantic. Robert M. Pirsig has labeled the two modes classic and romantic:

6. Ibid., p. 24.

7. S. H. Butcher, trans., *Aristotle's Theory of Poetry and Fine Art*, Introduction by John Gassner (New York: Dover Pub., 1951), p. xli.

51

AUTHORIZATION—BELIEF SYSTEMS

*A classical understanding sees the world
primarily as underlying form itself. A romantic
understanding sees it primarily in terms of
immediate appearance. . . . The romantic mode
is primarily inspirational, imaginative, creative,
intuitive. Feelings rather than facts
predominate. . . . The classic mode, by
contrast, proceeds by reason and by laws. . . .
which are themselves underlying forms of
thought and behavior.* [8]

The intellectual (Pirsig's classic) believes that systematical reasoning is the key to an ordered universe. He (or she) may conform totally or partially to Plato's original proposition that one must turn one's back on the senses in order to contemplate life in the abstract, or the Divine. The goal of the intellectual is to achieve an ordered Perfection. He fears and distrusts emotions, habitually controlling his own and others' feelings. Because any emotions are uncomfortable, even incomprehensible, to the intellectual, he will avoid feeling them however possible. Because of his constant intellectualizing, he tends to judge other people rather than empathize. He (or she) cannot comprehend why not everyone is able to control their feelings, and regards anyone who exhibits emotions openly as weak, inferior, or even crazy.

The romantic concentrates on a sensory approach to life. Logic is suspect, and the strictly rational life becomes both a bore and a trap. No one is more romantic than the perpetual hobo, swinging away into the sunset on the caboose of an endless train. The romantic, like the flower child of the sixties, does what he feels like doing, rather than what he (or she) thinks he should.

In his discussion of innocence, Rollo May describes the romantic attitude of the younger generation: "Technology consists of a complex system of tools that ought

8. Robert M. Pirsig, *Zen and the Art of Motorcycle Maintenance: An Inquiry into Values* (New York: Bantam Books, 1974), pp. 66–67.

52

AUTHORIZATION—BELIEF SYSTEMS

to extend human consciousness. . . . But in our day—so the younger generation feels—technology does just the opposite; it shrinks, dries up, depersonalizes human existence."[9] So the romantic seeks to personalize human existence, to concentrate on the details of life, to explore life through the senses, and to respond with feelings to the here and now. The romantic includes those who seek answers through mysticism and the occult as well as those who believe that through faith the answers will be handed to them. The romantic might also be one who rigidly clings to his or her faith and refuses to allow any hint of logic to weaken or repudiate that dogma.

These two approaches have created an abyss in philosophy which has not yet been bridged. In discussing the two modes, Friedrich Heer uses the examples of Peter Abelard and Bernard of Clairvaux, two twelfth-century men who represented on the one hand reason, and on the other faith:

> *The controversy between these two men revealed an abyss: . . . European thought from this time onwards cannot be understood without taking note of these dialectical efforts to reconcile or separate faith and knowledge, reasons of the heart and rational understanding; the two have finally become so diametrically opposed that Christian believers regard scientists as professional unbelievers.*[10]

The two approaches are not entirely antithetical to each other. Ideally one would be able to solve problems logically, using rational powers of intellect, *and* to employ, at other times, a sensory approach to life. More often, however, we get stuck in one mode and assume that philosophical bent to the exclusion of

9. Rollo May, *Power and Innocence: A Search for the Sources of Violence* (New York: Dell Pub. Co., 1972), p. 61.

10. Heer, p. 107.

AUTHORIZATION—BELIEF SYSTEMS

the other. Fixed firmly in our beliefs, we then disparage those who do not have the same ways of thinking or the same perception that we do. We may become rigidly intolerant as romantics, even as those who predominately use intellect as their avenue of understanding. The romantic may regard the intellectual as a dud, a drudge, and a bore, one who cannot possibly appreciate the nuances of feelings, while to an intellectual a romantic might appear frivolous, flippant, and empty-headed.

Another facet of romanticism apropos to the context of this book is that which was artificially created in the twelfth century apart from the emerging romanticism of the eleventh. To the increased interest in feelings, evidenced by the growing popularity of the poetry and music of the troubadours, Eleanor of Aquitaine added her own philosophy and set of rules. By so doing she inverted the time-honored positions of men and women and set in motion forces we still contend with today.

Eleanor's romantic also sought to personalize human existence, to emphasize feelings rather than the intellect. But this romantic included in her (or his) philosophy the inflexible belief that woman should be designated a position above man in the hierarchy of importance, with love of her held to be the highest good, even the pathway to salvation. This romantic developed a rigid set of precepts about women and men, and created inviolable rules of behavior. This romantic, born of necessity and inspiring millions throughout the centuries, provides us today with the hoax of romance.

Since the twelfth century two camps have been established. One is that of men, supposedly intellectual, nonfeeling, and tough. The other is that of women and men of feeling, supposedly emotional, weak, and nonthinking. The battle lines have been clearly drawn. According to the Greek philosophers, the Christian church, and societal tradition, man was mind; woman was emotion. As mind and body were believed to be separate and distinct entities, so were men and women. Men gave orders, fought battles, and attended to busi-

AUTHORIZATION—BELIEF SYSTEMS

ness. Women were subjugated to the home, there to preside over feelings. With Eleanor, these beliefs were solidified into dogma. From that time on, women were regarded as arbiters in the area of personal relationships. The battle of the sexes has indeed been just that, with women assigned the weapons of feeling and men those of thought, each trying unsuccessfully to convince the other of the superiority of their respective armaments.

The hoax of all this is that the romanticism we know, which stems from the courtly love system of the twelfth century, is a belief system comprised of rules and arbitrary regulations—*shoulds*. The romantic, man or woman, is as stuck in his or her belief system as is the nonfeeling intellectual or that kind of romantic who rigidly adheres to a faith. The romantic is not in contact with feelings, other than the ones approved by an inherited code, any more than is the intellectual. The rules set forth by the romantic code do more than dictate behavior; they actually prevent a person from having free access to feelings. It follows then, that the romantic, like most intellectuals, uses a pattern of learned concepts that have been integrated into an overall belief system and *not* feelings to function in life situations.

The code of romance stipulates that women are more emotional than men. Even this is more a conventional belief than fact. The reason men experience less emotionality than women in our culture is mainly because they have been propagandized by the romantic code to believe they should not feel certain emotions. Nor are women given permission to express, or feel, certain other emotions. Women have been role-trained to repress anger, aggressiveness, feelings of competiveness, elation, even excitement. Having been given permission by society to be emotional human beings up to a point, however, women have also been taught to believe that they should not, even cannot, use their intellectual powers. Women believe so strongly that they cannot think, many *will* not. I know about this belief from my own experience. It took me thirty-five years to realize that the head on my shoulders could do more than grow hair. Cultural messages corroborate the belief. When society gives women messages that their nonthinking behavior is expected and acceptable (for example, the dumb-blonde joke), they get further confirmation that their societal role is appropriate, and they continue to act the part.

Men have been taught to be far more controlled than women—stronger, tougher, more rigid. They have been permitted to express the more aggressive feelings, but they've been role-trained to repress their pain, fear, tenderness, helplessness, and any sign of "weakness," which is often equated with any of the preceding feelings. I know that men have about as much potential as women to experience all of their feelings; in believing that they should not, however, men (and controlled women) have learned to bury their feelings inside themselves. Continually repressing their feelings as a matter of habit, they will eventually succeed in not being able to feel at all. So when men or women say, "I don't know what I'm feeling," they may not be lying. They may truly not know what their feelings are at that moment; they may not realize they *can* feel! The same could be said of women and their powers of rational thinking!

I have enormous respect for the power that we human beings have to create or destroy ourselves, to win or lose, succeed or fail, live or die. We can do almost anything we set out to do, given the appropriate attitude. True, our core feelings may prevent us from willing our way to success or contentment—feelings that may be left over from childhood experiences of trauma, neglect or overprotection. I respect even that ability with which we hold down these feelings; we repress ourselves in order to survive. Our only way of surviving a traumatic childhood may have been to forget it entirely, to block out early memories and the resultant, sometimes excrutiating, pain of feeling. We can repress feelings by telling ourselves consciously that we shouldn't feel that, or that we can't feel it. We can also block painful memories unconsciously by the process of gating. Arthur Janov explains:

56

AUTHORIZATION—BELIEF SYSTEMS

> *. . . too much feeling becomes transmuted into its*
> *opposite—no feeling. . . . A person could take one*
> *reprimand or one humiliation, but too many of*
> *those cause him to split away from his feeling self.*
> *A psychologically "dead" person is not one with*
> *few feelings but rather someone with great*
> *amounts of repressed feeling.* [11]

He summarizes this, saying, ". . . too much intensive input means pain, the gate then shuts off more input, and the person is driven to avoid the situation."[12]

Whether our repression of feelings stems from the unconscious gating process, or from consciously telling ourselves that we shouldn't feel, the result is the same—no feelings. We may not necessarily have had a traumatic childhood, yet may suffer from "psychological deadness" just the same. Our parents may have been normal (whatever that is), loving parents, yet if they gave us continual messages on repressing our feelings—messages approved and long accepted by our society—that's just what we did. I hear these messages all the time. Once, in a movie theatre, I heard a mother and father talking to their son:

CHILD
"Can I have some popcorn now?"

MOTHER
"No, not yet. You can't be hungry already, you just ate."

CHILD
"But I'm hungry for popcorn."

11. Arthur Janov, *The Anatomy of Mental Illness: The Scientific Basis of Primal Therapy* (New York: Berkley Pub. Corp., 1971), p. 50.
12. Ibid.

57

AUTHORIZATION—BELIEF SYSTEMS

FATHER

"No, you're not. You should have eaten your lunch; then you wouldn't be hungry. Say, your teacher told me about your not eating lunch last week at school? You'll never grow up big and strong if you don't eat right."

CHILD

"I don't like their lunches; they taste yukky."

MOTHER

"Don't say that. They fix good lunches for you at school. I should know; I read their menus all the time. You should be grateful for what you get."

CHILD

"I hate them."

FATHER

"Shame on you. If you say that again I'm going to wash your mouth out with soap." (Child starts to cry.) "Now don't cry. Stop that! Everybody's looking at us. Don't be a big sissy. If you keep that up I'll give you something to cry about." (Child chokes back sobs.)

MOTHER

"That's my brave boy. You're a big boy; you don't need to cry like a baby. Now be good; sit still and watch the movie."

Exaggerated, you say? Not at all. I hear messages similar to this raining down on the heads of children every day. In this instance I didn't have to turn around to picture the big people dwarfing the child between them, instilling their messages into his head for years to come: "Don't feel your feelings," "Don't think your thoughts," "We know better than you because we're bigger," all of which add up to, "Don't be who you are; be who and what we tell you to be!"

Since we fear being abandoned

58

as children if we don't have our parents' acceptance, we all adapt in some way to their messages. We conform to the image they draw up for us, or we rebel against it, still using that image as a basis for our rebellion. Either way, we seek their approval. So if our parents tell us to repress our feelings (Don't cry. . . . You're a big boy. . . . Now be good. . . . or tell us to think only what they want us to think (Shame on you. . . . You should be grateful. . . . If you say that again I'm going to. . . .), that's probably what we'll do.

Once grooved in our brains the messages are there for life—unless we decide, in the process of our growth, to turn them off. The messages can be overt, loud and verbal, or nonverbal, subtle and hard to decipher. Whatever their form, they can be discovered and rooted out like the noxious weeds they are. Some of mine that I've discovered are: "You're stupid," against which I rebelled by getting a Ph.d.; "Act your age," which I conformed to by acting very grown-up, even as a child; "You're different," which I accepted by feeling that I didn't belong anywhere.

The most debilitating message of all, underlying all the rest, is: "You're not good enough," or "You're bad" (which amounts to the same thing). This message, a core concept in our system of romance, is interwoven into our entire cultural way of thinking. Setting up a lifelong internal battle, that message ensures that we either desperately try to prove how good we are, or conform to it by proving that we are indeed bad. Any sense of confidence and inner security we were born with is eroded away from within by our continual vacillation between the two extremes.

These pervasive messages on goodness, like black clouds, hover over many of us in the form of negativism. I can usually find such a message behind my doubts. For example, if I say to myself, "I doubt I can do that," I can find a message in my head *preceding the doubt* which tells me, "You're not good enough to do that." I'm also aware that when I doubt someone else I'm expressing a critical message about that per-

59

son. I'm not accepting him or her, nor am I giving that person permission to exist in the here and now. I'm setting up a standard of goodness for that person, an expectation, and I'm attempting to control.

I discovered how subtly controlling doubts can be one day when a woman said to me, "I admire you so much for doing all you've done and raising your baby at the same time. I could never have done that." I felt uncomfortable with her words, but couldn't understand why. After I thought about it I realized that I was feeling controlled. Why should I have felt controlled, I wondered, when she had expressed her own doubt? Wasn't that her problem? I answered myself, not entirely. When she had verbalized her self-doubt, I felt a subtle hook. At first I'd felt tempted to tell her that of course she could do all the things I'd done if she'd wanted to. But I've learned through hard experience to shut my mouth tight when I feel an urge to rescue someone, and in this case I did. Then I had a momentary urge to agree with her and say, yes, she was right; I knew all along she was the type who could do nothing at all. I fought this urge successfully too, telling her that I felt uncomfortable with her words instead. I realized that I hadn't felt complimented at all by what she had said to me. I felt used. She was setting me up to reassure herself about how good she was, and how well she could have performed if she had wanted to. She sought my approval because she couldn't accept herself.

The opposite of doubt is acceptance, whether of oneself or another person. If I accept you, I give you permission to be yourself; I have no need to control you. I don't need to either criticize you or rescue you. I can respond to you in the present and expose my own vulnerability to you. When I accept myself I do the same. I accept my "bad" feelings along with the "good" ones, my craziness, my hatefulness, my manipulations. I give myself permission to exist without worrying about my basic goodness. I allow myself to feel vulnerable without trying to be strong, to feel helpless without trying to be brave, to feel scared without covering it up with anger. I know I don't have to act out those painful feelings, so I can safely allow myself to

60

experience them without having to act them out; I know they won't last forever. If I don't know exactly what they mean, sooner or later I'll figure out what my feelings are about and what they are telling me about my external situation. My feelings, whatever they are, validate my inside self and my outside world. Without such validation I'm stuck with my self-doubt, and I cut myself off from my feelings. Doubts, suspicions, cynicism, distrust, defeatism, belittlement, negativism—all these are expressions of the biased standards we've been taught to live our lives by—and all these contribute to our slow (or sometimes fast) destruction by deadening our inner selves. All of these are, and always have been, part of our romantic training.

Scientists are now discovering that there is a difference between our thinking and our feeling processes inherent in the very structure of the brain. In the explosion of experiments within the last three decades, they have explored and probed the brain in order to understand how this little understood organ of ours works. They've found that we actually have two brains, which they call split-brain, or bicameral (twin-chambered). The right side of the brain is the older in evolutionary terms and is nonverbal, more intuitive, artistic, and oriented toward spatial concepts; the left hemisphere is verbal and analytical, logical and talented in such subjects as mathematics and verbal skills. I find it tempting to equate the romantic (the feeling person) with right-brain activity and the intellectual (the thinking person) with left-brain activity, and there is a certain amount of evidence to support this concept. Right-brain predominance does seem to be what we term "feminine," while the left brain seems to specialize in the so-called "masculine" traits. The two hemispheres communicate with each other over a common bridge called the corpus callosum, but each seems to have its specific tasks. One author explains:

If you reach into your pocket with your left hand and, without peeking, make a list with your right hand of what you've found, your brain faces a

61

AUTHORIZATION—BELIEF SYSTEMS

*complex communication task. The information
from your left hand is relayed first to your brain's
right hemisphere (the right hemisphere serves the
left side of the body, and vice versa). But since
vocabulary and writing skills are specialized in
the left hemisphere for most people, the
information must be transferred there before you
can assign names to what you have found and
write them down.* [13]

You can understand the difference in your own split-brain by
doing the following exercise. If you have learned to rigidly control your feelings, you may experience nothing during this exercise. But if you are able to turn off your thinking process you may
be able to feel a difference in the two sides of your body, understanding from that the difference in your brain itself.

Sit in a comfortable position
with your hands separated. Close your eyes to block out the
distractions of your environment. Now imagine that you go into
your right hand and become that hand. Describe to yourself in
detail what you feel as your right hand. Let your imagination go;
you don't need to be realistic. What do you feel as right hand?
Stay with this for a minute or so.

Now go into your left hand. Im-
agine that you become your left hand; describe to yourself how
you feel as your left hand, and how you differ from the right hand.
Stay with this experience for a couple of minutes.

Go back into your right hand
now, and again become right hand. Imagine some movement you
might like to make as the right hand and toward whom or what
you would like to make that movement. What would you do if you
were the right hand? Stay with this for a moment.

Now go into your left hand. Im-
agine a movement you might like to make as the left hand and

13. Monte S. Buchsbaum, "Tuning in on Hemispheric Dialogue," *Psychology Today*
(January 1979), p. 100.

62

AUTHORIZATION—BELIEF SYSTEMS

whom or what you would do that to. Stay with this until you're finished. Then open your eyes. Do this exercise before reading further.

I've found, in doing this exercise with people in my classes, that about 80% of right-handed people have feelings of strength, direction, ability, aggression (the more "masculine" traits) in the right hand. Often the right hands feel bigger, more powerful, abler. If the person has repressed anger, it's likely to show up in the right hand, or on the right side of the body. Many people have expressed wanting to hit, slap, or even stab someone when movement in the right hand is suggested. Some people I've worked with have repressed so much anger they've actually crippled themselves. One woman could not write with that hand when she began therapy because of what she thought was arthritis. In this exercise she was amazed to discover that she felt like stabbing her mother with a huge knife. She had never, she said, realized she was even angry at her mother. After she had expressed that previously unacknowledged rage her "arthritis" disappeared and she could use her right hand to write with for the first time in years. Other people I've worked with have held in such anger they've developed bursitis, or so much numbness in their right arm they could barely move it.

People have expressed different feelings about their left hands, saying that hand feels lighter, more delicate, weaker, even helpless (the more "feminine" feelings). Some have said it feels passive, inert, or numb in comparison with the right. The left hand often has feelings of tenderness or prettiness; women are often aware of their polished nails or the wedding rings on their ring fingers. Many people have felt that their left hands wanted to caress a loved one, hold someone, or stroke a pet. Some have expressed wanting to make light, airy movements, such as playing a piano or painting an abstract.

AUTHORIZATION—BELIEF SYSTEMS

Although the great majority of people experience similar feelings in right and left hands (men and women alike), true left-handers may feel the opposite of what others feel because of a difference in brain structure. Since feelings change from day to day, each person may experience different feelings in either hand, depending on what he or she is feeling at the time. Generally, however, and with a majority of people, the feelings that I've listed are the ones that are expressed time and again.

Although I've found no significant difference between men's and women's feelings in this exercise, studies have indicated that women's brains generally have more lateralization than men's. Verbal and spatial abilities are more likely duplicated on both sides of a woman's brain, while a right-handed man is more likely to have his speech center on the left with spatial skills on the right. One author says:

> *Because women's hemispheres may be less specialized for spatial and linguistic functions, it may be easier for them to perform tasks which combine the two in a single activity, such as reading or understanding a person's behavior from his or her facial expression, body language, and words. Men's brains . . . may make it easier for them to keep separate cognitively different activities done simultaneously, such as running a drill press while talking.*[14]

Karl Pribram and Diane McGuinness, Stanford neuropsychologists and researchers on sex difference in brain activity, have characterized man as a " 'manipulative animal' who tends to express himself in actions, while woman is a 'communicative animal,' who prefers to receive, remember, and transmit signs

14. Daniel Goleman, "Special Abilities of the Sexes: Do They Begin in the Brain?" *Psychology Today* (November 1978), p. 51.

64

AUTHORIZATION—BELIEF SYSTEMS

and symbols to others."[15] Their conclusion is that, in general, the greater exploratory behavior evidenced by men "suggests a kind of curiosity that leads to success in problem-solving tasks that require manipulation," whereas women, in general, show more sensitivity to touch and sounds and their "greater interest in people also shows up in better empathy."[16]

Scientists are careful to include the words "in general" in any discussion of differences between the sexes, for certainly there is a wide range of differences and varying degrees of mental abilities. Even if the studies showing evidence of differences due to sex are correct, however, I believe that we have a far greater discrepancy between sexual roles, due to our cultural attitudes and our belief system. Our social mores provide men with one role, women with another, and that, I am convinced, creates more of an immediate problem than the degrees of difference in our brain structures. To explore our social mores from a slightly different point of view, consider the concept of authorization.

In his hypothesis on the history of consciousness, which he correlates with brain structure, Julian Jaynes postulates that preclassic men obeyed voices of authorization in order to function within their civilizations. These voices, he theorizes, were spoken first by actual kings and priests and were heard thereafter by ordinary men in their minds. It was as if the actual words or general directions were imprinted on their brains. Men didn't have to decide which course of action to take with this internal kind of programming available to them. The voices in their heads would tell them what to do, just as if their kings or gods had spoken.

These bicameral, or preclassic men heard their voices on the right, or nondominant side of the brain. Through the development of language the left, or dominant, side of the brain began to take precedence. As the left side

15. Ibid., p. 56.
16. Ibid., p. 59.

65

AUTHORIZATION—BELIEF SYSTEMS

of the brain became more highly active, Jaynes postulates, the voices of the gods began gradually to recede. Man began to lose his directives, which he had previously obeyed without question. The more authoritative voices dimmed, the greater need he had to use his developing powers of rationality. With the evolution of consciousness, man developed, albeit agonizingly, his powers of choice.

Jaynes further theorizes that some modern men, called schizophrenics, relapse into their bicameral minds with auditory hallucinations, and that this type of slip is available to the rest of us. He says, "Most of us spontaneously slip back into something approaching the actual bicameral mind at some part of our lives. For some of us, it is only a few episodes of thought deprivation or an instance or two of hearing voices."[17]

I believe hearing voices is a much more common phenomenon than Jaynes indicates, an all too frequent occurrence for all of us. Like Jaynes, I believe we are not yet fully conscious, that we still have access to the vestiges of our bicameral minds. But I would call his "voices of authorization" the voices of parents in our minds. In describing the experiences of schizophrenics, Jaynes states that some patients are not sure ". . . whether they are actually hearing the voices or whether they are only compelled to think them, like 'audible thoughts,' or 'soundless voices,' or 'hallucinations of meanings'."[18] He also says that for some patients, the voices call from one side or the other, from the rear, from above and below, and that ". . . very often the voices criticize a patient's thoughts and actions."[19]

I find nothing novel in this. Dozens of clients have told me about hearing their parents' voices criticizing them, seeming to come from one side of their body or

17. Jaynes, p. 404.
18. Ibid., p. 90.
19. Ibid., pp. 89–90.

66

the other. I have had similar experiences myself. I used to hear the voice of my own parent coming down on me from above my right shoulder. "Get off my back," I would say when the voice got too strident, if it would not, if the "me" part would continue to rant at the "I" of me, I would end up with an aching neck and stiff back. Other people have described hearing the voice of a parent coming from the top of their heads, from their temples, or from behind them. Using the terms of Transactional Analysis, I call these voices, "Parent tapes," or tape recordings in our minds of the voices of the parents or parent figures we remember from childhood.

Sam Keen, who interviewed Julian Jaynes, also believes that our "voices" are still with us, saying:

> *I wonder if we have really left the bicameral mind*
> *so far behind. Don't most people still hear voices?*
> *Isn't consciousness a theater filled with inner*
> *dialogue? And what is conscience but the*
> *introjected voices of the parents? And what are*
> *guilt and shame except the fear of disobeying*
> *voices we once heard? And therapy? The cure is to*
> *learn to hear the silent voices, to recover the*
> *unconscious admonitions of the super-ego–the*
> *gods of our childhood.* [20]

These still present and all too strident Parent tapes give us the authorization to act as we do in the form of *shoulds* or *should nots*. If we've adapted to our parental expectations we believe our shoulds are right. If we've rebelled against them we believe our shoulds are wrong, but we may spend the rest of our lives struggling against them. Either way we'll suffer from doubts and defeatism, destroying our volition with negative criticism in our minds. We may have had enough permissions in childhood to be

20. Sam Keen, "The Lost Voices of the Gods: Reflections on the Dawn of Consciousness," *Psychology Today* (November 1977), p. 142.

67
AUTHORIZATION—BELIEF SYSTEMS

able to ignore such messages, or we may have matured enough to realize we can survive without listening to them any more; if so, we are fortunate, indeed. If we do listen, our parent messages—as well as messages from our society—give us authorization for our behavior, just as Jaynes's bicameral men received authorization from their gods and kings. The difference between us and those ancient men is that we have more rationality and ability to choose.

We have more ability to grow and change, to learn to hear those silent voices, "the gods of our childhood." Our growth involves unblocking memories and ungating against pain. We may fight growth because in unblocking these painful memories we sometimes encounter pain in a very physical sense. But as individuals must, even painfully, discard repression in their quest for awareness, so too must the race. Collectively, evolution seems to be toward consciousness. We must, in order to become consciously aware, confront the history of our dogmatism. We can then decide to stop listening exclusively to our voices of authorization, although perhaps one can never entirely silence those voices in times of stress.

I've found that I can successfully turn off my negative, critical Parent tapes most of the time except when I'm overtired, sick, pressured, or undergoing some life stress. Then the voice of authorization in my mind scourges me unceasingly: I can never do anything right; I'm too stupid to know better; I should grow up and quit feeling sorry for myself; I don't count. Understanding how my own "loud thoughts" (as some of my class members have described their voices) are activated by stress, I read with interest Jaynes's theory on what caused the "guidances of the gods in antiquity," *and* the hallucinations of modern-day schizophrenics. He says, "It has now been clearly established that decision-making (and I would like to remove every trace of conscious connotation from the word 'decision') is precisely what stress is."[21]

21. Jaynes, p. 93.

68

When the ancients needed to make decisions they listened to their voices and obeyed. As we become more conscious and aware of our choices, those inner directives recede, leaving us free to choose but still accountable for our actions. If we decide to act contrary to our inner voices, we may suffer their chastisement. If I oppose my Parent tapes by trying something unfamiliar, for example, the old voices may start up: You're going to fail. Afterward they keep on: You did that wrong; you can't do anything right; you should have known better. With such strident opposition to my attempts, I have at times decided not to try at all. It has seemed easier to allow my tapes to dictate. But is it? As I pointed out in *Act Yourself*, our emotions are greatly influenced by our beliefs. If we act according to our shoulds continually, allowing them to be in full charge of our lives, we are not in touch with the real world. We may suffer more when life changes occur than one who accepts reality for what it is.

Any change in life situations causes stress when decisions must be made: graduation, marriage, childbirth, loss of job, divorce, death of spouse, retirement, moving. Whether we move up the ladder of success or down, we encounter stress. We may try to avoid making a decision but find ourselves taking a certain course, because if we don't it's a decision of sorts anyway. We're caught between obeying our inner voices or suffering the results of our rebellion. If we obey, we may find stress because our beliefs render us out of touch with reality; if we rebel, we suffer the disapproval of our mental voices.

Changing our beliefs causes stress as well. How comforting it is to cling to archaic belief patterns. Although they may cause misery, they're at least known. Anything new, on the contrary, is threatening because of its unfamiliarity. So deciding that one's beliefs are invalid and that changes need to be made causes pain, perhaps even more pain than putting up with a miserable marriage, a life-threatening habit, or an incapacitating self-image. For that

69

reason, most of us need to be forced to change by our own frustration or an unrelenting other person. Change hurts; stagnating hurts. It's like that sign on the wall of a psychiatrist's office: "Either way, it hurts!"

Of course we can refuse to change by blaming somebody else. I've labeled anger based on shoulds "phony," because it's a reaction to one's own beliefs rather than a straight, gut-level response to whatever is happening in the present. Another word might be "safer." It's safer to blame somebody else; then the angry one won't have to admit being in the wrong, or change in any way. Anger based on beliefs is a strong and righteous position—if I can convince you that you're at fault I won't jeopardize my own security. I won't have to feel vulnerable. I can intellectualize my grievances against you—accuse, rationalize, complain, and defend. I won't risk feeling my own internal pain. And I won't have to suffer the stress of change by challenging my own belief system.

Who wants to get beyond blaming someone else, behind the secure coverup of anger to experience one's own hurt, pain, and fear? It's no fun to find a bellyfull of sadness, loneliness, and apprehension. And who wants to challenge one's beliefs? That's not so great either—to find that the beliefs one has built a life around are wrong, and years have been wasted because of those fallacies. But we *can* do it, and survive. We can risk confronting our entire belief system, risk changing our ways of relating to others in light of our new awareness. We can confront our romantic ideal—even if it hurts!

Romance—our authorization to relate to one another as we do, our shoulds that tell us to behave only in societally approved ways. We need to challenge that authorization, to rip it apart, leaving only those parts that we want to keep in awareness and discarding the rest as garbage. I'm with J. W. Krutch, who says, "The romantic ideal of a world well lost for love and the classic ideal of austere dignity seem equally ridiculous, equally meaningless when referred, not to the

70

temper of the past, but to the temper of the present."[22] I'm for responsiveness in relationships, not shoulds. And I'm for giving men and women equal permission to think and to feel, not as intellectuals or romantics but as individuals.

We've believed, according to our romantic code, that we *should* find love through marriage, that life *should* bring us happiness. When people don't behave as we expect they should we suffer. When our children don't act as we believe they should we resent them. When our lovers disappoint us, we despair. But why do we search all our lives for love and happiness? Why do we castigate ourselves and others when we don't find what we expect? Why *should* we idealize relationships and people at all, and what happens to us when we do? A brief look at the history of romance will provide us answers and help us understand how concepts developed by a culture eight centuries ago still affect our society of today. An examination of our origins will help us realize how we still use, and are used by, the authorization provided by romance.

22. Joseph Wood Krutch, *A Krutch Omnibus* (New York: William Morrow & Co., 1970), p. 13.

71

AUTHORIZATION—BELIEF SYSTEMS

4. THE HISTORY OF ROMANCE

ORIGINS OF THE ROMANTIC CODE IN TWELFTH-CENTURY FRANCE.

For centuries after the fall of Rome, Europe suffered through barbarian invasions, famine, poverty, and disease. With feudalism, political and economic order began to be restored. As the threat of war in Europe diminished and the economy stabilized, feudal lords and their subjects gained in wealth. Conditions were such, as the twelfth century approached, that men could once more concern themselves with pleasures and matters of the mind.

The women of the feudal aristocracy attained a status such as women had rarely before reached, evidenced by the variety in their dress, their accomplishments, travels, and activities. They went to festivals and fairs, rarely chaperoned, on pilgrimages, and even on the crusades as a part of their husbands' retinues. Despite the civil laws and theological doctrine of the time stressing woman's innate inferiority, many medieval women ruled not only their men but their kingdoms as well.

Although clerics were the acknowledged superiors in arts and letters, women were more likely the ones to receive education in refinement while their husbands labored in the marketplace or fought on the battleground. But average men were becoming better educated, too. The general mood of the twelfth century populace was an increasing interest in the written word, poetry, and song. A new literature began to evolve which showed a different emphasis than the mere recounting of well-known tales. The tendency of the new literature was toward introspection and awareness of man as an individual. In some respects the man of about A.D. 1200 resembled his ancestors; he had the same spirit of violence, abrupt changes of mood, and preoccupation with the supernatural, but in two ways he differed profoundly from his predecessor. "He was better educated. He was more self-conscious."[1]

1. Marc Bloch, *Feudal Society: The Growth of Ties of Dependence* trans. L. A. Manyon, (Chicago: University of Chicago Press, 1961), p. 106.

75

THE HISTORY OF ROMANCE

Troubadours sang their novel renditions of older epics and lyrics throughout Europe, no longer focusing on men's deeds but attempting to analyze their heroes' feelings. For a century, from about 1150 to 1250, the troubadours taught manners to their aristocratic hosts along with the songs, and instilled in them refinement. Their influence gave the aristocracy a taste for formal elegance and the game of wit. More important, "they evolved the courtly concept of love by applying their code of chivalrous conduct . . . to the relations between men and women."[2]

A favorite subject of their epic poems was the life of King Arthur. In their attempts to establish a legitimate history, several chroniclers had created a fantasy that gradually took on an aura of reality in the minds of the people. Arthur, the traditionally Celtic king, was the epitome of the old British kings who banded their people together against foreign invaders before the Norman Conquest in 1066. The collection of stories about Arthur, Percival, Lancelot, and the Grail was welcomed by people throughout Western Europe.

Along with increased interest in education and the new romances was a general resurgence of religion. A growing reverence for the Virgin Mary was especially noticeable. "The cult of the Virgin is the most characteristic flower of medieval religion,"[3] and was inextricably bound up with the institution of chivalry. As chivalry grew and became accepted as a cultural institution, so too did worship of the Virgin. Cathedrals were built in her honor, pilgrimages were made to her shrines, and, in churches not wholly hers, chapels were dedicated in her name. She was already supreme by the eleventh century and remained so until the end of the Middle Ages.

The widespread worship of the Virgin Mary was particularly influential in increasing the status

2. Heer, p. 177.

3. Eileen Power, "The position of Women" in *The Legacy of the Middle Ages*, ed. G. C. Crump and E. F. Jacob (London: Oxford University Press, 1927), pp. 404–5.

76

of women. As reverence for Our Lady in heaven spread, so too did adoration for the lady on earth. "The cult of the lady was the mundane counterpart of the cult of the Virgin and it was the invention of the medieval aristocracy. In chivalry the romantic worship of a woman was as necessary a quality of the perfect knight as was the worship of God."[4] This incongruity in viewing women on the part of both the Church and the aristocracy apparently bothered no one. That woman was viewed as basically flawed in her intelligence, and tainted by Eve's original act of rebellion toward God, did not prevent her from being worshiped as the earthly representation of the Virgin in heaven.

The laws of the Church and those of feudalism were opposed to each other and sometimes clashed. The clergy often found themselves in conflict with laymen. Whereas the clery would have been content to have their flocks worship the Virgin in heaven, men preferred women on earth. Certainly worship of the Virgin helped to moderate the barbarism of the early knights, but living women helped even more.

The Church did give women a status that civil law did not. Basically, the doctrine of the Church was founded on the same belief as civil law, that man was woman's superior, not only in physique and status but in brainpower as well, and that woman had been placed on the earth to serve man. But the Church went beyond civil law in its doctrine; it enforced monogamy, insisted upon a single standard of morals for both sexes, and defended woman's right to the inheritance of property.

Into this twelfth-century renaissance—a time of awakening, self-awareness, prosperity, and increasingly liberalized treatment of women as well as men—came one who would shift the philosophy of the time ever so slightly, and, in so doing, change western European concepts for centuries. Perhaps at no other time than that particular

4. Power, p. 405.

century could she have been as effective, for she was granted stature by her aristocratic birth, privilege by the new status of women, power by her inherited lands, and position by marriage to royalty. Eleanor of Aquitaine would use the concepts developed by her male contemporaries in a new way. She would place woman next to God, in the seat of judgment over man's spirit if not his soul.

We cannot consider the development of the courtly love tradition without understanding Eleanor and her life, for the politics of her time, her philosophy, and the events of her life were intertwined with the formation of that code of manners we know as romance. Morton Hunt says, "It was her fortune to . . . bring courtly love from Provence to the royal courts of both France and England and help it grow from a literary fad into a seriously practiced way of life."[5]

Eleanor was born in about 1122 in Provence, in the south of France. She was the granddaughter of William IX, count of Poiters and duke of Aquitaine. William, a writer of song and verse, created the first of the new-style love lyrics, and manners to match. He was the first troubadour whose work has come down to us. Because of him and the immediate acceptance of his poetry among his contemporaries, historians generally concede that romance began in eleventh-century Provence. Despite the Church's disapproval of his obscene poetry, echoing Ovid and moorish Spain, William's style of flattering ladyloves through delicate verse spread rapidly throughout France and, later, Europe.

Eleanor inherited her grandfather's temperament, his passionate love of life, and his predilection for poetry, along with his immense domains. At that time Aquitaine stretched from the Loire river in France to the Pyrenees in Spain, from the Central mountains of the Auvergne

5. Hunt, p. 152.

78

to the Atlantic ocean, with Provence as its core. Provence had been shaped by influences far different from those of northern France and the rest of Europe. Greece, Spain, and the Near East had left their marks. So had the religious ideas of Gnosticism and the Orient. Northern France, with its more stringent religious atmosphere, regarded Provence with suspicion, fear, and even hatred because of its emphasis on freedom of the spirit, which manifested itself in poetry, enjoyment, and the arts of love.

The uneasiness of the northern French toward those in the south still persists. When I visited France fifteen years ago I read about "sultry" Languedoc, a region of passion, poetry, illicit love, and languid beauties. (I wonder now if "languid," from a northern French point of view, equates Languedoc with laziness.) Traveling through Provence, I kept my eyes open for this ubiquitous passion, but it remained hidden. Frankly, the south of France seemed very much like the north, except that it was warmer and less tamed through agriculture. The inhabitants seemed friendlier than the ones from the industrial northern cities, but the people I met didn't offer me any illicit love. No one proposed to educate me in the ways of love, as had a Parisian. I wasn't followed to my hotel, as in Rome; patted on my posterior, as in Milan; or pinched in approximately the same spot, as in Venice. Now I realize that the fame of Provence is a leftover, along with romance itself, from the time of Eleanor eight centuries ago. Reputations die hard.

Eleanor had quite a reputation herself. She was not unique among medieval women of her time in her travels, education and accomplishments. But because of her inheritance, intelligence, and good looks she was singular in her magnetic appeal.

Her passionate approach to life, a combination of inherited temperament and her upbringing in Aquitaine, made her life tempestuous. At fifteen years of age, the richest heiress in western Christendom, she was married to

79

Louis VII of France, a quiet, pious man. In Paris, Eleanor found a life far more rigid in its religious traditions than the one she had known in Provence. Eleanor was never one to accept convention. She accompanied her husband on the Second Crusade and, according to rumor, had an affair with her uncle, Raymond, prince of Antioch. Eleanor wanted to remain in Antioch, but Louis had her seized in the middle of the night and forced her to return with him to France. From that time on clergymen castigated Eleanor, but her vassels and contemporaries loved her all the more. Her reputation increased as she grew older, because of her many rumored love affairs.

Her relationship with Louis grew worse when Eleanor, unable to conceive for many years, gave birth to two daughters in a row instead of a male heir. By this time Eleanor was thoroughly tired of Louis. Still a desirable match at thirty because of her personal attributes and her vast inheritance, she looked for another husband. She found him in Henry II of England, almost twelve years her junior. Divorcing Louis, she married Henry and went with him to Angers. There she recreated a court of music, poetry, and aristocratic manners as she remembered it from her native land.

During the next fourteen years Eleanor bore Henry eight children, two of whom later became kings of England. But her relationship with Henry deteriorated as well. Like many medieval lords, Henry had a roving eye. No household maid was safe from him, and his vassals knew enough to keep their women out of his way. Eleanor was not particularly upset by his actions; she knew about love affairs. But Henry developed a relationship with a woman named Rosamund Clifford which both persisted and became public knowledge. Henry's relationship with "the fair Rosamund," as she was dubbed, was not just another affair; it was serious. It may well have been one of the most costly affairs in history. Eleanor was hurt and angry at Rosamund's replacing her in Henry's affections. She had toler-

THE HISTORY OF ROMANCE

ated his previous escapades, but this was different. In her bittnerness, she decided to break with him openly and returned to her native Poitiers, determined to start a new life for herself. With her she took her third son, Richard (later called the Lion-Hearted), whom Henry had appointed duke of Aquitaine at eleven years of age. Eleanor remained the real power behind the title.

Because of her unique status as former Queen of France, present but absent Queen of England, the actual ruler behind the title of one of France's richest territories, Eleanor gradually found herself entrusted with the training and safekeeping of most of the children of aristocratic value west of the Rhine and north of the Pyrenees. Her household in Poitiers came to include not only the children of her two estranged husbands, Henry II and Louis VII, but it was also a nursery and academy to other prospective kings and queens, princes and princesses, dukes and duchesses, and other high-born heirs.

At that time the custom of lateral instead of vertical inheritance of fiefs predominated in most of France. This tradition provided that land be passed from brother to brother rather than from father to son. Many young men found themselves landless and unemployed, ambitious yet footloose, and still dependent on their uncles or brothers for income. The only hope these men had of retaining their aristocratic birthright was by acquiring a wealthy, well-born bride. They willingly went, therefore, to Eleanor's newly established court for training in the arts of courtly life.

They badly needed such training. With the discipline of courtly manners just becoming known, the knight was not far removed from the barbarians who had overrun Europe just a few centuries earlier. In theory, the knight was a religious, gentle man. He was supposed to protect women and the poor, defend the Church, speak the truth, and pursue infidels. In practice, in wars and in tournaments, he was a killer.

Faced with the lack of an established tradition in her new court and surrounded by her young and boisterous charges, Eleanor needed help in developing some plan of discipline. She sent for her first daughter by Louis VII. Marie, countess of Champagne, was raised in the sophisticated courts of Paris and Troyes, polished in courtly manners and in royal discipline. She came to Poitiers determined to help her mother set up their own code of manners.

Although Marie's background had included training in several courts, none provided an exact precedent for what her mother needed at Poitiers. So she and Eleanor devised a plan that would enable them to control their wild bunch of titled young people. The regime they developed was not entirely original but was yet highly innovative in its interpretation of existing ideas. Amy Kelley explains:

> *What the countess obviously needed for her royal academy was not advice for penitents, but a code of manners to transform the anarchy and confusion that confronted her into something refined, serious, and decorous, a code to give currency to her own ideals for an elect society to be impelled not by the brute force that generally prevailed, nor by casual impulse, but by an inner disciplined sense of propriety. . . . And upon what could one ground a code of chivalry save on the classic and universal theme of love?*[6]

Marie and Eleanor used the framework of the Arthurian legends to give authenticity to their novel code of manners. It was a

6. Amy Kelly, *Eleanor of Aquitaine and the Four Kings* (New York: Random House, 1950), p. 205.

82

natural choice, for interest in the tales had been growing rapidly through the years, partly because of Eleanor herself and her role as England's Queen. When Eleanor and Henry had arrived in England to establish their Angevin empire, their main obstacles were the king in Paris and the pope in Rome. They deliberately fostered interest in the legend of King Arthur in an attempt to undermine the old idea of a Holy Empire, with Charlemagne its patron saint. By helping to establish Arthur as a legitimate king, ties to the papacy, the king in Paris, known as Charlemagne's successor, and to the French, called the "people of Charlemagne," would also be weakened.

As Arthur's legend became more accepted the *chanson de geste*, which propagandized the cult of Charlemagne, was steadily replaced with the *roman courtois*, extolling the virtues of Arthur and knightly courtesy. The latter also conveniently linked Henry II and his Angevin ancestry to the earlier Celtic king. Into this new literature Eleanor inserted elements of courtly love as she had learned them from her troubadour grandfather, William, and the more relaxed customs of her native lands in the south. Friedrich Heer explains:

> *Europe's conversion to the courtly way of life, the birth of the* roman courtois *and the flowering of troubadour poetry were all intimately connected with Eleanor and the rise of the Angevin Empire. . . . The day when monks and clerks were the custodians of a man's soul was past; a man's hope of felicity now lay in the hands of his* dompna *(Provencal for domina), his lady.*[7]

Before she came to Poitiers, Marie, with the ancestry of her great-grandfather and her mother behind her, added her own

---

7. Heer, p. 165.

touch to the growing body of Arthurian legend. She suggested the theme of the greatest love story of the time to her court poet at Troyes, Chretien. Under her guidance and patronage, Chretien de Troyes wrote the "Knight of the Cart," or "Lancelot." Chretien tells us in the poem that the countess gave him both the subject matter of the poem and the manner of treatment, and that he was just carrying out her intention. The entire poem, in fact, "is an elaborate illustration of the doctrine of courtly love as it was introduced into northern France by Eleanor and Marie."[8] Chretien's poems also contained elements of the then popular works of Ovid. Perhaps even Ovid's return to popularity may have been influenced by Eleanor's and Henry's political aspirations in their attempts to obscure the conspicuous image of Charlemagne.

The *romans*, exemplified by Chretien's works as well as others, were efforts to aid man in his search for enlightenment. Through his worship of a woman, man gains access to his soul; through his love for her he becomes wiser, more sensitive, more scrupulous as a person. He goes through danger and temptation in his quest for inner awareness; he sins, errs, even experiences madness. But his guiding light and ultimate salvation is woman. And through his service to the god of love, exemplified by his vassalage to his particular lady, he becomes ennobled.

The concept of vassalage contributed to the courtly love system. During feudal times in Europe vassalage established a legal and symbolic bond among men and between families in a society where mistrust was the rule. To be the "man" of another man gave some protection to the vassal and was a source of strength to the lord. The word "man" expressed the personal dependence of the vassal on his lord and

8. Andreas Capellanus. *The Art of Courtly Love*, Intro. and trans. John Jay Parry (New York: W. W. Norton & Co., 1941), p. 14.

THE HISTORY OF ROMANCE

was at first applied to persons of all social classes. (In later medieval times vassalage became an upper-class institution.) The vassal voluntarily entered into a contract wherein he would give his lord counsel, financial aid, support, and military service, although some of these varied from country to country. The lord in turn would support his vassal by giving him a fief, offices, and positions at court and accepting him as a retainer within his own household. A ceremonial act of homage cemented the bond between the two, with the vassal kneeling before his lord and promising to become his man. The tie created a mutual bond between the two and, "its reciprocity touches on what was a fundamental medieval concept, particularly in Western and Central Europe. The relationship was a contractual one binding both partners equally."[9]

When the courtly love system was developed, the concept of vassalage, by then integrated into the thinking of Europeans, was naturally included. In explaining courtly love, Lewis says:

> *There is a service of love closely modelled*
> *on the service which a feudal vassal owes to his*
> *lord. The lover is the lady's "man". . . .*
> *The whole attitude has been rightly described as*
> *"a feudalization of love."*[10]

It seems an overstatement to assert that Eleanor and her daughter, Marie, set out to establish their court of love at Poitiers in a deliberate attempt to control men for control's sake. But it may be closer to the truth than not. Some authors insist that they did so quite deliberately. Friedrich Heer states:

9. Heer, p. 36.
10. Lewis, p. 2.

85

. . . Andreas' treatise is informed with the pulsating energy and passion which drove the women of Eleanor's entourage to create their own world and attempt the dethronement of masculine oppression and mastery. Courtly love was a practicable way of rebelling against the prevailing social moeurs, and was consciously adopted to serve this end.[11]

It is obvious, however, that Eleanor used for her own purposes a tradition which had been evolving in Western Europe for some time and which expressed political concerns as well as the increasing quest of people for self-awareness. Eleanor, with the help of Marie and other women around her, set out to change the direction of the existing philosophy in order to meet her immediate needs at Poitiers. She inserted her own and Marie's ideas into the evolving interests of her contemporaries, and because of her exalted status those ideas spread rapidly.

Their purpose was not the indulgence of uncontrollable passion. On the contrary, they wished to educate their untutored young charges through a strict discipline. These young men and women who peopled their royal court were to be ennobled by teaching them higher precepts, and love was the goal and agent of their education. It was one of those accidents of history that the time, the place, and the means were all ready and waiting for the cult of woman to evolve. Eleanor and Marie simply brought the existing elements together to create their Court of Love.

It was a court in every sense of the word, where women sat as judges upon a raised dais and listened to specific cases of love that men, the suitors to the court, brought before them. The judges, of course, were Queen Eleanor

11. Heer, p. 172.

and Marie, along with other noblewomen: Isabella, countess of Flanders (a niece of the Queen); Ermengarde, countess of Narbonne; Emma of Anjou; and others. References in Andreas' book suggest that even Marie's sister-in-law, Adele of Champagne, then queen of France, participated in the court. After hearing the case and expounding on the rules of courtly love, the ladies would give their decrees according to the merits of the case, rendering their judgments on whether the courtier loved his lady in conformance with the rules.

Some scholars have rejected medieval evidence for Eleanor's Court of Love, considering it a poetic device; others insist it occurred only as a formal piece of playacting. Today, most accept its existence but still debate its seriousness. Whether it had a recognized legal function or met in mock-legal parody of a court, however, is unimportant. The fact was that Eleanor's court, serious or quasi-legal, provided a method of examining and establishing a novel code of behavior. Morton Hunt emphasizes its significance:

> . . . men and women met in the Court of Love on terms of mutual respect to explore . . . their relationships to each other. This is the importance of the Court of Love, and a measure of the profound alteration beginning to take place, at the top level of European society. . . .[12]

Undoubtedly Eleanor and Marie were well aware that their Court of Love and the new direction their philosophy gave to the existing code were at odds with the beliefs of the rest of their society. After all, women were still chattel property, and the judgments of Eleanor's court were sheer feudal heresy, subversive of the society around them. They knew that, as women, they

12. Hunt, p. 155.

87

were not really mistresses of their situation, that men still regarded them as inferiors in fact, and as booty to be won, bought, or stolen. They also knew that in their feudal society marriage was contracted for political and commercial reasons, and that for many young men marrying a rich wife was the only way to become a landed aristocrat. Perhaps for that very reason the verdicts given out in their Court of Love did not concern marriage at all. Love was an emotion between a man and his mistress, with or without the knowledge of her husband. Marriage was regarded not as an outcome of love between two individuals but as a barrier to it. Indeed, in the philosophy of Marie of Champagne, marriage precluded love.

Inherent in Marie's thinking was the mutualism implied in the code of vassalage. The right of resistance applied to both the lord and his lady; if one broke faith the other was no longer obligated to serve. Such was not the case with marriage, where a woman, although the possessor of wealth for which a man might marry her, was still regarded as his inferior. It took more than a breach of faith to dissolve a marriage where property and intricate alliances were involved. So the two conventions did not complement each other in the eyes of these medieval women, although Andreas ambiguously says, "Marriage is no real excuse for not loving."[13]

The rulings given out in the Court of Love weighted the scales in favor of the woman. Although the suitor had the right to appeal, it did him little good, for the force of love itself was so great that he could not resist. The lady was the one who had the power to withhold or bestow her love, the one to be sought after, and the one to be the final arbiter of the validity of the love. The lady was therefore not only the equal of her suitor but, once ensconced on her pedestal, his acknowledged superior. Men were to serve her, as feudal vassals served their lords. And through service to their ladies, through

13. Capellanus, p. 184.

THE HISTORY OF ROMANCE

being instructed by women wise in the rules of love, men were to find the higher elements of their souls.

Eleanor's court lasted for only about six years. News of her unorthodox philosophy and methods of disciplining her young charges reached Henry II in England. Henry was disturbed by rumors that Poitiers was the meeting place for aristocratic rebels who opposed his rule and that Eleanor was subverting his own sons. In 1174, Henry finally decided to act. He raided Poitiers, scattering the rebels and taking Eleanor prisoner. He had her put in a tower in Salisbury, where she stayed for fifteen years, refusing to divorce him and finally emerging triumphant when Henry died in 1189.

After Henry disbanded the court at Poitiers, the ladies and their courtiers went back to their respective homes. Marie returned to Troyes, where she continued, in a small way, her mother's social experiment. She also encouraged her court poet, Andreas Capellanus, to write down and codify the rules that had been the basis of judgments rendered in her mother's court. Andreas wrote his book about 1184. From a date given in its contents, May 1, 1174, which was toward the end of Queen Eleanor's reign at Poitiers, it is evident that the book's intent was to furnish a picture of life in her court. It's also apparent that Andreas received more than suggestions about the book's style and content from Marie of Champagne. John Jay Parry, in introducing Andreas' book, says:

> *The other features of the book, including the exposition of courtly love, are, I am sure, due to Countess Marie and her associates. The style, it seems to me, rises at times above anything of which Andreas is capable, as though he were writing from dictation.*[14]

14. Ibid., p. 20.

89

THE HISTORY OF ROMANCE

Andreas, under the direction of Marie, used Ovid's poems as his model and source, faithfully copying the format but using prose instead of verse. There was one other glaring difference. What Ovid wrote in jest in *The Art of Love*, Andreas presented in all seriousness in *The Art of Courtly Love*. Although he could not have helped but understand Ovid's poem for the tongue-in-cheek manifesto that it was, he wrote his own book not satirically, like his sophisticated predecessor, but deadpan. Following Marie's philosophy and desire to codify what had been handed down as judgments in her mother's court, Andreas wrote a new treatise on manners. His book twists Ovid's ribald and irreverent rules of conduct in the game of love into a new concept. In Ovid's work, man is the master, using all of his arts of seduction to take woman for his own pleasure. The man is encouraged to seduce, beguile, and manipulate—anything to get his way with a woman. (Women also are encouraged to manipulate, but more in the vein of serving—or servicing—their men.) In Andreas' book the reverse is true; the woman is the mistress and the man is the slave; his only goal in life to worship her, to serve her, to honor and protect her. Through Andreas' work, woman is placed on her pedestal at last, her power absolute.

Ovid, born in 43 B.C. into a Rome not yet ravaged by barbarians from without and decadence within, was an intellectual and a sophisticate. He composed a series of poems satirizing his fellow citizens, which they appreciated in the vein he intended. One of these, *The Art of Love*, ostensibly instructs men and women in a lengthy but witty discourse on the rules of love. The truth is that Ovid was kidding. Love, to Ovid, was not sacrosanct. It was rather a fact of life, a necessary part of living, as natural a function as breathing or eating—a source of pleasure, despair, excitement, and hilarity. In his poem Ovid subtly conveys the idea that love, and the sexuality that accompanies it, is a healthy joke to young men (and women) and a snickering memory to those too old to join in the chase. His underlying meaning was not lost on Romans, who accepted it as an elaborate piece of satire on one of the world's oldest and most engrossing subjects. C. S. Lewis says, "The very design of his *Art of Love* presupposes an audience to whom love is one of the minor peccadilloes of life, and the joke consists in treating it seriously—. . ."[15]

Ovid's poem was sensual, satirical, and very popular. He pretended to lecture young Romans on their behavior, telling them how they should act if they wanted to seduce their girls. He told them how they should behave, as well as how to dress, speak, look, wash, even sigh. He went into exquisite detail, telling the men that they should be clean and tanned, brush their teeth, get haircuts, cut their nails as well as the hair in their noses and ears, and keep their breath sweet. He tells them to look pale:

> *But a pallor is right for the lover, a suitable color:*
> *Prithee, why not pale? that's the complexion for*
>   *love. . . .*
> *Thinness is also good, a proof of sentiment; also*
>   *Do not think it a shame wearing a hood on*
>   *your brow.*
> *Lying awake all night wears down the bodies of*
>   *lovers,*
>   *All that passion and pain—how can you help*
>   *but grow lean?*
> *Be a pitiful sight, if it helps to accomplish your*
>   *purpose,*
>   *Let anyone who observes say, "The poor*
>   *fellow's in love."*[16]

He also addresses women, giving them rules similar to those he had given the men, satirical in content but suited, of course, to their unique role. Like the instructions he gives men, he tells women how to use the techniques of sexual artfulness:

15. Lewis, p. 6.

16. Rolfe Humphries, trans., *Ovid: The Art of Love* (Bloomington, Ill.: Indiana University Press, 1957), pp. 127–28.

91

What a girl ought to know is herself, adapting her
method,
Taking advantage of ways nature equips her
to use.
Lie on your back, if your face and all of your
features are pretty;
If your posterior's cute, better be seen from
behind. . . .
Let the woman feel the act of love to her marrow,
Let the performance bring equal delight to the
two.
Coax and flatter and tease, with inarticulate
murmurs,
Even with sexual words, in the excitement of
play,
And if nature, alas! denies you the final
sensation
Cry out as if you had come, do your best to
pretend.[17]

Ovid's poetry was an expression of his times, for love was regarded in a totally different way than it is today. So were women. The ancients took women for granted as a necessary but often tedious part of life. Women's duties were to take care of the home and the servants, to bear and raise the children, to provide a certain amount of companionship, and to take care of men's sexual needs. Beyond that, the ancients concluded that love and friendship occurred almost exclusively between men, who loved each other in the most virtuous of manners (as well as in the most unvirtuous).

At least in the literature of the period, men regarded women on the same plane as their household possessions or their slaves. Aristotle assumed that women were inferior to men (for that reason it was worse to kill a woman

17. Ibid., pp. 176–77.

than a man), although he admitted that occasionally conjugal relations might rise to the same level as friendships between men. Other ancient writers treat the love of women as either an orgy of playful sensuality or as an accepted part of the domestic scene. Sometimes love was portrayed by the ancients as a tragic madness, almost a disease that strikes men and women alike. One of those so afflicted by love in its tragic sense was Medea. People prayed to the gods to be spared the kind of love that might turn them from sanity to self-destruction.

Andreas' book advocates that men seek out the kind of consuming love the ancients might have called madness. His rendition echoes Ovid's ribald poetry, but with the punch line taken out. To Andreas, as to Queen Eleanor and Countess Marie, love was no joke. Andreas stresses again and again the power of love for good: "O what a wonderful thing is love, which makes a man shine with so many virtues and teaches everyone, no matter who he is, so many good traits of character.[18] Through love, he insists, men learn courtesy, cleanliness, honesty, humility, courageousness, and generosity. Everything, in fact, that makes a man (and a woman) virtuous, is either granted him or enhanced in him by the power of love. And who is it that enables man to find love, and ennobles him in the process? Why, woman, of course—the bestower of sacred favors, the sought-after, worshipped, adulated, desired but seldom attained high priestess of love: woman, who, on her pedestal, holds the whip of love over the willingly bowed back of her troubadour lover.

Andreas lists certain attributes that tell the lover how to behave if he is in love.

Every lover regularly turns pale in the presence of his beloved.
When a lover suddenly catches sight of his beloved his heart
*   palpitates.*
A man in love is always apprehensive.

18. Capellanus, p. 31.

93

He whom the thought of love vexes eats and sleeps very little.
Every act of a lover ends in the thought of his beloved.
A true lover considers nothing good except what he thinks will
    please his beloved.
A lover can never have enough of the solaces of his beloved.
A true lover is constantly and without intermission possessed by
    the thought of his beloved.

He tells lovers that the one unmistakable sign that one is in love is jealousy:

He who is not jealous cannot love.
Real jealousy always increases the feeling of love.
Jealousy, and therefore love, are increased when one suspects his
    beloved.
A slight presumption causes a lover to suspect his beloved.

Andreas also lists certain axioms about love for the benefit of lovers wondering if they're "in love."

It is well known that love is always increasing or decreasing.
No one can love unless he is impelled by the persuasion of love.
Love is always a stranger in the home of avarice.
When made public love rarely endures.
The easy attainment of love makes it of little value; difficulty of
    attainment makes it prized.
A new love puts to flight an old one.
If love diminishes, it quickly fails and rarely revives.
Love can deny nothing to love.[19]

The signs of love, according to Andreas, are jealousy, obsession, compulsion, apprehension, and fear. All one need do is check for these factors to ascertain true love. If anxiety and jealous fear are present, assuredly one is in love. Then the lover may serve the

19. Ibid., pp. 184–86.

beloved as long as love persists, for, says Andreas, love denies nothing to love. In denying nothing, the lover gives away his or her power of choice, assigning it to love.

By making love the force that can create or enhance the Good in man, Andreas substitutes love, and its agent, woman, for God. No longer does man have to seek the Good, or God, as he did in Plato's day. Nor does he have to quest intellectually for Perfection. All he has to do is wait for love to strike and for love's signs to be revealed to him (or to her) through the emotions. He doesn't have to think about it, only wait passively for love to arrive. Once it grips him the lover is compelled to follow love's dictates. He cannot escape, so he might as well submit to love's power, stronger by far than his own.

The final judge of love must be woman, since she is the interpreter of love's affairs and instructor of its precepts. Man must turn to woman as love's agent in order to reach salvation. In accepting love as the final goal and the pathway to the highest good, man rejects any other pursuit as unworthy. Love for a woman transcends everything else in life—business, war, world and state affairs, or relationships with other men. Without love, man has no way to achieve goodness of any kind. Love itself has become, in Andreas' scheme of things, the Perfection all men should seek and their very reason for living. Love is suddenly all that matters. Amy Kelly says of this upside-down philosophy of women:

> *The code of Andre gives glimpses of a woman's notions of society different in essential respects from the prevailing feudal scheme, which was certainly man-made. In the Poitevin code, man is the property, the very thing of woman; whereas a precisely contrary state of things existed in the adjacent realms of the two kings from whom the reigning Duchess of Aquitaine was estranged. The sheer originality of Marie's scheme can be grasped by trying to imagine Henry*

95

Fitz-Empress (or Louis Capet for that matter) transformed by its agency into the beau ideal.[20]

The existing code was turned upside down by placing woman over man, as well as by her method of controlling him. Instead of making a man fear for his life if he did not behave appropriately, the new code appealed to his sense of goodness. If a man did not maintain the proper attitude toward his beloved, obeying her abjectly as any vassal did his lord, he would suffer the loss of love. He must be well mannered—good—in order to keep her.

Andreas, with Ovid's example before him, sets down some of the minute detail that tells lovers how they should behave:

> *Every man should also wear things that his beloved likes and pay a reasonable amount of attention to his appearance–not too much because excessive care for one's looks is distasteful to everybody and leads people to despise the good looks that one has. If the lover is lavish in giving, that helps him retain a love he has acquired, for all lovers ought to despise all worldly riches and should give alms to those who have need of them. Nothing is considered more praiseworthy in a lover than to be known to be generous. . . .*[21]

Women also are instructed throughout Andreas' book in how to act to keep their lovers: In speaking to a lady, a man says:

> *From your opinion it seems clear to me that with you the care of the clothes is more pleasing than the adornment of good character. This, as you know, detracts from your own good character, for*

20. Kelly, pp. 207–8.
21. Capellanus, p. 152.

96

ill-bred women put all their reliance on showy
clothing, but noble and prudent women reject
showy clothes unaccompanied by good breeding
and think that only the cultivation of good
character deserves respect in a man.[22]

He further instructs her, "you should seek more lofty subjects for discussion, so that your nobility of birth will be apparent and your good sense will be recognized not only from what you wear and the way you walk but even from what you say."[23]

Like Ovid, Andreas stresses that lovers should manipulate their ladies to ensure their love. Unlike Ovid, Andreas is serious. He does not, like the earlier poet, playfully chide his fellow citizens about how they *do* act. Preacher-like, he instructs them in how they *should* act:

He who wants to make a real test of the faith and
affection of his beloved should, with the greatest
care and subtlety, pretend to her that he desires
the embraces of some other woman, and he should
be seen near this woman more often than he has
been. If he finds that this upsets his beloved he can
be sure that she is very much in love with him and
most constant in her affection.[24]

He also tells women what they must do when lovers waver in their affection:

. . . she must be careful not to let him know her
intentions and she must hide her real feelings and
by careful dissimulation make it seem to him
that she is not distressed by the upsetting of their

22. Ibid., p. 113.
23. Ibid., p. 114.
24. Ibid., p. 158.

THE HISTORY OF ROMANCE

> *love affair. . . . If the woman sees that she is
> getting no results by this method, she must very
> cautiously pretend that she is thinking about the
> embrace of some other man, so that the lover . . .
> may become jealous.*[25]

Despite Andreas' reliance on Ovid, the difference between the two was enormous. Both authors viewed love as existing outside the marriage bond, to be sure; beyond that and the fact that Andreas used Ovid's poem as a format there was little similarity. Hunt says:

> *Andreas shows the woman not as the prey, but the
> predator, and man not the conqueror, but the
> conquered; as for the nature of the conquest, Ovid
> was candidly and plainly speaking of
> intercourse, . . . while Andreas carefully and
> specifically urged his readers to control their
> lusts. . . .*[26]

The immediate and widespread acceptance of Andreas' book shows too the immense difference between the society of Ovid's time, whose members could roar with appreciation at their poet's ribald treatment of an accepted joke, and that of later medieval times, when love was becoming sanctified. Hunt states that Andreas' work was not "just a guidebook to a complex amusement; it was the manifesto of an emotional revolution."[27]

Eleanor's social experiment had an unprecedented effect on the philosophy and ethics of the rest of Europe. Using her Court of Love as an example, other courts similar in design flourished. Aristocratic women, some of them

25. Ibid., p. 160.
26. Hunt, p. 158.
27. Ibid., p. 161.

Eleanor's daughters and relatives, became influential in spreading the new gospel of love. The poems of the troubadours contain many references to courts maintained by high-born ladies in France and Italy. As many as sixty women at a time sat in judgment on cases submitted to them at some of these courts. Thousands of people participated. At one court alone, held in 1283 at Florence, Italy, a Court of Love was held which lasted two months and was attended by a thousand people.

After Eleanor and Marie left the dais and their Court of Love had disbanded, Andreas' treatise and the poems of the troubadours continued to spread the new philosophy. Andreas' book (popular throughout Europe), the songs of the well-traveled troubadours, and the tales of the poets gave the new ideas rapid dissemination. As the new concepts became accepted, woman began to take on an aura of legitimacy, but not equality. Women were certainly not men's equals, either in literature or in daily life. Although still generally viewed as men's property in the flesh, however, women in theory were beginning to change from objects of denigration into images of worship. As one historian says, "The process of placing women upon a pedestal had begun, and whatever we may think of the ulitmate value of such an elevation . . . it was at least better than placing them, as the Fathers of the Church had inclined to do, in the bottomless pit."[28] A subtle change occurred in the minds of the people of Western Europe which was to continue down to the present. It was, for that time, as great a change as if suddenly, secretly, God had been renamed "She."

The doctrine of romance that started with William, duke of Aquitaine in the eleventh century, rose to new heights with his grandaughter, Eleanor, queen of England in the twelfth. The concepts were sung about by the troubadours, written about by poets such as Chretien de Troyes and authors such as Andreas Capellanus. These novel, even

28. Power, p. 405.

99

THE HISTORY OF ROMANCE

revolutionary ideas were eagerly grasped by people throughout western civilization, and they are with us still. C. S. Lewis points out that "an unmistakable continuity connects the Provencal love song with the love poetry of the later Middle Ages, and thence, through Petrarch and many others, with that of the present day."[29] Lewis continues:

> . . . the most revolutionary elements in it have
> made the background of European literature for
> eight hundred years. . . . Compared with this
> revolution the Renaissance is a mere ripple on the
> surface of literature.[30]

The alteration in the existing belief system of medieval men and women, as expressed by their literature, was gradually to alter their behavior in daily life, and that of others throughout the centuries. Writing about Thomas of Britain, who, he states, wrote *Tristam and Ysolt* for the favor of Queen Eleanor or one of her family, Roger Loomis says, "There was the new social creed of chivalry and courtly love, which spread so rapidly throughout Europe that the doctrine of the inferiority of women has never had the same standing since."[31]

Certainly such a philosophy had effects on peoples' lives even then. Eileen Power says, "It is obvious that a theory which regarded the worship of a lady as next to that of God and conceived her as the mainspring of brave deeds, a creature half romantic, half divine, must have done something to counterbalance the dogma of subjection."[32] Counterbalance earlier beliefs it did; balance them it did not. The factors in the history of romance caused the pendulum to swing

29. Lewis, p. 3.
30. Ibid., p. 4.
31. Roger Sherman Loomis, intro. and trans., *The Romance of Tristam and Ysolt by Thomas of Britain* (New York: Columbia University Press, 1951), p. xvii.
32. Power, p. 406.

100

far past the middle mark to the opposite side, where it has hovered for centuries. Women became not men's equals but creatures known by a double standard, oppressed on the one hand because she was still man's slave, adored on the other because she was his inspiration. She and the men who have alternately used and served her have had no common ground on which to relate to each other except an indeterminate and ambiguous truce. Each sex has had to sort through differing standards within his or her own code, as well as puzzle out the diametrically opposed values of the opposite sex. Is it any wonder that the battle of the sexes, fought in a ground mist of confusion, has resulted in a stalemate for both sides?

Today we are finally beginning to understand the destructiveness of the two separate standards the code of romance had foisted upon us. We are at the point of being able to let the mist rise and see our way clearly, without our clouds of confusion to deter us. We can now let go of those ancient concepts intended to keep women on a pedestal with men standing guard underneath. Women can step down from their pedestals so that they can stand side by side with men for the first time in history. We can throw away those roles, developed originally for personal and political expediency, and know each other as separate, but equal individuals. We can dispense with Eleanor of Aquitaine's artificial and arbitrary code of romance.

101

5. CONCEPTS CREATE OUR IMAGES

OUR SELF-IMAGES DICTATE THE WAY WE BEHAVE.

With the twelfth-century alteration of the existing code, the concept of love changed from a healthy joke, as in ancient times, to that of a sacred ennobling experience considered necessary to man's (and woman's) growth as a spiritual being. Before Eleanor of Aquitaine and her daughter, Marie of Champagne, established their Court of Love, woman was regarded as the property of man, to be dealt with as he wished. After the Court of Love disintegrated and their concepts circulated throughout the country, the theory began to crumble although the actuality persisted. Man, in literature and fantasy if not in fact, became the property of woman. Man had to pursue, worship, and plead with woman for her favors. Man became the supplicant, woman the ruler and judge.

As the new concepts were accepted, the status of women improved immensely. Granted new identity under the courtly love system, women became worthy of men's respect. No longer just slaves, women became elevated to a position unknown before that time, that of "ladies." Men began to treat women differently, according to their novel image as objects of adoration. In the time preceding acceptance of the romantic code, men believed that women owed them love. With the reversal in philosophy, men became the debtors. They began to seek women's approval, attempting to win the love of a lady through good deeds. As a consequence, women gained a great deal of power. While still restricted by societal standards from acting on their own, they were increasingly able to manipulate men emotionally to act for them.

Men too received a bonus from the new system. Prior to the appearance of courtly love, men had been restricted to a hierarchal system with a rigidly established order. Although individual deviation from the rules of feudal society was common, it was not sanctioned; men served other men along certain proscribed lines. Individual feelings counted less than the rules that had been developed through the cen-

105

turies. The courtly love system gave impetus to a change in that long-established order, enabling men to make decisions according to their own feelings rather than to defer rigidly to the will of some superior.

Had the romantic concept remained a theory apart from the reality of our relationships, it might have continued to exert a positive influence on men and women. Had people continued to regard romance as an inspiration, an ideal of perfect manners, and a lovely but unreachable fantasy, perhaps our lives today would be different. But romance became integrated into our belief system. Far from remaining an abstract ideal, it became an expected way of relating to each other in Western society and an undisputed part of our etiquette.

None of this happened in a day. Concepts create changes imperceptibly and in time. Yet, once formulated, concepts continue to spread, as contagious in their own way as germs. Although twelfth-century communication methods were limited, the ideas circulated quickly, broadcast by song and verse, by manuscript and royal decree. What average man and woman had the education and authority to challenge the edict of their king and queen? So the novel ideas gained intellectual acceptance first, gradually changing the emotional content of interactions between living men and women, as well as literary figures.

Because of the nature of communication itself, the romantic code could not have remained a theory apart from actual relationships. Julian Jaynes points out, "Word changes are concept changes and concept changes are behavioral changes."[1] Words are powerful tools, not only indicators of experience but creators as well. Jaynes speculates that words and the languages resulting from them are determinants of culture, each dependent on and resulting from what has gone before. Particular concepts build cultures, not the reverse. He

1. Jaynes, p. 292.

106
CONCEPTS CREATE OUR IMAGES

says, "each new stage of words literally created new perceptions and attentions, and such new perceptions and attentions resulted in important cultural changes which are reflected in the archaeological record."[2] Words create awareness, expand mental horizons, and enlarge upon our prior conceptions. Words open the door to new perceptions, within one's own mind and without, to another's. Both words and communication open the self to change.

Another author states that learning, and through it, culture, came about by means of language, both verbal and silent. He says:

The development of language and technology, an interrelated pair, made possible the storing of knowledge. It gave man a lever to pry out the secrets of nature. It was the necessary condition for that burst of creativeness which we think of as culture in the highest sense.[3]

By communicating our concepts to another person and by allowing his or her concepts to filter into our consciousness through language, we can change. Communicating is sharing; taking another person's ideas and feelings into oneself and giving one's self—opinions and emotions—to that other person. Using words to share our concepts, we bridge the distance between two people and open ourselves to change. So people in times past communicated new concepts to each other, and changed in the process.

Prior to the medieval creation of woman as an image to be adored, women in ancient times were taken for granted, as necessary though inferior partners on the

2. Ibid., p. 132.

3. Edward T. Hall, The Silent Lanugage (New York: Doubleday & Co., Anchor Books, 1973), p. 58.

107

CONCEPTS CREATE OUR IMAGES

domestic scene and off, in seriousness or frivolity. Certainly they were never thought of as better than men. But from the twelfth century on, women were enthroned, still inferior to men in some respects but vastly superior in others. Woman in the abstract was granted an ethereal quality that removed her from the condition of original sin imposed on ordinary, earthly women. Woman was, in romantic song and literature, more than human, less than divine, but tending toward the heavens. Like Eleanor, however, living medieval women were not above having their own flings outside of wedlock; it was, indeed, a condition of the romantic code. Although the clergy might object, the "ladies" could be as lusty and earthy as their men in actuality without tarnishing the ideal itself.

The attitude of the troubadours had begun as a practical solution to a common dilemma. Prohibited by warrior husbands from getting too close to their wives, the troubadours were restricted to singing about their ladyloves from a discreet distance. As time went on, their practicality became literary convention.

Adoration of the Virgin Mary was important to the development of the image of the lady. Our Lady in heaven was held up as the proper model for girls and women to emulate. Some women, such as nuns, did so as exactly as they could, dressing in her ancient style of dress and following what they believed were her personality traits—serenity, humility, and passivity. Other women may not have gone to the extreme of confining themselves in convents, in cowls, and long robes, but still tried to adopt similar personality attributes. Modeling their mental images on the Virgin's example, real-life women developed the belief that in order to be a lady, one must be calm, sweet, controlled, and sexually pure.

Chastity, in particular, has been long considered a quality necessary to being a lady. Because Mary was a virgin, both before and after conceiving a child, women believed that earthly sexuality leading to conception was

CONCEPTS CREATE OUR IMAGES

not an accepted part of spirituality. Ordinary women could not emulate the Virgin Birth, but they could follow the Virgin's example in spirit. They could not be actually chaste in body and still have children, so many ladies settled for the mental image. As the centuries went on and the image became entrenched in people's minds, women accepted spiritual otherworldliness as their appropriate role and acted out the part. If they granted their husbands sexual favors, they held themselves back from enjoying themselves while participating. Sexual activity was tolerated only for procreative purposes; otherwise it smacked of sin or wongdoing.

By the eighteenth century in America, fashion dictated that ladies be in delicate health and have their bodies all but hidden from view. Certain bodily parts were considered evil; sexual desire was forbidden, and any display of sexual feelings on a woman's part, even with her husband, was a sign that she was wanton. Ladies were to be protected from men, and from themselves. For a time in the nineteenth century, the practice of clitoridectomy was common, in an attempt to make sure women would not experience sexual feelings.

So the concept of refinement and spiritual purity was translated from a twelfth-century theory into latter-day actuality. By adopting the image, women clothed themselves in what they believed were the behavioral accouterments of the Virgin. They became purer in outward demeanor than those medieval ladies who developed the ideal ever thought of being. The theory, become philosophy, resulted in behavioral changes that we in our present society have inherited. Women, and men too, have developed certain attitudes that prohibit acceptance of all bodily parts as equally respectable. Many still hold the beliefs that bodies are bad and feelings are evil, and both should be tightly controlled and hidden. Others believe that our bodies are generally all right but some of our bodily parts are bad, and it's not permissible to touch or to be touched there.

When I consider such messages

109

they seem ridiculous: It's okay for men to shake hands but not to hold hands; for a man to kiss a woman's hand but not to touch her breast; for a woman to hug the top part of another person's body but not get too close below the waist. It's okay if we rub our eyes, scratch our ears, tickle our feet, or fold our arms across our chests, but not okay to touch our breasts or genitals. It's all right for many people to feel sensations in the upper half of their bodies but not in the lower. Although these prohibitions may seem silly, we can and do follow our training by numbing certain parts of our body or suffering guilt for what we do feel. Some of us turn ourselves off generally so that we feel little or nothing throughout our entire bodies. Ann T. was one of these.

Ann came to see me because of what she'd briefly explained on the phone was a marital problem. She reluctantly entered my office and sat down, her feet tucked under her as if she wanted to run.

"What's the problem?" I asked.

"I don't know if I can talk about it," she said.

"Okay," I said. We sat there for a few minutes while Ann fidgeted. I've learned that I can outwait more comfortably than a client can wait.

"It's incest," she said, after a very short time.

The story she told me was by inference rather than words. Her grandfather had molested her when she was eleven years old. Shortly afterwards her cousin had coerced her into "playing doctor."

"How long did this go on?" I asked.

"Oh, just the one time with my grandfather and a couple times with my cousin," she answered quickly.

"What did your parents do?" I asked.

"They didn't know anything

CONCEPTS CREATE OUR IMAGES

about it," she said. "I couldn't have told mother; she wouldn't have believed it about her father. And she would have died of a broken heart to hear what my cousin did; she loved him. Father wouldn't have believed me about either one of them."

"Did you ever talk about sex in your family?" I asked.

"No. I don't even remember asking about it," she said. "I remember when I started to menstruate; it happened shortly after the other incidents, and I thought I was being punished. I managed to tell my mother something; I can't remember what. She gave me a book to read, and I figured out what was happening from that. She told me nothing though, not then or since."

"Your father didn't talk to you about it either?" I asked.

"Never," she said. "All he ever said was, 'Don't let the boys catch you behind the woodshed,' but that was when I was older."

"What did you think about it when you were young?" I asked.

"I really don't think I did," she answered, "or if I did at all I thought it was bad. I know it was a taboo subject in our house, and even if they never told me in so many words I felt that certain parts of my body were bad. I've never dared look at those parts, let alone do what some people do."

"Masturbate, you mean?" I asked.

"Yes. That's seemed to me the greatest of all sins, worse even than having sex with a man. I don't know where I got that idea because I don't remember my parents telling me that. I just know there were some things we didn't do, and we didn't have to talk about them to know what they were."

"Sounds like your family behaved very properly around each other," I said.

111

CONCEPTS CREATE OUR IMAGES

"Yes, we did. We never went around in our underclothes or anything like that. And we didn't touch each other. We're not huggers like some families. I never even saw my parents kiss. I guess that was why it was such a terrible shock when my grandfather and cousin did what they did."

"How did you deal with it?" I asked.

"I stayed away from both of them from then on. Mother never understood why I didn't want to be around grandfather, but he knew. Shortly after that we moved, and I never saw either of them again."

"But you never forgot it," I said.

"No, I never did." She sighed heavily. "It's ruined my life. I've been afraid of men ever since. I did get married in my late twenties, and we have two children now. But I'm more and more turned off by sex, and my husband's patience is wearing thin."

"Have you ever felt turned on sexually?" I asked.

"No, never," she said firmly.

Her resolute decision to stay out of touch with her feelings indicated more than what she had told me. I suspected that those experiences were not all that had influenced her.

"How do you feel about your mother?" I asked.

"I love her very much," she said. "We get along well. She never gets angry at me the way some mothers do with their daughters. If she's upset with me, she's very calm about letting me know. She's a very nice lady."

"How about your father?" I asked.

"Everybody loves father," she said. "He's always joking, never takes anything seriously. Actually he's a lot like mother, very stable."

112

"And you?" I asked. "Do you ever get upset?"

"Yes, but I don't show it. We've never believed in moods in my family," she said.

"What would your parents have done if you ever threw a tantrum?" I asked.

"I don't know, I've never tried," she said. "I suppose I knew they wouldn't permit that."

I saw a pattern emerging that revealed Ann's strong beliefs about feelings—in her case, about not feeling. She didn't want to feel, to go through the upset of expressing her emotions. She had her parents' examples in her mind as the right way to act. She had no permission from either of her parents to express her feelings directly and believed, as they did, that controlling oneself meant being stable and being a lady—like her mother. She knew, moreover, that neither of her parents would support her if her behavior was different from theirs, or if she told them something contrary to what they believed.

Ann had blocked not only sexual feelings from her awareness, but her whole range of feelings. When I pointed out the reasons, however, she had a hard time accepting the cause. She believed so firmly that her parents' way of behaving was correct that she had difficulty substituting the word "control" for "stability." She held onto her complaint that her childhood experiences were the only cause of her problem. She insisted on blaming her grandfather and cousin for their behavior twenty-five years previously. They were responsible, she insisted, for her frigidity. It wasn't her fault that she felt the way she did; it was theirs!

I half-expected Ann to discontinue therapy after our first session because of other clients I've had who believed strongly that they shouldn't feel. Many such controlled people have come to one or two sessions, then simply stop coming. I've checked with some of these people to find out why they've discontinued therapy, and some have expressed fear of going any farther into their feelings.

113

CONCEPTS CREATE OUR IMAGES

"It hurts too much," one person told me. "I just don't want to get into that!"

Another said, "I feel too foolish when you ask me what I'm feeling. I'm too embarassed to talk about it."

But I'd underestimated Ann's determination. She had decided that she valued her marriage enough to expose herself to the dangers of feeling. She persisted, coming to therapy sessions off and on for two years. She started to experience her feelings slowly. At first she felt nothing when I pulled various Gestalt exercises out of my therapeutic bag. But little by little she began to experience feelings in her body.

"What are you feeling?" I asked one day as her eyes filled with tears.

"I'm afraid," she said, remembering a long-buried childhood scene. "My head hurts," she added.

"Just let that happen," I said.

"I don't want to feel that," she said. "It hurts."

"Nobody does," I said. "But it's safe to feel it now; stay in touch with the feeling and let it go when it will." By allowing herself to reexperience it, she found that the feeling left as easily as it had come.

As Ann got in contact with her feelings through therapy, she began to feel more in her daily life, even during sex. She also began to understand her reasons for turning herself off. She realized that her childhood decisions about feelings had as much to do with her frigidity as the sexual molestations she experienced when she was eleven. Actually, her decisions had been made at a much younger age than that. As far back as she could remember she had been told not to cry loudly or express her anger outwardly, to act "like a lady," to "calm down," and to "grow up." She knew her parents expected her to control her behavior, and she did. She controlled her feelings along with it. The more she permitted herself to feel, in therapy, the less

114

afraid she became of her strong feelings, her anger, and her excitement. Instead of telling herself to calm down, as she had done all her life, she began checking for her feelings, then allowing herself to experience them.

Gradually, as Ann permitted herself to get in touch with all of her feelings, her relationship with her husband improved. Ann has told me that she cannot let herself go entirely yet, and she would not initiate a sexual encounter. But more and more, she's said, she experiences exciting feelings in her body during sex. And although she feels she has a long way to go, both she and her husband are delighted with her increased responsiveness.

I've known several women with experiences similar to Ann's. Some of these women have been molested sexually as children by friends or relatives, many by their parents. Some have had one traumatic experience, others have suffered years of abuse. I haven't known any who have come through such experiences unscathed. Many of them, like Ann, don't want to talk about it or remember it in any way. Even though it happened years before, the memory still floods them with anguish. Like Ann, they've numbed their bodily feelings. And, like her, these women have invariably had other messages that influenced their physiological deadness. Although the memories are to blame in their minds for their general state of numbness, the overall pattern of childhood messages and their early decisions about them is congruent—"Don't feel," Along with that, they've been told verbally or wordlessly, *"Those* parts of your body are bad and if you have feelings there, *you* are bad!" So, with the great power of their minds, they have turned off all feelings, and numbed their bodies into generalized frigidity.

Many of us have had prohibitions on feeling, even though we may not have suffered sexual abuse when we were little. As we move toward the twenty-first century we become more accepting of our feelings, sexual and otherwise, but many of our beliefs remain confusing. I've had to confront my own attitudes to begin to accept all of my bodily parts

115

CONCEPTS CREATE OUR IMAGES

as equally worthwhile. I know I still have, and convey, some hangups. I became particularly aware of this one time when I saw my daughter "tickling herself," as she calls it, in her bath. Until then I'd had ambivalent feelings about what she was doing, but, not knowing what to say, I'd said nothing. I'd hoped the whole issue would go away. Of course it didn't, and she seemed to be doing it more and more. When she was six I noticed her giving me fearful, guilty looks when I'd interrupt her, and I became aware that my face was strained and tight. I knew I didn't want her to grow up feeling guilty about her body and thinking that masturbation is bad, as I did. It took me thirty-five years to find out that it was not only okay, but through masturbating I could relieve my own tensions without having to find a man, whether I liked him or not, to do it for me. I discovered a sense of self-sufficiency I didn't have before, which helped me doubly appreciate a good man I chose because I wanted *him.*

I decided that I'd better share my feelings with my daughter, before the guilt she was displaying became permanent. The next time I noticed her masturbating I said, "Honey, I just want to tell you that what you're doing is okay. Sometimes I know I've given you angry looks, and it's because I was told when I was a little girl that tickling myself was bad. That's my problem. But what you're doing is all right. And you know something else? Sometimes I do it too!"

"You do?" she said, and her eyes got wide. "When?"

"Sometimes when I'm in bed," I said.

"Oh," she said, and that was all. But I haven't noticed her doing it as much since then.

Permission is such a potent force! Once we have permission, we can quit struggling. I didn't mean to have my daughter quit masturbating; its all right if she keeps on for the rest of her life, feeling okay about herself. But my giving her permission relieved her struggle so she, and I, can

116

CONCEPTS CREATE OUR IMAGES

go on to other things. We don't have to stay locked in a silent battle, with her behaving in the way she knows I disapprove of in a reverse effort to get my approval. When I gave her permission, she had no further need to struggle. She has my permission to be herself.

Permission to be oneself, to exist—acceptance of one as he or she is—is an all powerful factor in change. The most valuable gift one person can give another—a child, friend, lover, or oneself—is permission to be. Permission establishes a place in the universe, grounds one to the earth, and centers one's being. With permission to be—no matter who we are—we belong.

Permission is a part of the communication process. If I don't permit you to be yourself, if I try to control you in some way, you will not want to open up to me. You won't feel safe in exposing your innermost feelings to me. And you should not. You should rightly close off and barricade yourself from me because I'm trying to take over your personal territory—yourself. But if I simply accept you as yourself, you can let your guard down whenever you are ready, let my new concepts into your perception, and commit yourself to change.

Commitment is an underlying force in change. Many people have asked me, "How do you motivate someone else to change?" I have never had a good answer for that one.

"You don't," I've said often, "if the other person doesn't want to change." The more one pushes, the more the other person will be likely to rebel. One can nag, bitch, scream, demand, plead, reason, or forcibly try to control another person, but that person will probably resist, dig in, and refuse to budge. Remember the folk tale about the wind betting the sun that he could get a boy to take off his coat? The more the wind blew, the tighter the boy wrapped his coat around him. When the wind gave up, the sun began to shine. Soon the boy took off his coat, motivated by the warm rays of the sun. Maybe the

117

CONCEPTS CREATE OUR IMAGES

sun's way is the only sure way to motivate someone else to change. Give that person warmth, acceptance, permission to be—and he (or she) may commit himself to change.

Through working with Ann T. and scores of others, I can understand the power of commitment within the process of change. Commitment allows participation in the decision-making. Without commitment, one may not be motivated enough first to make the decision to change, then to continue the process. One may not want to expose feelings openly to another person, or to accept any new concepts in place of unworkable beliefs. Ann was motivated to come to therapy in the first place because she was committed to her marriage. Unlike some I mentioned who discontinued therapy because it seemed so risky, Ann was also committed to her own growth. She didn't blame her husband for all of their problems; she was willing to accept responsibility for her share. Even though I challenged her entire belief system with new concepts, though I confronted her feelings and childhood decisions, she was still willing to risk changing herself and her behavior. She continued to come to therapy sessions because she was ready to grow.

Each person has his or her own point of readiness. This point, which varies with each individual, depends on one's inner conviction that he or she will survive change. A person may decide on an intellectual level to change in some way. For example, an obese person decides to diet. But on a subconscious (feeling) level, the decision may be quite the opposite, a wee inner child voice crying, "I'm too scared to go hungry!" And the left hand surreptitiously reaches for a cookie while the right isn't watching. So being ready to give up something that has helped one survive is also a part of commitment, and hence of change. No matter what one might gain by changing, there is also something one stands to lose. If the individual feels that he or she needs that defense to survive, then that person will not give it up no matter what the gain.

Ann was ready to risk giving up her self-control, which in her belief system was called stability

CONCEPTS CREATE OUR IMAGES

She could commit herself to change because she felt inwardly that she would survive. She had permission to quit being so stable. I did not tell Ann she *should* change, any more than I would tell someone he or she should diet. Shoulds activate the rebellious kids in all of us, bringing out the typical response, "I won't if I don't want to!" I substituted permission messages for the old restrictive ones Ann had received from her parents, and she used them to free herself from her own control. I would give similar messages to overeaters ("It's okay to quit eating and to feel!"), to drinkers, gamblers, compulsive shoppers, pill takers, or nonstop talkers. These defenders are similar in that they are all attempting to numb their bodily feelings.

Ann gave me permission too, by accepting me as I am. She didn't feel threatened by me, nor I by her, so we could both perceive each other without expectations of how the other should be. Our mutual acceptance enabled her to let down her barricades of mistrust and allow my new, albeit threatening, concepts into her awareness. It allowed me to speak freely without evading issues, as I sometimes find myself doing when I'm feeling judged. She was not trying to impress me, or hide from me, nor was I with her. We were both sharing experiences, beliefs, and feelings openly, trusting that neither of us would belittle, criticize, or judge the other.

This climate of mutual acceptance enabled both of us to feel safe. Without such acceptance on both sides, our communication would have been blocked. If one of us had not accepted the other, or her words, no mutual interchange would have taken place. We could have talked and talked, as if one was speaking Greek and the other Latin. Communication in that case would have been decidedly a one-way street. Neither of us would have understood the intent of the other's words. Although the words would have been heard by our ears and registered by our intellects, no inner penetration would have taken place. The words could not have been perceived.

Mutual acceptance means that no controls are necessary. One person is willing to perceive

119

another person as he or she is. No barriers need be thrown up because neither needs to guard against the other. If I accept you, and I feel that you accept me, I need have no fear that you will hurt me, nor do I have to control you because I'm afraid. I do not have to judge you, or accept your judgments of me. We can hear the meaning behind each other's words, and feel heard.

Acceptance and its concomitant, permission, enhance communication with oneself for similar reasons. If our own internal voices of authorization, the parent messages that each of us hears in our minds, are accepting and approving, then we have permission to behave according to the way we feel. But if those internal voices are disapproving, rejecting, or ridiculing, we may adapt to them with guilt, or rebel against them resentfully. If the voices do not approve of us, then it is not safe to let down our mental barriers. We must keep the blockade up for our own protection. The voices tell us what we should do, and we try hard to comply. But if we do exactly what they demand, we give up our sense of self.

Without an internal feeling of being accepted for what we are, we vacillate between obedience and rebellion. "I want to lose weight," says the overeater, translating from his or her parent message, "You *should* lose weight." But, feeling far safer with a blanket of fat as an emotional coverup against the internal reprimand, "You're bad; you should be better than you are," the overeater will cling to the old defense. Hearing the "you should" rightly as control, he will not comply, for giving in would mean giving up an essential part of himself, an inner sense of territory. To comply with that control would mean adapting to the image the parent messages demand, and becoming a nonentity, a nobody. So the commitment, the decisive force in motivation, is never allied with the overeater's verbal, intellectual decision to change (his or her "want" to want to quit.) Nor does the overeater feel a sense of mastery over his body; with the Parent tapes in control he has no sense of ownership. Since he has never really assumed control of his body, he can make no inner commitment to change. Thus the overeater, the drinker, the pill

120

CONCEPTS CREATE OUR IMAGES

taker—whoever defends against feelings—has little choice. With nothing to cling to in his or her helplessness but the old habit, that person will continue the struggle to gain acceptance by eating, drinking, popping pills, defending, all the more.

Perhaps commitment is such a potent force in self-motivation and in communication because of our brain structure. Visualize, in our split-brains, the feeling of commitment coming from the right side, while the "you should" voice is verbalized on the left. We may understandably feel that we're fighting against ourselves, in deciding to change. The two sides of our brains are literally fighting it out between themselves. They may continue to fight throughout our lives because of the authorizations imposed on us in childhood, and because of our needs to fight those controls in order to find our feeling selves—our own identification. A woman verbalized this recently when she said, "I understand the split-brain theory very well. That's how I've felt all my life. One part of my head has been battling the other part. Everytime one part of me has wanted to do something, the other part says I shouldn't. And when it tells me I should do it, I don't want to. So I've done nothing—all my life!"

The authorizations given us by our romantic concepts are shoulds too. Romance permits us no acceptance of each other as people, but ensures that we are controlled by our respective images. When women expect to be more fragile than men, more in need of protection and delicate treatment, they control themselves by their own ideal of fragility, as they are controlled by men's expectation that they live up to the image. If they act contrary to their image they call themselves bad, and, depending on the area, men label them accordingly. In the sexual area, men may label women fast. Men may call women sluts because they act in ways the men consider improper toward and with other men. Directed toward themselves, the actions might be described in a more positive manner. Still, the image demands decorum. How can a man continue to worship a woman who steps down off her pedestal and acts as

121

men have been permitted to act for centuries? How can he look to her for his pathway to salvation if she acts the same way he does? How can he depend on her for inspiration in goodness if she displays sexual feelings openly, along with anger or aggressiveness?

In the belief that she should act like a lady, the woman may control herself so tightly that she tenses her entire body. She may appear poised and serene, but in reality her body may be rigid and nonfeeling. She may not let herself get excited, raise her voice, or express any strong emotion outwardly. She may slow down to a walk everytime she feels like running and whisper when she'd like to scream. Eventually, she will no longer feel like running or screaming at all. She may be not only rigid and controlled, but frigid and nonresponsive, believing that she is being ladylike.

She may also believe that she should be helpless. She may expect that men should open doors for her, hold her coat, stand up when she enters a room, buy her lunch, bring her gifts, work for her, even fight for her. She has been trained for so long to let men do things for her that she no longer believes she can do them for herself. When men don't fulfill her expectations, a woman such as this is devastated, believing their servitude to be her right. These women may, through their feelings of helplessness, angrily blame men for keeping them dependent. But men aren't to blame, any more than women are. We have all been programmed by the romantic tradition for so long that we've accepted the roles. We have formulated our self-images on that creed and molded our lives to fit it.

Women have been taught that it is improper for them to exhibit aggressiveness. They've been taught to repress themselves, unlike men who are taught as little boys to channel their aggressive drives into competitive activities. So women become sneaky, showing aggressiveness, if at all, in devious ways. Women learn to twist men around their little fingers, as they did dad, but, believing still in their traditional roles, they don't come out openly with their anger, their wants, their competitive drives. They moan that there are not enough

122

CONCEPTS CREATE OUR IMAGES

women executives, but how can women compete with men for these positions if they've been taught to act helpless and let men take care of them?

If women have suffered in the business world because of their inner concepts of themselves as ladies, man also have suffered in their relationships. Men have accepted the image of strength and manliness. A man may not express fear or feelings of helplessness, because he's been taught to believe these are weaknesses. He may never reveal his tenderness because he holds firmly to the belief that it's wrong to show feelings like that, even to those closest to him. He may surreptitiously brush away a tear during a sad movie, but he won't cry if he hurts; he has been taught that it's wrong to feel sorry for himself. He believes he has to be tough and protect the "weaker" ones around him, his women and children. And by suppressing all expressions of feeling except those that relate to his toughness, he becomes frigid in the emotional sense of the term.

Lack of communication is blamed in a majority of divorces today, but how can men communicate with women, or with other men, if they won't discover what they feel? If communication means sharing with another person, and being open in expressing feelings, men are licked before they start. They cannot reveal their inner feelings openly to anyone because of their very images as tough, resourceful protectors. Their inner voices of authorization tell them they should not appear weak, so they keep up the barriers and guard others against their unaccepted feelings, even while their women wail that their men won't talk to them about feelings. Our romantic code has taught us that men are the doers and protectors, and women often marry them for that very reason. Only afterward do the women complain that the very strength they were attracted to in the beginning seems like a trap after marriage. The women do not want to be rescued out of their rightful sense of identity and independence. They want to be supported emotionally, and the men don't know what they mean.

Romance has taught men to take

123

CONCEPTS CREATE OUR IMAGES

care of women. So men try, but they've interpreted that rule in strictly material terms. They support women by working for them and their children. They also try to take care of them emotionally by *not* sharing problems with them. Men rescue women by not expressing anger because they've been taught that women are too delicate to withstand their wrath. So men bury their anger, taking it out on their own insides, or working it out in their businesses because they've been taught, "never complain, never explain." Their wives might be pleading with their husbands to share their concerns. The women might even beg their men to please express their anger so that they, the women, will know where they stand. But the men have been so imbued with the romantic concept of upholding women with strength and bravery that they stoically refuse. "Nothing's wrong," they say. "I don't want to hurt your feelings." And saying that, many of them walk silently out the door for the last time, away from their wives, suffering their strength in loneliness while their women die inside from the anguish of not knowing why.

Men and women in America have created separate realities out of our pervasive training in romantic sensibilities. Each lives his or her life based on separate images, according to different rules. The voices of authorization in the minds of men and women tell us to act in rigidly defined, entirely different ways. Those voices tell us to follow the rules of what's "right" and what's "wrong," to create impossible expectations of each other rather than respond with feelings in the here and now. We do not have to question the values our voices impart to us. We accept them; everybody believes them; it's always been done that way. By adapting to our socially approved concepts, we behave in certain predetermined ways, changing the actual structure of our bodies and perhaps our brains as we do so. We act out whatever roles we've been taught to play, and our physical selves conform to our mental images.

Romance has been such an integral part of our present society for so many centuries that we can hardly imagine any other attitude. So natural has our roman-

124

tic point of view seemed to us that until recently we have not questioned our western version of love. Certainly, not being able to formulate the question, we haven't found any answer! C. S. Lewis says:

> . . . a glance at classical antiquity or at the Dark Ages at once shows us that what we took for "nature," is really a special state of affairs, which will probably have an end, and which certainly had a beginning in eleventh-century Provence.[4]

Nowhere in ancient times, before the concepts of courtly love became popularized, do we find evidence of that form of romance that we in modern-day America take for granted. We find it hard to visualize the other world that existed before the coming of romance. We have been taught the ground rules for so long—preached at, sung to, advertised, and proselytized romance—that we can hardly conceive of a world without it. To imagine a world without romance is to shift our minds to a different plane. "We must conceive a world emptied of that ideal of 'happiness'—a happiness grounded on successful romantic love—which still supplies the motive of our popular fiction."[5]

To let go of those images imposed on us by our romantic heritage, we *must* visualize another world. Not the ancient world that existed before Eleanor of Aquitaine came on the scene, for that had its own drawbacks. Not that known in eastern civilizations, such as Japan or India, where courtly love has never gained widespread acceptance. We must create another, less rigid, in which we can break free of our romantic imagery and know each other without our traditional roles to confuse us. Until we let go of our romantic concepts we have no way to break down the barriers between us, to quit fighting the battle of the sexes. Don't we know by now that it is

4. Lewis, p. 3.
5. Ibid., p. 4.

125

CONCEPTS CREATE OUR IMAGES

not sex we're fighting about at all? We are warring over romance! The concepts of our romantic belief system keep us fighting the battles that maintain the war. To negotiate the treaty that will end the war, we need to find out what it is we're really fighting about. We need to uncover the rules of romance. One of those rules is that we should find happiness through our romantically founded, and often ill-founded, marriages.

CONCEPTS CREATE OUR IMAGES

6. THE RULES OF ROMANCE: HAPPINESS

THIS RULE GUARANTEES SUFFERING
AND *UN*HAPPINESS.

The twelfth-century concept of romance, exemplified by the Court of Love of Eleanor of Aquitaine, extolled love as the highest virtue. Although its interpretation has varied through the centuries, the basic theme has remained unaltered; today love is still generally regarded by us in the present day as the goal of life, the panacea for all ills, the hoped-for solution to all problems. When it proves otherwise as a result of one of life's hard lessons, we are genuinely surprised. It rarely occurs to us initially that love may be an inconsequential goal, only a highlight of life rather than its totality.

How could we know differently, without experiencing the reality of love for ourselves? We've been taught the rules of romance since birth and have unquestioningly accepted them. How can we, when we are young and inexperienced, defy our culture? We cannot know, without having tasted the bitter dregs of romance, that its promises are empty dreams and its siren song only a badly composed, half-remembered melody? Its hope has been with us for so long; how can we know that the promise of happiness implicit in romantic love holds a hidden set of chains? Yet even though we pray that love will solve our problems and our romantic dream will blissfully materialize, we believe in the chains.

We still hold some of the same beliefs as those long-gone people of the twelfth century. They believed:

> . . . *love was resistless in power; it absorbed the lovers nature; it became his sole source of joy and pain. So it sought nothing but its own fulfillment; it knew no honour save its own demands. It was unimpeachable, for in ecstasy and grief it was accountable to no law except that of its being. This resistless love was also life's highest worth, and*

129

THE RULES OF ROMANCE: HAPPINESS

*the spring of inspiration and strength for doing
valourously and living nobly.*[1]

Andreas Capellanus tells us, in words that still have meaning to
us eight centuries later, "Love gets its name (*amor*) from the
word for hook (*amus*), which means 'to capture' or 'to be captured,' for he who is in love is captured in the chains of desire and
wishes to capture someone else with his hook"[2] Andreas compares the lover to a poor fish, netted by the irresistible power of
love. Even today we believe firmly in our defenselessness against
love. We anticipate love's ensnaring us with "chàins of desire;"
once caught we'll have no power to free ourselves, but must, like
the fish, remain hooked. Our popular phrase, to "fall in love,"
conveys that reminiscent weight of "resistless" power. We
realize we can choose *not* to marry someone, but who can choose
not to fall in love? Somehow the power of love seems great enough
to sweep one "off his feet," as we say. And what happens to the
love once he (or she) is swept? "Love conquers all," we answer,
which means in essence, "Don't think about it; don't acknowledge
your indecision and your qualms; stay helpless, hopeless, and
hooked."

In ancient times, people feared
such an irresistible love, thinking it would lead them into madness and despair. Today we seek it, believing that such a love
comes once in a lifetime, that it's "true love," and our source of
salvation for all time. We believe still as Andreas did when he
wrote in 1184, "a true lover would rather be deprived of all his
money and of everything that the human mind can imagine as
indispensable to life rather than be without love, either hoped for
or attained."[3] Love, from the twelfth century on, changed in the
minds of western men and women—from insanity, a healthy joke,

1. Henry Osborn Taylor, *The Mediaeval Mind: A History of the Development of*
Thought and Emotion in the Middle Ages, vol. 1 (Cambridge: Harvard University Press,
1959), p. 590.

2. Capellanus, p. 31.

3. Ibid., p. 30.

130

THE RULES OF ROMANCE: HAPPINESS

or a domestic necessity to the highest good. Love became not only an ennobling experience, but the one and only source of happiness. In our time love has been inextricably linked with another powerful determinant in the search for happiness—marriage. Therein lies the source of many of our current problems.

One of the most pervasive and destructive concepts of the romantic fantasy in our society is that we will find happiness through love—that we should be happy, and that marriage will automatically ensure us that happiness. We envision perfect love, with marriage as our final goal from early childhood. Women in particular are led to believe that once they find their man, all their problems will be solved. Men also look toward love as a solution to unhappiness, not considering they may need more than the right partner to give them a sense of fulfillment. Other intangibles may be necessary: feelings of competence, importance, usefulness, interest, confidence. Men and women may both need to accomplish something they consider of worth—along with finding love—to bring a sense of completion to their lives.

Often, however, because of our inane romantic beliefs, we deliberately pick the *wrong* partner to accompany us on our marital way. If we do not realize our mistake on the day of our wedding (some of us do!) we find out soon afterward. Yet we usually stick with that partner, knowing we are wrong for each other, knowing that two wrongs do not make a right, that two resentful people do not make for a harmonious relationship. We stay together, demanding that the other person make us happy. Even in our incompatibility we insist that the other person change to fit our idea of the perfect mate, and provide us with the dream of happiness we've been taught to expect from marriage.

We cannot conceive of that dream of happiness as only an elusive fantasy. Since childhood we have been encouraged to believe in its tangible existence. We've looked for happiness as a permanent state of being, and we are continually disappointed when we find it has evaded us once

131

THE RULES OF ROMANCE: HAPPINESS

more. We have not been taught that feelings are temporal, that the more we seek out one feeling, the more it will elude us. We have not been taught that if we attain happiness for a short time it will disappear when we become angry, hurt, or grief-stricken. We may become happy again, to be sure, but the feeling will never last forever. No one has the power to fix a feeling permanently in time. All that human beings can know as a certainty is change. People change, feelings change, and if one is happy, then that too will change. I often remember the words of the old Persian philosopher who was asked for advice in bad times. "Even this will pass away," he responded to his questioner. And in good times? The same applies.

With change as our only known reality, how can we find permanent happiness in anything? Yet the rules of romance suggest that we'll find that permanence. They tell us that we should be happy. We should seek happiness, expect marriage to make us happy, and, in particular, believe that our lovers have the power to give us happiness forever. If we don't find that perfect dream of happiness, we not only blame our partners for not making us happy, we also blame ourselves. I've heard many people say, "I've got everything a person could ask for—a good wife (or husband), beautiful kids, good job. Why am I not happy?" They don't consider they may have many reasons for feeling the way they do; they may resent their partners bitterly and lack any intimacy between them. Or they may be frustrated by countless other problems: finances, career, relatives, location, ill health. One man, recently divorced and under tremendous job pressures but in the middle of a searing love affair, told me, "I can't understand it. I've got this gal who loves me and she's good for me, unlike my ex. I really care for her too, but it doesn't seem to be enough. I'm still unhappy." Others, like him, have expressed similar disappointment with love. Yet, no matter what their other frustrations or negative feelings, they expect that if they have love and/or marriage, they should be happy.

Our underlying belief in the irresistible power of love also assures us that we have no choice in

132

the matter. Love strikes and impales whom it will with Cupid's arrow. The lover is helpless to resist its power. We have no ability to help ourselves, but most succumb to love. If the lover is not the person we visualized, or if the love does not feel quite right, we still have no choice. We must submit to the power of love because, as the saying goes, "It's bigger than both of us." After love hits, we believe, along with Andreas, that we must suffer: "Love is a certain inborn suffering derived from the sight of an excessive meditation upon the beauty of the opposite sex, which causes each one to wish above all things the embraces of the other."[4]

Two opposite and therefore unattainable concepts are set up at once as a basic premise of romance: that love is the only path to happiness, and that love automatically brings suffering. It may seem impossible that one can be happy and suffer at the same time, but we believe it. If we're unhappy in what we assume is true love, we castigate ourselves for not being happy, as we *should* be. But our unhappiness itself appears as a sure sign that we are in love. If one cannot get the beloved out of his or her mind, if the thought of losing the beloved brings anguish, if the lover is in agony while away from the beloved, then he or she can be sure it is true love. Ridiculous? Not at all. I've heard similar ideas expressed hundreds of times by friends and clients. I used to hold these beliefs myself in my romantic days. We've accepted the obsessive quality of love in our day every bit as much as Andreas (who calls it excessive) did in his.

Love is increased, says Andreas, if it's hard to achieve: ". . . it is said to increase if the lovers see each other rarely and with difficulty; for the greater the difficulty of exchanging solaces, the more do the desire for them and the feeling of love increase."[5] And, of course, the more difficult it is, the more one is bound to suffer, the more helpless

4. Ibid., p. 28.
5. Ibid., p. 153.

133

THE RULES OF ROMANCE: HAPPINESS

one is to resist that suffering. Andreas says, "if one gets easily what he desires he holds it cheap. . . . On the other hand, whenever the possession of some good thing is postponed by the difficulty of getting it, we desire it more eagerly and put forth a greater effort to keep it."[6] So our very desire to find happiness through love causes us suffering when we don't have it. Too often, it causes us suffering even when we do.

The kind of "excessive meditation" on the beloved that Andreas stresses, which supposedly indicates to us that we're in love, is, in my mind, fascination. I took years to discover that being fascinated with someone is extremely destructive to me as well as to a relationship. When I am fascinated with another person I discount myself. And, telling myself my feelings don't count, I lose contact with what is going on in my own body. Being so out of touch with myself, I am unable to make any decision at all on the basis of what I'm feeling about the other person. Certainly, of all questions, this is the one we need to ask ourselves if we're wondering what we feel about someone: "What do I feel inside my body when I'm with this person?" There's no other way to know.

When I am fascinated, I have all of my attention on that other person; I am thinking about and evaluating him (or her), using concepts given me by my romantic upbringing: he's so smart, or attractive, handsome, charming, etc. At the same time I am comparing myself with that person unfavorably: I'm not as smart, attractive, and so on. All the while I tell myself how fantastic that person is, I criticize myself. And when my negativism results in self-castigation I tell myself all the more that he is great, and I am worthless. If I have feelings of anger, hurt, or fear, I will bury them inside and work myself deeper into my self-made mire.

Our propensity for carrying such a love into marriage cements us in destructive, though often enduring, relationships. If we fall in love with someone

6. Ibid., p. 99.

fascinating, think obsessively about that person, suffer a great deal, and have difficulty obtaining love from our loved one, we may consider marriage. It is the logical next step in our society. After all, we are told that marriage is the answer to everyone's prayers. So we make a permanent decision on the basis of a temporal romantic infatuation, then whip ourselves into living by that decision for years afterward. The more obsession and suffering we go through, the surer we can be, say our romantic contemporaries, that we're in love. And when we marry, our temporary obsessions, our heretofore transient sufferings, become permanent.

Marriage does not change the feelings of the people who've undertaken that "logical" next step. It will quite likely intensify them instead, sometimes to the unbearable point. If their love was founded on romantic concepts alone, the couple is in trouble. The feelings won't go away by themselves, so the partners are stuck with all the suffering, all the obsession, all the powerlessness and helpless feelings that originally told them they were truly in love. They're stuck, in effect, in a symbiotic relationship.

A symbiosis is a mutual dependency, a complementary relationship that can occur between people, animals, or other living creatures. In human relationships a symbiosis is normal, healthy, and life-sustaining for the child in the first few years of life. As the child gets older, the symbiotic need for care and nurturing will lessen if the parents, particularly the mother, provide adequate caring. The parent will be able to let the child go as the child expresses a desire to break away and establish his or her own identity. But if the relationship has been traumatic, if the child has not been permitted to progress through each stage of growth with adequate nurturing, then both parent and child will feel compelled to clutch each other tighter as time goes by. At the basis of the symbiosis is a terrible need on the part of both parent and child, a need to be filled.

Far from leaving behind such

135

symbiotic relationships when we leave our parental homes, we naturally continue to look for what we know. So if our symbiosis has bonded us to our parents with suffering and misery, we tend to seek out a relationship similar to the one we left behind. We may not like it, but it seems familiar to us, so we cling to the new one as tightly as we had clung to the old. No matter how many partners we know, if we haven't let go of our childhood needs, we will continue to seek out relationships patterned after our original symbiosis.

We may even stay with a partner who is absolutely, incompatibly wrong for us, fighting continually, but believing our disharmony is love. Others will confirm our belief. "Lover's quarrels," they say, and accept our misery as proof of love. We hope the quarrels will not go on and keep hoping that somehow we can change that other person into the ideal lover we want—as we wished to change our parents and never could. We stay in the relationship, noted only for its daily bickering, and hope that sometime soon our partners will change. How long do we stay? It depends on how long we can control our feelings. I managed for five years with my former husband, and cannot remember one day without a fight. I've known others who've stayed for thirty years and are still hanging in there, hoping.

Trained to discount our feelings, we try to use our power of reason to think through our problems and resolve our misery. So we think, and then we think some more. When logic fails to penetrate our confusion, we end up going back to those rules on which we have modeled our lives—the rules of romance. Those rules tell us we were right in marrying for the reasons we did; love and marriage should automatically follow romantic fascination. The rules tell us that if the relationship does not seem right, it's not because we chose the wrong partners and have grown to dislike them; it's because love soured, or our partners have changed, or the romance has gone out of the marriage. Because the rules justify our behavior, we may keep trying for many more miserable years, denying the

136

THE RULES OF ROMANCE: HAPPINESS

reality of who our partners are and what we feel when we are with them, still hoping that he or she will change to fit our dream.

But the rules are wrong. The truth is that romance encourages destructive symbiotic relationships. Romance encourages people to love each other on the basis of their needs. Instead of permitting people to love each other for *who* they are, the romantic concept dictates that people love one another for the happiness that each can get from the other person, encouraging each to lean on the other until both grow weary from the burden. Romantic love, in our culture, sucks lovers dry, drains every bit of good feeling from each person for the sake of the other, suffocates both. Nancy Friday says:

> . . . *our culture confuses symbiosis and love;* but when we are grown, symbiosis and real love are mutually exclusive. . . . *In a symbiotic relationship, there is no real concern for the other person. There is just a need, a craving to be connected, no matter how destructive.*[7]

Our belief that this need can be satisfied through love is based on our centuries-old acceptance of the concept that only love can make us happy, and only a lover can supply us that love.

If we were unfortunate enough to have such a traumatic or abusive childhood that we have tremendous unresolved inner needs, no present-day relationship will ever satisfy our internal longings. Our only hope, in such a case, is to explore our own feelings, and there are many ways to do this; therapies and classes and workshops are available today to help people reexperience their childhood feelings and let them go. But if we believe implicitly in our romantic training, we'll never work on our own growth. We will only look harder for some lover to supply us with the good feelings that we did not get from

---

7. Nancy Friday, *My Mother, My Self: The Daughter's Search for Identity* (New York: Dell Pub. Co., 1978), p. 69.

137

THE RULES OF ROMANCE: HAPPINESS

our parents, substituting a grown-up symbiosis for the childhood one we didn't really leave behind.

We will get into romance, and then marriage, picking a partner because he can supply us with the strength we lack; because she can make us into the fun person we would like to be; because he or she can make us happy. Down deep we'll continue to believe that we are powerless to find these attributes in ourselves, helpless to achieve happiness for ourselves. We will keep right on believing that only our lovers can make us feel good, and that if we do not it must be their fault for not giving us what they should. We will blame each other for not making happiness our permanent and unalterable state of bliss.

Some of us believe so strongly that we *should* be happy that we con ourselves into thinking we are when we really are not. We have an amazing ability to disguise our feelings when we want to, convincing ourselves that we feel one way when we really feel quite the opposite. Several clients who have persuaded themselves in this way that they were happy have come to me when their relationships suddenly evaporated. They had believed in their mutual happiness until one morning they woke to find their partners gone. Lillian M. was one of these.

Lillian came to see me for chronic depression. Her husband, she explained, had recently announced that he didn't love her anymore and wanted a divorce. He moved out the next day. She was stunned by this, she said, because they had been so happy. She had had no idea previously—none, she insisted—that he was unhappy with her. They had been married for ten years, she told me, and all those years had been good. She wanted nothing more than to have him come back.

I had a tough time believing all that; in fact, I couldn't buy it at all. When I asked about her history, Lillian told me she'd first married a surly, critical man who resented her inability to give him sons. She had married him to get away from a home situation that seemed intolerable, but

138

found that her married life was even worse. When Ross came along, Lillian was ready to find someone else. She had thought Ross handsome and considerate; he said all the right words and offered to take her anywhere she wanted to go. She told herself how lucky she was to find a man like him, and kept on telling herself that for years afterward. She did not deserve to have such a good man, she told me.

"Why do you put yourself down so much?" I asked.

"I don't know," she said. "I guess I've always had an inferiority complex."

"Do you think your husband is superior to you?" I asked.

"Oh, yes," she said quickly. "He can do everything I can't; he's charming and witty and the life of the party. I can never think of anything to say. Everyone likes Ross."

"Except you," I said.

"Oh, no, I still love him very much," she said. "I just want him to come home."

"Aren't you angry with him for walking out on you?" I asked.

"No," she said. "I'm hurt, but I can't be angry with him. He must have had his reasons."

"What are they?" I asked.

"I don't have any idea," she sighed. "I can't understand why he left. We've been so happy, and now he says he wants a divorce."

"Does he have someone else?" I asked.

"I don't think so," she said. "He said there's no real reason; he just doesn't love me anymore. He wants to be my friend, but he doesn't want to live with me anymore. I can't stand the thought of living without him. There isn't any point to going on anymore."

"Are you thinking of killing yourself?" I asked.

139

THE RULES OF ROMANCE: HAPPINESS

"I've thought about it a lot lately," she admitted.

"How have you thought of doing it?" I asked. (I get even nosier than usual whenever anyone mentions the possibility of suicide.)

"Oh, maybe drive into a brick wall or something," she said. "But with my luck I'd just get crippled for life, so I suppose I'd never do it."

"I'm glad about that," I said. "I don't want to take you on as a client if you're planning to kill yourself. I haven't lost anybody yet and I'm not about to now." I asked her to promise me that she wouldn't commit suicide until our next meeting, with our contract renewable at that time. She reluctantly agreed.

"You do have options other than killing yourself, you know," I said, "even though you can't see them now. There are other men in the world, too."

"I don't want anyone else," she said. "Just Ross."

"Do you mean to tell me you were so happy with him that you could never be happy again with someone else?" I asked.

"Yes," she said firmly. "Our life together was perfect."

"I can't believe that," I said. "You mean you never got angry at him?"

"Sure, I got mad at him occasionally, but I wouldn't tell him about it," she said.

"Why not?" I asked.

"I was afraid he'd hit me," she said.

"Did he ever really hit you?" I asked.

"He used to hit me a lot when we first got married. Finally I left him for two months, and after I came back he never hit me again. But I guess I was always afraid he might. I never dared tell him when I was angry."

140

THE RULES OF ROMANCE: HAPPINESS

The rest of her story came tumbling out. It was not long after their marriage that Lillian discovered Ross was an incorrigible liar. It wasn't that he *could* not tell the truth, but he *would* not tell it if he could help it. He would much rather embellish and exaggerate a fact until she rarely knew what was the truth and what was not. Still, he whispered sweet words in her ears, words she desperately wanted to hear. He told her how beautiful she was (she had always thought of herself as ugly) and how much he wanted her with him (she had felt rejected by her own family). As the years went on, he stopped flattering her and said very little. When he spoke to her at all it was only to find fault with her. Lillian excused him by telling herself he was right, because she was usually to blame anyway. She pushed his harsh words out of her head and refused to acknowledge the fact that he lied to her. She wanted so desperately to be happy, and she was still fascinated with Ross.

"He spoke so beautifully," she said, "sometimes I didn't even care if it was a lie. I loved to listen to him."

"Didn't you ever think that Ross might not mean all those things he said to you?" I asked.

"I know that I did," she admitted, "but I was so hungry to hear someone talk to me like that. I mean, Ross talked to me about beauty—sunsets and poetry. All my former husband talked about was how the crops were failing or what was wrong with the pigs."

"What did you feel later on in your marriage?" I asked.

"Later Ross got very critical. He wanted me to keep the house just right, and if I didn't he always found something to criticize," she said. "I still didn't care though. I thought I was lucky to have him."

Gradually in our therapy sessions Lillian was able to admit the reality of her marriage. It had not been the perfect relationship she had originally told me it was. Lillian realized that she had buried her own resentment by

141

catering to her husband. Her repressed feelings did not let her off lightly. She suffered from continual migraine headaches and back pain. After about two months of therapy she reported that she felt better than she had in years, rarely had headaches or pain, and her depression had lifted. True, some days were worse than others, especially when she caught herself saying the same old things: about how lucky she had been to have a man like Ross, how well he had treated her, how handsome and well-spoken he had been. But when she heard herself repeating the old clichés and realized they had not fit the reality of her marriage for years, perhaps ever, she stopped saying them.

Throughout her marriage Lillian followed the concepts of romance as she had learned them. Her parents had taught her that a good wife should do her best to please her husband, no matter what his request. In the area of sex, Ross reemphasized her parents' advice. He told her early in their married life that she was never to say no to sex, and she never had. But often, she admitted, she felt nothing.

"He expected me to turn into a passion flower the minute we got into bed, no matter how badly he'd treated me during the day. I couldn't do that. But I never refused him."

Ross, in turn, criticized her all the more because of her lack of response. Superficially, Lillian tried even harder to please him, but their relationship continued spiraling downward. She could never do enough for him; indeed, the more she tried, the more he seemed to resent it. And as Lillian's own resentment grew, her efforts to please her husband became empty gestures of appeasement. Toward the end of my notes on Lillian's case I noticed the words "Trying to please is trying to control."

Control is inherent in any relationship problem. Whenever people meet, they maneuver to establish order in their relationships. When two or more people meet for the first time, when a new person enters into an existing order (such as an office), or when people change, their relation-

THE RULES OF ROMANCE: HAPPINESS

ships must be adjusted. If they do not reach agreement on their respective positions, they will continue to conflict with each other. Only when they arrive at a mutually agreed upon order do they have stasis, or rest. They can agree on respecting each other as adults, or they can agree that one will submit to the other's dominance in a symbiotic, child-parent way. As long as both accept it, however, the relationship will go on. More often than not, in our society, the partners continue on in manipulative, draining symbioses rather than open, intimate, and satisfying relationships. Both partners may be unhappy, yet they endure their misery because they don't know how to change it.

We can initiate or maintain control in any number of ways. One of the most subtle ways is trying hard to please the other. When one person is trying to please another, he (or she) is attempting to impose some control so that the other person will behave in a predictable manner. He is trying to arrange the future so the other person will act as the pleaser wants. The pleaser can then react with a well-rehearsed behavior pattern, adapting his behavior according to prior beliefs, and expecting that the other will do the same. Pleasing in this manner is manipulating someone else without having to respond to that person with feelings.

Nevertheless, we believe without question that we should try to please our partners. We're barraged on all sides with the rightfulness of pleasing. Recently I heard an actress on television say, "I want to be the best I can for my husband. I like to please him because he makes me so happy." Pleasing each other and making each other happy is commonly accepted by us as the only way to go!

I cannot count the number of people I've worked with who believe implicitly in the notion that they should always try to please others to maintain a smooth relationship. They believe that they should *not* reveal any negative feeling they might have but instead "put on a happy face," always. We have all been taught this; pleasing one's lover is an integral part of the romantic concept. Not only does Andreas

143

imply that a lover should try to please his beloved out of fear of losing her, he states unequivocally that a lover is compelled to do so in the very name of love:

> *Men find it easy enough to get into Love's court,*
> *but difficult to stay there, because of the pains that*
> *threaten lovers; while to get out is, because of the*
> *desirable acts of love, impossible or nearly so. For*
> *after a lover has really entered into the court of*
> *Love he has no will either to do or not to do*
> *anything except what Love's table sets before him*
> *or what may be pleasing to the other lover.* [8]

Pleasing someone else is not only manipulating another person by controlling, it is also being controlled. Again, romance sets up an impossible situation for us. Two people trap themselves together in the name of love, willingly submitting to each other's control. I shudder to think of the hidden rage generated from the very beginning by such a tender trap. Nor can we see our way out of it. Anytime someone submits in helplessness and tries to please the other person because he or she *should*, anger is bound to be bubbling underneath the surface. We have no freedom of choice in such a setup; we *must* please because we are in love, and that's all there is to it. And if we don't? Then either the expectations of our partners in love may manipulate us back into line, or our partners may walk out because we are not being good and proper lovers. If the latter is the case, the one who is not being "good" just lucked out! That person has been *freed*, like it or not!

Too often, the pleaser cannot stand the thought of being lonely, and so gets back into line and continues the game. Such a subtle, hostile game! It goes like this: If the pleaser is a woman, she may ask her partner—not express her desire in a straight forward manner, but ask in a roundabout way—"Would you like to go out to eat tonight, dear?" Her part-

8. Capellanus, p. 71.

144

ner may respond naively, "No, I'm too tired; let's stay home." The pleaser feels irritated with her partner because she really wanted to go out, so she starts criticizing him in her own mind: "He's always too tired to go out; can't he see that I need to get out occasionally? He's a drag." The partner picks up her irritation and feels uneasy, realizing that she wanted to go out, so the next time she broaches a request he may say, "Whatever you want, dear." Again she is irritated, because he is not giving her the right answer. She wanted him to respond enthusiastically and suggest a restaurant. Even if he had, he would have been wrong, however, because he had not named the right restaurant, and again she would be irritated. There is no pleasing a pleaser.

Or, if the pleaser is a man, he may try to do what he thinks his wife would like. For example, he changes the living room furniture while she's off on a trip. He has heard her say she likes Danish modern, so he junks the old and buys a full set of modern furniture. When she comes home he waits for her praise but hears instead, "What have you done? You've changed the furniture. I hate it!" "But dear," he says indignantly, "I was only trying to please you!" The pleaser is angry, but safe. He didn't have to discuss his idea openly with her; he could go ahead and act on his assumptions. He had control of the situation and his partner. And the old furniture, which *he* probably disliked, is gone, with the new furniture, which *he* likes, in its place.

Trying hard to please a person usually amounts to nothing more than trying to get the other person to give us what we want. It may mean maneuvering that person into making a decision, or it may mean projecting our own desires upon the other person in the form of assumptions. A pleaser ostensibly strains to do what he or she thinks the partner wants, but the pleaser's own desires are uppermost in mind. The pleaser doesn't have to take a stand by expressing a direct opinion, but can wait until the other person makes a suggestion; then (zap! gotcha!), "You're to blame." The bottom line to the pleaser's justification is the most devastating of all: If the partner finally

145

has enough and confronts the pleaser with, "Why didn't you tell me you wanted to go out to dinner?" or "Why didn't you tell me you hated our furniture?" the pleaser will say, in a total disregard of his or her partner's existence, "But dear, I didn't want to hurt your feelings!"

I am aware that when I'm with a pleaser I feel an instant, subtle irritation at his or her request. I have a tendency to respond negatively while criticizing the person mentally: "Why can't he decide?" If I hook into the pleaser's request in this way, I usually feel a sense of guilt and reverse myself by trying to outplease the pleaser. The conversation might go like this:

PLEASER
"What would you like to do tonight?"

ME
"Nothing." Then, feeling guilty, "Ah, what would you like to do?"

PLEASER
"Anything you would."

ME
"How about a movie?"

PLEASER
(Zapping me.) "There's nothing good playing."

After I try to outplease the pleaser I end up thinking that nothing I can do is right for that person, and feel guilty for trying—all very appropriate feelings in such a situation. I confuse myself by thinking, "But he is being so good by trying to please me, I shouldn't be angry." If I buy that trip, I'm stuck with my feeling of guilt and insecurity, and the pleaser is stuck with his (again!) very appropriate thought, "Nobody can please me." Color me blue, but color the pleaser, finally and despairingly, lonely.

When one decides to stop being a pleaser, disregarding the ancient rules of romance, the two

146

partners may experience agitation for a time. Feelings are so unsettling. Responding, the opposite of controlling, is often very upsetting. Sharing with each other what each feels at the moment means becoming vulnerable to the other. Through being open, each takes the risk of being hurt by the other person. Sometimes the underlying fear is, "If I make a decision and it's wrong, you'll hate me," or, "If I told you how I really felt, you might leave me."

Responding is also upsetting because the agitation goes on in one's own head, as well as with a partner. We are so circumscribed by our internal rules that we may suffer a great deal of agitation by rebelling against them. I have a hunch that many marital fights are not so much between partners as within our own minds. For example, a woman may fight her husband's shoulds fiercely, but her very vehemence is caused by her internal conception of herself. If he tells her not to act in certain ways she may rage at him, yet hear her own internal voice of authorization echoing in her mind, activated by her husband's expectation and corroborating it, "Ladies don't act that way!"

Pleasing, on the other hand, may give the outward appearance of serenity to a relationship. When a person uses parental and societal authorizations as a basis for behavior, he or she does not have to think about or experience feelings at the moment. Long-established habit makes that unnecessary; one just behaves the way one should, the way it has always been done, and there is no agitation. One doesn't have to respond in the here and now, but can behave according to predetermined beliefs. The pleaser usually expects, however, that because he or she is trying so hard to accomplish his or her fantasy of what the partner wants, the partner should reciprocate. When the partner, being displeased, does not, the pleaser, more than resentful, is full of righteous rage. But expressing those feelings is prohibited in the pleaser's catechism. The feelings get pushed down inside, making the surface of the relationship look as placid as a summer lake, while the depths boil and seethe. Many couples hold themselves under such rigid con-

147

trol that they never get upset with each other outwardly. They prefer to stay closed off from each other—untouchable, calm, and sedate. Then one word may set off a storm, and the hateful feelings bubble up, pouring out from that bottomless sea. Even if the eruption never occurs and they manage to keep their feelings hidden, they will never be able to share openly with each other. They will end up as pleasers must—lonely, isolated, and alienated.

Lillian had been lonely in her relationship with her husband, but she had not admitted it to herself during all her married years. Their lack of open communication had become apparent shortly after they got married. Ross had started to play golf on weekends, and he continued through out their years together. At first he played on Sundays; then, as the years passed, he also played on Saturdays and holidays. When he wasn't on the course he would sit in the clubhouse drinking beer and talking to his friends. Lillian did not play golf although she would have been willing to learn. Ross didn't ask her. He went his way, she went hers, and she futilely, silently wished he would spend time with her.

"I can see now that I resented his staying away all those weekends," she said. "It seemed to me at times that he was trying to keep away from me, but he would never admit it. He wouldn't even talk about it. When I asked him why he wouldn't spend his weekends with me, he'd tell me not to push him too far. So I just kept telling myself that if I really loved him I should try to please him by not being a nag."

Her acquiescence didn't take away her loneliness or her gnawing sense of resentment. There was no way she could express her anger to Ross. He would not listen; he did not want to talk about it; he would not sit still to hear her out. If she tried to tell him what she felt, he would swear at her and leave the room. So Lillian was stuck with her feelings which, the more she repressed, the more she suffered from depression and bodily ailments. As for sex, she did not deliberately withhold it; she had never refused Ross after his warning

148

early in their marriage. But, feeling angry, even though generally unaware of it, she turned off sensually. The result was a state of sexual numbness that persisted no matter how often she decided to please him. Despite her "trying" to please, her unemotional response to Ross gave him no pleasure.

Had she known what her feelings were and dared to express them, Lillian might have had a satisfying relationship that would still be a marriage. She and Ross could have had ten years of warmth and caring to remember instead of the frustrating and isolated years that each had spent with the other. Or, she might have found out very soon that she had no relationship at all. They could have gone their separate ways and saved ten years of their lives for other, more satisfying, companions.

Our acquired romantic concepts keep us from being straight with each other, or for that matter with ourselves. Through trying so hard to please others, we often tell them what we think they want to hear. We edit our speech so that it comes out softened, tempered, twisted in meaning. We assume we know how another person will receive what we say, so we say only what we think the other will approve of. We deflect questions, not wanting to take the risk of answering directly. We distract the other person from the truth by going off on a tangent. We don't communicate what we actually feel to the other person; we say we don't want to hurt that person, when what we really mean is that we don't want to take the risk of being hurt. Andreas says, and we still believe it, "A lover is afraid to do or to say anything which might for any reason make his beloved angry or give her a grievance against him."[9]

This smacks of symbiosis and control, not responsiveness. The lover is trying to control the beloved and arrange the future. As children, many of us behaved the same way, afraid to say anything to anger Momma and incur her wrath. Then, we were probably very much in touch with our

9. Ibid., p. 190.

149

real world. If we had no permission to express our feelings openly, we would have been crazy to try. We would have let ourselves in for our parents' anger, which for a small child is worse than the wrath of God. We might have even jeopardized our place in the family home. Children have been given away to the courts or to foster homes, or abandoned, if the parents thought they were unmanageable. So the symbiotic relationships that sustained us in childhood were necessary then, even if they were destructive for us. We needed then to adapt to our parents, however we could, in order to survive.

After we have grown up and left home, we *have* survived. We no longer need to maintain that tie to our parents, or adapt to our fantasy of them through our lovers. What will our lovers do if we tell them what we're really feeling? What is the worst that could happen? Our lovers could die of a broken heart on the spot! But how many people have that tender a heart? They could get mad and scream at us, and we could die! But how many of us are that fragile that we would die from fright? Our lovers might reject us! Now we get down to the heart of the problem: We fear being rejected by our lovers—just as we were afraid of being rejected by our parents when we were small (and may still be when we're big). We are scared of rejection even when we are so angry that we may be considering leaving our partners. Even then we won't be straight with what we're feeling, because the habit of a symbiotic relationship is so strong. We still try to please the other by hedging about our feelings, still trying to suck approval from the stern parent that the other, in our internal reality, has become.

We are afraid to show any feeling at all different from the one the partner expresses. We fear showing any separateness, any sense of self. Even in a miserable relationship, or one on the verge of breaking up, we fear causing any division between us. We prefer, though suffering our own internal rage, to appear united. Nancy Friday says:

In a symbiotic marriage, you feel protected,
close–in fact, so close that no separation can be

150

tolerated. . . . I've heard this kind of marriage called "the long quiet walk, hand in hand, to the grave." A psychiatrist I know calls it the "tit-lined coffin."[10]

We are afraid to "make the other person mad," so we withhold our own feelings. Such grandiosity, as if we are godlike and have the omnipotence to cause someone else to feel one certain emotion! Such pomposity, as if we alone are the focus of everyone's emotions! How, in truth, can anyone "make" someone else feel something? We can *influence* someone to feel an emotion. People can respond to what we do with a certain feeling and react to our behavior in a predictable manner. But it is *their* feeling, and *they* can have it. Their feelings are *their* responsibility.

When we can start allowing other people to own their feelings, and admit the ownership of ours instead of blaming others for "making us feel," then we can stop pleasing. We can stop maintaining our symbiotic relationships by deferring to our partners. We can separate ourselves from our partners enough to please them only when we truly want to, not when we think we should and not when we're projecting our own desires on them. We can be totally straight about our feelings.

I remember confronting Dan S. on his beliefs about pleasing his wife, gradually helping him to see that he would not hurt her (nor himself) if he told her what he felt. Before we talked, he had few language tools to express his feelings. Whenever he and his wife had an argument, he told her what he thought about her, and she told him what he could do about it! She would fly into a rage, and the battle was on. He would usually try to pacify her, unsuccessfully holding his own anger inside. Their conflicts ended in stalemates, with Dan usually racing out the door in a fury and driving off, with nothing resolved. When Dan came to see me he was ready to either end the marriage or find a mistress.

10. Friday, p. 411.

151

THE RULES OF ROMANCE: HAPPINESS

"What would you like to say to her?" I asked him.

"I'd tell her she's a nag and a bitch and to get the hell off my back."

"Isn't that what you've been telling her?" I asked.

"Well, yes, and all I do is make her madder. Then she starts screaming at me, and I can't stand that. I'd do anything to avoid that kind of conflict, and yet that's what it always comes down to."

"What would you say if you were to tell her what you felt," I asked, "not what you were thinking, but what you were feeling?"

"I'd tell her I was angry at her for trying to change me into somebody I'm not," he answered promptly. "I'd tell her I get scared when she screams at me, then I'm afraid I'll hit her, so I run."

"Why don't you tell her that?" I asked.

"She'd think I was weak if I did," he said. "She'd never forgive me."

"She might not," I admitted, "but wouldn't it be worth the risk? You're thinking about breaking up your marriage now. How about being straight with her first?"

"All right," Dan reluctantly agreed, "I'll try, but it won't be easy."

"It never is," I said.

But he did it. He wrote me a note of appreciation later which said, "My problem was that I was trying to please my wife, and I would do anything to avoid a conflict. Since I saw you, my wife and I have had some battles that would have just killed me before, but with my new language I could finally understand what was going on. It hurt, all right, but at least we both think we're on the right track. And I don't have any of those crazy ideas anymore about a mistress!"

152

THE RULES OF ROMANCE: HAPPINESS

From the tone of his note, I could see that Dan had finally quit trying to please his wife. He had decided to stay and fight, verbally, whenever they got into a conflict. He had risked telling her openly what he was feeling. By being straight with her he could convey to her that he felt she was trying to change him. He had hated her attempts to make him over into her ideal, but he hadn't been able to explain his feelings in words she could understand. From his note, I could see that they were learning to speak the same language.

Isn't this another aspect of our romantic fantasy? We fall in love not with the person as he or she exists in the here and now, but with our ideal of that person. We look at the other person as if we are wearing reflective glasses. When we gaze into our lover's eyes we see, staring back at us, the image we hold in our own minds. As the romantic fantasy fades, and our image of that person begins to blur, we blame our lovers. It is all their fault. They didn't live up to our expectations. Romance has gone; our illusions have flown away; the honeymoon is over. But why is it that we blame our lovers when we should blame our own beliefs—the concepts of romance that we've blithely accepted all these years as the truth?

We do not consider, while "falling in love," that marriage is a day-to-day merger of two separate people who have feelings, thoughts, and desires of their own. Marriage means living with another human being through winter snows and summer heat, through good feelings and petty hassles, through job hunting and home maintenance and arguments with and over children, friends, and relatives. Marriage is two people deciding to live together—usually, though not always, under the same roof; it means a continual negotiation over territory—sharing it, giving it, and taking it. Marriage contains little romantic fantasy, but is simply a living arrangement certified by society.

A good marriage is that in which the good feelings more than merely balance the bad. When the moments of contentment, camaraderie, and joy tip the scale to the positive side—outweighing the anger, irritation, and

153

THE RULES OF ROMANCE: HAPPINESS

disappointment—then the relationship is constructive and worthwhile. If the scales constantly tip to the negative side, the relationship has turned into a destructive and stagnating one for the former lovebirds. The partners then need to consider what changes are possible and what options each has to alter himself, herself, or the relationship itself.

The romantic vision that we picture before marriage floats in our mind's eye as our ideal kind of life. Undoubtedly, our partners have a different picture in their heads. Sooner or later on a lazy, unplanned day, after or even during the honeymoon, one lover will ask the other, "Honey, what should we do today?" If the partners are open with each other, the beloved will express his or her desires and feelings in a straightforward manner, not withholding by trying to please, but being direct: "I'm restless today. I'd like to go for a long walk in the woods." The partner may want to go to a concert, and say so. Then the two will need to negotiate on who will go where and when, and what each feels good about doing. But a pleaser will say deviously, "Whatever you like, dear." Or the pleaser will make an assumption about what the partner wants and will usually be wrong. The pleaser will feel resentful for not having satisfied his or her own desires and will be sure to displease the partner, who may have honestly wanted some straight feedback.

If both believe in pleasing each other at all costs, neither will get satisfaction out of the relationship. Because they are continually straining to do what each thinks the other wants, they live in a fantasy world. Neither really knows what the other wants, but each will fantasize about the partner's desires, then act on those fantasies, whether or not the partner likes it. If the partner objects, the pleaser slides through another skirmish in what may be a long battle, with the characteristic cry, "But I'm only trying to please you." And the marriage may succeed or fail because of that battle cry and how the couple decides how to spend an afternoon.

The marriage will certainly fail if the couple bases the entire relationship on their romantic fan-

154

tasies, "falling in love" with each other in spite of their separate and invariably divergent ideals and living their daily lives according to the rules of romance. Even if they stay together as a couple, the marriage itself can't help but fail in terms of intimacy between the two partners. The myth of romance will ensure that the couple experiences alienation, resentment, and loneliness for most of their time together.

How can they *not* feel angry with each other? The rules of romance assured them that they would be happy once they got married. All their lives they had believed in these rules, waited for the day they would get married, and looked to marriage as the answer to all their problems. Then they fell in love, and immediately the pain and suffering began. Yet they were confused, for the romantic code offers suffering as the gauge to check out their level of love: If they feel anxious, fearful, and distraught when they think of their beloved, then they can be sure it is the real thing!

The longer such a relationship goes on, the more confused and filled with negative feelings the couple becomes. Each might try to take responsibility for his or her own feelings, saying, "What's wrong with me, that I can't appreciate what I have?" But it is hard to take all the blame for one's own bad feelings. Resentment and anger, no matter how well hidden, are like limpets looking for a rock to fasten to. And the most convenient, closest rock happens to be the head on the pillow next to one's own. It is much easier and more tempting to blame one's problems and bad feelings on that other head.

Then the mutual blaming rapidly spirals the couple down toward total alienation. "If only it weren't for you," each thinks, "I'd be happy." Of course, they may be right, and that's the hard part to decide. Would each really be better off without that convenient other person on which to blame his or her problems? Or would each person again cast about for a new romance on which to hang his or her fantastic expectations of an ideal marriage? If they truly would be more satisfied apart, if they have grown enough as individuals to look

155

for a freeing kind of love instead of their present suffocation, if they seek a relationship based on sharing and companionship and caring for another as a person instead of a symbiosis, then the couple would do well to give each other a goodbye kiss and go their separate ways. But if they would separate only to hook immediately into another symbiotic relationship, then they might just as well stay together and work on their own growth as individuals.

Happiness is not a goal to aim for. Its very elusiveness prevents our finding it for long. As I said in my previous book, *Act Yourself*, the fairy tale ending "and they lived happily ever after" would be much more apt if it were phrased "happily sometimes after."[11] Love should not be pursued in the expectation of happiness. Without that impossible goal to disappoint the lovers, love can bring good feelings—zest, energy, relaxation, excitement, gratitude, caring—a sense of joy and contentment. Love can also bring anger, irritation, and hurt—but if these are immediately expressed they will only temporarily dampen the positive feelings. The joy won't be rained out for long but will shine again, like the sun, once the cold and negative feelings are expressed.

Love and romance, in my opinion, are opposites. Love has many connotations: to need, to be of service, to use, to be used by, to care for, to take care of. If any of those meanings imply that one partner is controlling the other in any way, it's not love at all but hostility. When people say, "I love you," they may mean, "I want to eat you up, to ingest you, to have you fill up the emptiness in my belly." They may mean, "I want to hurt you," or, "I want you to hurt me like my parents used to." They may mean, "I want to absorb you into myself so that I can live through you." Do these meanings really indicate love, or, more appropriately, use of another person for the satisfaction of one's needs, one's symbiotic, unfulfilled childhood desire to suck out satisfaction from an internally present parent?

11. Jo Loudin, *Act Yourself: Stop Playing Roles and Unmask Your True Feelings* (Englewood Cliffs, N. J.: Prentice-Hall, Inc., 1979), p. 100.

156

Love that is free of hostility means caring enough for the other person to allow him or her to go, without strings attached, or to stay if he desires—freely—to remain. A freeing kind of love allows the other person to exist as he or she *is*, thinks and feels, without prior expectations about how things *should* be. Tender feelings, which we equated with romance, are the caring, sentimental, or passionate emotions that any of us can have, given the proper mood and setting. But romance itself means controls and strings—chains, even—to make the other person behave in certain predetermined ways. Romance means expectations and fantasies and shoulds; it means suffering and helplessness and bad feelings. Romance also means jealousy, and that's another part of the story.

157

7. MORE JEALOUSY

IN THE NAME OF JEALOUSY WE DESTROY
OUR RELATIONSHIPS.

Our romantic vision beckons us on continually in the quest for the good life. In the United States we are preoccupied with our dream of happiness, and we have different ways of finding it. Some wait; they spend their entire lives working hard, raising their families, saving their pennies, making meticulous plans to relax during their promised "golden years" in comfortable retirement homes. Some chase, striving hard to be happy, rich, famous, or perfect, according to which fad is currently "in." Others believe they have no other purpose but to breeze through life, letting others do the deeds and produce the goods while they float, butterflies on the wind, through what everyone else sees enviously as the "good life."

I have met many of those who have pursued happiness, but I have not known any who found it. I have seen them basking in the sun, playing in the surf, drinking by the pool in magazine ads. In real life the ones who have waited have found their golden years turned into gray misery by poverty, fatigue, or ill health. I've seen the chasers turn into workaholics, alcoholics, or sickaholics—the number of migraines, ulcers, and heart attacks can be directly correlated to their incessant running. And the butterflies? Well, I have never known a butterfly yet whose cocoon of happiness didn't turn in winter into a frigid and coffinlike trap.

I do not think I know, come to think of it, any completely happy people. I am not a happy person myself. Sometimes I'm happy—I sing from sheer joy, or I giggle over a neat memory I've got tucked away in a secret corner of my brain, or I see or smell or hear something that fills me with a sense of wonder. *Sometimes.* Other times I am angry, pissed off, not a bit nice, and all too ready to let everyone around me know about it. I feel bitchy at times, suffering from my personal version of paranoia; raging, snarling, feeling crumby, and crabby—if I were undersea I'd walk sideways and wave my claws around. Other times I'm depressed. I sit in a heap, wondering what in the

161

MORE JEALOUSY

world is the matter with me that I cannot get off my backside and do something—and at that moment I can't. It is not that I will not; my will has failed me, my sick body or repressed feelings are dragging me down, and there is nobody to pull my strings. So I sit helplessly and glower.

I'm not happy *all* the time—maybe not even *half* the time, but *sometimes*. I have an image in my head that says I am scholarly, grown-up, and a hard worker, yet I operate out of my childlike self much of the time. Even in my most serious workshops and classes I have an enormous amount of fun. I can remember many times that I've acted like the silly child I've been told I shouldn't be, and enjoyed every minute of it. The older I get, the more I let my parent messages and resultant inhibitions go, the giddier I can be. I used to be so rigidly grown-up that people thought I was poised. At a workshop several years ago, a woman said to me, "I feel very hostile to you because you seem so poised and sure of yourself." I thanked her for telling me that; it took courage. Since then, both that woman (who has become a staunch friend) and I have become less rigid. She has shown it by letting go of her hostility, and I my poise. Sometimes now I feel like a wet noodle, whether I'm speaking to a hundred people or one. I do not hold myself stiffly anymore; I may stutter and stammer, but it doesn't particularly bother me. If I feel like crying, I cry; if I want to giggle, I do. In my last workshop, I felt very adaptive toward one participant. So whenever he would make a particularly dogmatic statement, I sat cross-legged at his feet. I spent quite a bit of time in that workshop sitting on the floor!

I realize now that I'm not serious, or poised, or grown-up, or crabby, or bitchy *all* the time. Nor am I happy all the time. Feelings change continuously; they don't remain constant. Knowing that, how can I continue to search for happiness as a condition of life? But in our society the carrot of happiness is forever under our noses, tantalizing us on. Do this, buy that, drink this, eat that, go here, or go there and you will be *happy*. I see laughing people in the ads, whiskey glasses in hand;

if I drink that product, the ad implies I can be happy. I visit stores filled with cakes and pastries, temptingly displayed; if I eat them, I can be filled with good feelings. If I smoke I'll find laughter and fun and camaraderie. If I go traveling I'll find love and companionship. If, if, if. The great consumer ripoff tempts me on with it's great "if." I'm like Alice, looking at all the tempting goodies that I should try if I want to find my way out of Wonderland.

What the ads don't tell me is that there is no way out. There is no door out of Wonderland, no escape hatch. If I drink too much I'll eventually die of cirrhosis, or, with a pounding head the morning after, be left wondering how so much fun can feel so bad. If I eat too much of those sugar yummies my rolls of cellulose will cause my heart to strain with exertion. If I smoke I'll get lung cancer, or emphysema. If I spend all my money on a ticket to the other side of the world, I'll realize after I get there that I have dragged all my rotten feelings along with me, and have dysentery besides. There is no way of evading life's problems or my feelings about them. I have real and appropriate reasons for feeling the way I do, even if I don't always know what they are. I can't escape my feelings forever. But romance tells me I should.

Our romantic code says that I should be happy forever, if I follow the rules. If only I act the way society says I should, the manners of which are specified by popular definition, I will find the goal I seek—total and continual happiness. Well, I'm not buying that pitch anymore. I have realized the nonsense inherent in our code of romance. Many people are still buying it, however, believing that through romance they will find the good life, happiness, the way out. They believe that if they do what they're told to do, eat the magic mushroom, drink the eighty-proof elixir, they will find the way out of Wonderland—home. Once there, they believe, they'll find perfect and limitless happiness. Meanwhile, they will know the road by the suffering they have as they travel along it. Some have even convinced themselves they deserve to cry a sea of tears

163

MORE JEALOUSY

forever, or that the dark forest path full of fear and anxiety is the only way there is. For romance tells us our very suffering indicates we've found love, the source of all happiness. Andreas says:

> *Therefore if one has difficulty in obtaining the*
> *embraces of one's lover and obtains them rarely,*
> *the lovers are bound to each other in more ardent*
> *chains of love and their souls are linked together*
> *in heavier and closer bonds of affection. For*
> *constancy is made perfect amid the waves that*
> *buffet it, and perseverance is clearly seen in*
> *adversities.* [1]

I agree that we appreciate things we work for more than those objects given us without any effort on our part. A boy values a bike he's earned through selling papers more than one his father buys with a check. He has had more time to anticipate having it, and appreciates it more when he gets it. I have had similar dreams, for instance, about my new sports car. Certainly I appreciated having it, but the minute I got it, I thought, "What next?" The challenge of getting rather than the satisfaction of having has driven me on from one thing to another, always looking for the "next." My fantasies of future goodies have prevented me from enjoying what I've had in the here and now. Yet romance encourages us to fantasize. The promise, the dream about a lover is more important than relating to him or her in the now. In our romantic tradition we talk about "getting" a lover, as if he or she were a possession to be bought and paid for. And what happens once we've "got" him? Then, quite likely, we create a new fantasy as our pride of ownership fades, and we go on to the "next."

Romance puts love on the same level as the marketplace, where one pays a stiff price for a desirable object and little for one that seems worthless. In his

1. Capellanus, p. 99.

MORE JEALOUSY

book, Andreas continues the medieval idea that women are chattel property, to be bought, sold, or stolen. He expands on that philosophy by suggesting that women are worth more if they deliberately keep the price of the goods high. In order to increase the price, to intensify the lover's "inordinate desire," the woman should make it difficult for the man to get her. Certainly she should not sell herself too cheaply or he will lose interest in her. She should even manipulate. Andreas tells us that to keep hold of a wavering lover a woman "must be careful not to let him know her intentions and she must hide her real feelings and by careful dissimulation make it seem to him that she is not distressed by the upsetting of their love affair. . . ."[2]

M.C. D'Arcy points out that intensity of suffering was, in the twelfth century, at the core of the romantic concept: "The ordinary woman in this feudal age was much more a chattel than an ideal, and yet side by side with her came the dream of a woman at the very vision or thought of whom the heart of man is wounded beyond curing."[3] Nor could the lover be cured by obtaining that vision in the flesh. Central to the concept of romance was the implication that lovers will suffer through their love, ending up losing that love or in despair. Andreas encourages lovers to increase their torment in order to intensify each other's desire: ". . . when love cannot have its solaces, it increases beyond all measure and drives the lovers to lamenting their terrible torments, because 'we strive for what is forbidden and always want what is denied us'."[4]

Even if the lovers get each other, however, they find torment and suffering. D'Arcy suggests that secretly we have a preference for being unhappy, and this love of suffering is written into the code of love: "This lies behind the silly sentimentalism of the romantic movement in Germany and the decadence at the end of the nineteenth century

2. Ibid., p. 160.
3. D'Arcy, p. 37.
4. Capellanus, p. 34.

165

MORE JEALOUSY

as well as the torments and ecstasies of the seventeenth century poets."[5] Symbols of despair—agony, loss, darkness, suffering, death—run as constant threads throughout romantic literature, and are interwoven with symbols of hope—self-awareness, understanding, perfection, love.

We have not let go of those threads today. Our attitudes about romance are shot through with ambivalence, the threads of both suffering and ecstasy. We still believe in suffering, thinking that love will increase if we hold ourselves off from it. Actually, love, in the twelfth-century definition of the term, had nothing to do with happiness. Nowhere does Andreas give the idea, nor do other romantic writers, that obtaining love will bring satisfaction and good feelings. The love that they proclaim as an ideal was a dream that could never be achieved. D'Arcy calls it, "love perpetually unsatisifed," a love that is goal and Grail but not one that can bring contentment or peace. We have clung to these concepts and still use them in our relationships. We particularly believe in increasing the suffering of our lovers by trying to make them jealous. Jealousy, we've been taught to believe, is a valid part of love.

Along with earlier romantics, we believe that if we can make our lovers jealous, we'll have certain proof of their love for us. As Andreas says, ". . . love cannot exist without jealousy." He goes on:

> *Now jealousy is a true emotion whereby we*
> *greatly fear that the substance of our love may be*
> *weakened by some defect in serving the desires of*
> *our beloved, and it is an anxiety lest our love may*
> *not be returned, and it is a suspicion of the*
> *beloved, but without any shameful thought.*[6]

Who would deliberately choose a love based on such a "true emotion?" Any lover would be miserable in a relationship like

5. D'Arcy, p. 37.
6. Capellanus, p. 102.

MORE JEALOUSY

the one described, agonizing that the beloved might leave. Filled with trepidation he would feel insecure and anxious about that love, but powerless to change the situation. The lover would suspect the beloved, distrusting everything she said or did. But, if he were a romantic, obviously he would know for sure he was in love; his suffering would prove it. He would (as I have in the past) undoubtedly make life decisions based on that surety. He might even convince himself he was "happy."

Andreas says, "He who is not jealous cannot love,"[7] defining the emotions of those who love confidently as mere "affection." Three aspects of jealousy must be present to make the emotion a "true" one. He states, "A truly jealous man is always afraid that his services may not be sufficient to retain the love of the woman he loves, . . . he is afraid that she may not love him as he loves her, and he is so tormented with anxiety that he wonders whether she doesn't have another lover. . . ."[8] With this definition of jealousy, Andreas dismisses the love of husband for wife as affection, since a man cannot truly be jealous of his wife. He explains: "But that this last aspect of jealousy is not proper for a married man is clearly apparent, for a husband cannot suspect his wife without the thought that such conduct on her part is shameful."[9] Andreas distinguishes between "real jealousy," which contains three elements, and "shameful suspicion," which does not. He concludes that because "real" jealousy containing the prerequisite three aspects cannot naturally exist between husband and wife, "love between them must necessarily cease, because these two things always go together."[10] He therefore assigns "affection" to married couples, with true love restricted to unmarried lovers.

Jealousy, in romantic terms, is not only the chief indicator of true love but, in Andreas' words,

7. Ibid., p. 184.
8. Ibid., p. 102.
9. Ibid.
10. Ibid., p. 103.

167

MORE JEALOUSY

"the mother and the nurse of love."[11] In my experience, jealousy is something quite different. I define jealousy in most cases as a fear of loss derived from one's childhood fear of being abandoned by his or her parents. The more traumatic experiences a person has had during those impressionable years of childhood, the more intense the fear of being left, even when that person is grown. If one retains archaic feelings of being abandoned (whether the parents actually left the child or not), and if one has not become aware of the origin of those fears, one will undoubtedly project the feelings into a present-day situation. The old panic will spill out toward someone today and the old feelings will dominate, being rationalized by the word "jealousy." The internal terror, actually from long ago, seems like a feeling of today, particularly when our fuzzy romantic thinking still encourages us to believe that jealousy is a normal and natural part of love.

Jealousy may destroy our relationships, making them acrimonious replicas of compatibility. Yet jealousy is inherent in our romantic code, is in fact its very substance. That archaic feeling in our guts, rationalized in the name of romance, encourages us to maintain our symbioses with our partners in clinging need, not freeing love. No matter that the original romantic code stipulated that married people could not love, reserving jealous love for the unmarried. We've long ago blurred the distinction between the two, assuming that true love normally leads to marriage and is continued within that sanctified state thereafter. No matter that Andreas differentiated between jealousy and "shameful suspicion." We've never explored the fine distinction between the two as did earlier romantics. To us jealousy *is* suspicion. And suspicion is fear, which, for most of us, returns us full circle back to our symbiotic need for mama.

How can we know the difference between need and love when the romantic code glorifies jealousy not only as a component part but as the one sure indicator of true love? Once we accept the premise that jealousy denotes love, we

11. Ibid., p. 101.

168
MORE JEALOUSY

set ourselves up in a syndrome of suspicion, mistrust, and doubt in which we project those negative feelings outward and influence our lovers to give them back twofold. Instead of helping us become aware of the actual origin of our doubts and insecurity—in our childhood—romance teaches us that this projection of feelings is appropriate if we are truly in love. We *should* fear that our lovers will leave us, and we *should* alter our behavior to ensure that they won't. So we're encouraged by the very code of romance to become pleasers, connivers, and manipulators of each other. We are taught to cling to our partners by whatever means of manipulation we have at our command because of our internal fear that without them we will be everlastingly lonely.

Whereas many romantics of former generations have welcomed loneliness as an opportunity to worship at the altar of their love, or grieve over its loss, we fear it. We have been imbued with the idea that loneliness is intolerable. Many of us would rather endure a turned-off relationship, even an actively miserable one, than try to make it on our own. Women in particular believe that they will not be accepted by society as a single person. They have been used to defining their worth in their own minds for so long as wife and mother, they cannot picture themselves as persons in their own right without a man. They are so afraid of being lonely that they will seek out a man to cling to in desperation, regardless of whether their feeling for him is positive or not. They would rather remain in a manipulative relationship than face life without a man to lean on. But isn't loneliness and the fear of being alone simply that old childhood fear of abandonment once more? "I want my mommy," we say as children. As adults we change it to, "I need a man," or, "I can't make it on my own without a man." Again, our fear of loneliness is exaggerated by romantic tradition. Marilyn French says:

> . . . *sometimes when you are alone, aren't you*
> *feeling sad mostly because society tells you you're*
> *not supposed to be alone? And you imagine*

169

*someone being there and understanding every
motion of your heart and mind. When if someone
were there he–or even she–wouldn't necessarily be
doing that at all? And that's even worse. When
somebody is there and not there at the same
time. . . . I think loneliness is the creation of the
image makers. Part of the romantic myth. The
other part being, of course, that if you find your
dream person, you'll never feel separate again.
Which is a crock.* [12]

Women are not the only ones inflicted with a fear of loneliness. Since they've been taught the same romantic fallacies as women, men are just as likely to be caught up in the fear of being alone. We are both, women and men alike, stuck in our respective romantic traps. I know several men who have expressed their frustration with wives who are, by their description, cold, unresponsive, even critical and abusing. Yet these men have stayed married to those women. (Twenty years was the minimum among those I've talked to.) Their common fear was verbalized to me by one when he said, "I've wanted to leave my wife since the day after we got married, but I'm afraid that I'll end up a lonely old man." So he stayed, as many other stay, rationalizing their torpidity for the kids' sake, alternating between misery and despair, yet remaining tied symbiotically to their no doubt equally miserable partners.

Such steadfastness of purpose does not always do the kids a service, as many children from strife-torn families can testify. They may be far better off if their parents would conquer their respective fears of loneliness and separate, thereafter to build more constructive lives either alone or with someone new. The rationale of remaining for the sake of the children may have more to do with the needs of the parent than those of the child. Still tied to his own parents, a man such as the one in the preceding example seeks nurturing from a nonexis-

12. Marilyn French, *The Women's Room* (New York: Jove Pub., 1977), p. 358.

170

MORE JEALOUSY

tent parent. Unable either to have his needs met or to change his behavior, he remains stuck, fluctuating between anger and despair, in passivity.

The importance of the passivity mechanism in maintaining symbiotic relationships has been explored by Jacqui Lee Schiff in her work with schizophrenics.[13] Passivity in this sense does not mean being passive; one can alternate between being inert or intensely active but essentially remain stuck in the situation and in the same type of behavior. Schiff outlines four steps in this mechanism: (1) doing nothing relevant to the problem; (2) overadapting to someone else; (3) agitating; and (4) becoming incapacitated or violent; that is, either becoming incapacitated through fainting, migraines, vomiting, etc., or exploding outwardly in violence. A person may be passive, then try very hard to adapt to the partner's wishes. After finding that overadapting doesn't create the expected behavior on the part of the partner, he or she escalates to being agitated. But that still doesn't bring the desired changes, so he or she may explode into violence, quit caring, or implode the feelings into bodily ailments. After violence or incapacitation the person will have released enough tension to revert to inaction again, and the whole process starts all over.

I have heard couples describe their passivity mechanism as a vicious circle, a constant fight, the same arguments happening over and over again. Nothing ever seems to get resolved, yet the two are aware that the fights have an unnerving familiarity. They may go on battling for years, however, in the hope that the other person will somehow change to fit their fantasies. In the interim, the doing-nothing step gets shorter and shorter, and the escalation to violence quicker. Maryann M. described her passivity to me as her "lack of control."

"I don't know what's wrong with me," she said. "I used to be able to control myself when I'd get

13. Jacqui Lee Schiff, *Cathexis Reader: Transactional Analysis Treatment of Psychosis* (New York: Harper & Row, Pub., 1975), p. 10.

171

MORE JEALOUSY

angry with Tom. I could forget about how I felt and go about my work, and pretty soon it would go away. That is, until I got mad again. I can't do that anymore. I'm appalled at my total lack of control. Now it seems like I'm angry all the time. I'm even starting to throw things. I'm terrified that one of these days I'll throw something harmful, like a knife, and connect."

Maryann was discounting herself and her own feelings, which is how many of us maintains passivity. We may discount ourselves or others, or our problems, their significance, and solvability. Maryann had certain pet phrases that she repeated to herself in discounting her feelings, such as, "That's too petty to get mad about," "I shouldn't feel that way," "Be nice," "You're bigger than that," or, "He's trying so hard; why can't I appreciate it and just be happy?" She was frightened by her mounting anger, however, which seemed to grow the more she criticized herself. Finally she decided to call me up for a therapy session, and convinced her husband that he should come with her. Tom sat quietly at first while Maryann poured out her frustrations. After ten years of staying home with the children, she wanted to go back to work. She had been a legal secretary before they got married; now she wanted to reenter the field. Tom wouldn't hear of it, she explained.

"He's afraid I'll meet other men where I work," Maryann said, "and I'll get involved with them. He's so jealous; he thinks everybody is out to make me. It's so ridiculous. I handled myself very well before we got married."

"Is that true, Tom?" I asked checking it out.

"Well, yes," he said. "But she doesn't know when she's leading a man on and when she's not. She doesn't know what happens out there in the world. She's too naive for her own good."

"I am not," Maryann objected. "Look, I'm over forty years old, and he acts as if men are about to rape me every time I go to the water cooler. What he's really objecting to is my talking to people."

172

MORE JEALOUSY

"That's right; you're too friendly for your own good," Tom said. "You'll talk with anybody, anybody at all. You don't even have to know the person and you'll be talking to him. You just don't know what men have in their minds when you act like that."

Tom assumed that all men thought about women in the same way he did, and he may have been right up to a point. Certainly men are taught the romantic concept that women should be provided for and kept in dependent positions. But not all men are as fiercely protective as Tom, nor are all as hung up on sexual issues. Tom held to the traditional belief that men and women, given the time and opportunity, could not resist acting out sexually with each other. He totally discounted Maryann's ability to distinguish between feelings and actions and assumed that she, like everyone else, was at the mercy of her "baser" emotions. Tom's outlook was decidedly puritanical, which spoke volumes about his own training in matters pertaining to sex. Tom not only denied his wife's ability to handle the situation if a man did proposition her, he distrusted her motives for wanting to return to work entirely. He felt comfortable only if she stayed at home, protected from the passions of the outside world and from her own.

Tom and Maryann were stuck in their passivity syndrome by continual discounting. Whereas Maryann discounted her own feelings, Tom discounted both her and the problem itself. He seemed to think that if only she stayed home and shut up, everything would be all right again. Maryann believed that if only Tom would let her get a job, everything would be all right. Since they both believed that the other should change, both had been powerless to alter their relationship. They had complained and criticized each other, escalating from passivity in what each regarded as a bad situation, to violence. Maryann was the more explosive of the two, and more verbal in her accusations of Tom, while he usually imploded his feelings into aches and pains. Yet when Tom did talk, he had little good to say about her, disapproving of everything she did that seemed out of

173

MORE JEALOUSY

his control. Their marital disharmony had been building for many years and only needed the spark of Maryann's discontent to explode. Tom's jealousy, which he readily admitted, was one of the factors that contributed to that disharmony.

"How come you're so jealous?" I finally asked, considering his jealousy exorbitant.

He acted irritated with me for asking such a dumb question. "Because I love her," he said. "I don't want to lose her."

I explained my theory of jealousy to them, that the feelings are based on childhood fears of abandonment. Tom fidgeted, but I asked him anyway, "How did you feel about your parents when you were a kid, Tom?"

"I loved them; they were always good to me," he said.

"Were you ever afraid that they would leave you, or did they ever?" I asked.

"No, never," he said quickly. "They were always there," and he would say no more about it.

I felt frustrated when Tom and Maryann left because it seemed to me that we had gotten exactly nowhere. We had not discussed options they might have, nor did I feel either of them was being completely open with me. But I have learned that I cannot change people; if change occurs at all, the individual is the one who must decide to accomplish it. Sometimes people need to mull over their problem for weeks or years before they can even talk about it, let alone arrive at the decision to change.

Maryann called me up a few days later to tell me that they wouldn't be coming back. "I'd like to," she said. "It did me a lot of good to be able to say things I've never said before. But Tom doesn't want to. He said he objected to some of the things you said. Actually, I think he felt too threatened."

"What about?" I asked.

"Well, for one thing he didn't like your digging into his past," she said. "He doesn't like to think

174

MORE JEALOUSY

about his childhood. He wasn't straight with you, you know. He had a lousy childhood. His father beat him a lot, and his mother never really wanted him. She ran around with other men and left Tom and his brothers all alone most of the time. He was an unhappy kid, but he can't stand to admit it."

"He's not the only one I know who doesn't want to dig into his past," I said. "Who wants to get into all that pain unless he has to? Have you two made any decision about your going back to work?"

"Yes," Maryann sighed. "I've decided not to do it. I know Tom acts the way he does because he loves me. And in his way he's doing it for my own good. He's got so many good qualities, but some of his attitudes drive me wild, like this thing about work. He said if I insisted on working he'd leave me. And he told me to stop acting so friendly with other men. I don't like it, but I'm just not ready to cope with raising two kids alone yet."

"Do you resent him for it?" I asked.

"You bet I do," she said. "But there's nothing I can do about it right now, at least nothing that I'm going to do."

"Okay," I said. "If you get too tied up in knots you know my phone number."

"Thanks," she said. "I might be giving you a call."

Another marriage headed for divorce in a few more years, I thought. Maryann felt helplessly trapped because she didn't think she could manage on her own. For the time being she was willing to submit to Tom's control by not getting a job or talking to people so much, but her acquiescence wouldn't take away her resentment. The more she submitted to Tom's orders, the angrier she would become. Tom was sitting on a powder keg. If he continued to insist that Maryann do what he wanted her to do, her obedience would be only temporary. Tom might think their marriage was fine because Maryann

175

seemingly went along with his commands, but sooner or later her hostility would explode. Maryann could cope in her passivity syndrome for a time, but she knew she was counting the days. Unless Tom changed his attitudes and Maryann changed her feelings about him, they were headed for an inevitable breakup.

They might not even make it that far. From Maryann's description of her mounting anger, she might indeed take after Tom with a knife during one of her explosions. If she did, Tom would do his best to calm her down as he calmed himself, never understanding that buried feelings boil away inside, persistently alive. The very reason that her feelings were getting so explosive was that she had no way to let them out. Tom would not let her talk to him about how she felt. He believed feelings should be hidden and forgotten. Whereas Maryann escalated her feelings to violence in the passivity syndrome, Tom escalated his to incapacitation. When the two of them became agitated enough to fight verbally, Tom got so upset he simply tuned her out. He would not fight with Maryann, so he either said, "I don't want to talk about it," and wouldn't, or left the room, leaving her raging at the silent walls. Tom would go for a long walk, and when he came back he believed he'd forgotten all about it. He could not understand why Maryann couldn't do the same. Tom didn't change his beliefs or his control of Maryann. His feelings were still there too; although he may not have been aware of them, they didn't change either. He still felt angry at Maryann, and he was still suspicious of her, no matter how much she superficially towed the line. Tom was still jealous.

I have no doubt that Maryann had a part in encouraging Tom's jealousy. She did not want to admit it, but when he tried to control her talking to other people, she talked to them all the more. She said she couldn't help it, that she was naturally curious about people, but I felt that she was rebelling against Tom's control, even going out of her way to start conversations. The madder he got, simmering silently, the more innocent she acted, insisting that she was only being friendly. Her attitude was, "Who, me? How can you think that about me?" Although she would deny it, she was being as hostile toward Tom

176

MORE JEALOUSY

as he was toward her. She may even have been unconsciously trying to play on his jealousy. Although she could not "make" Tom jealous, she, like all of us who live with another person for any length of time, knew which buttons to push to activate certain feelings. Maryann knew that all she had to do to "make" Tom a green-eyed monster was to strike up a conversation with a strange man. Then they would have a period of agitation, with the expected behavior ensuing on both sides; they would release their tension with the fight and deescalate to zero. Like so many other couples caught in the passivity cycle, their fights occurred about once a week.

After each one, they would convince themselves that they should keep trying, and they would stuff down the resentments until the next time. And all the time they were fighting, they both believed that they were acting out of love. Maryann believed Tom's heavy control of her was a reflection of his love. Like Peter, however, Tom was trying to keep her in a pumpkin shell because he was afraid to lose her. And Tom couldn't see that Maryann was being hostile while acquiescing to his control. She was using him as her meal ticket until she felt ready to go out on her own, and she never lost sight of that fact—but she didn't tell him that.

They both believed that Tom's jealousy of Maryann was caused by his love for her. They didn't come to therapy sessions together long enough for me to confront that belief. And Tom might not have heard me if I had. He did not want to change his beliefs. He wasn't alone in his obduracy, however. We in America have been conned by the romantic fallacy for so long that we persist in hanging on tightly to our beliefs, even when someone challenges them. We believe so strongly that jealousy is a normal part of love, few of us will listen when it is defined otherwise. We believe, as Andreas said so long ago:

The man who is in love is bound in a hard kind of slavery and fears that almost anything will injure this love of his and his soul is very much upset by a

177

slight suspicion, and his heart is greatly troubled
within him. Because of love's jealousy he is afraid
every time his beloved talks with any other man,
or goes walking with one, or stays out of sight
longer than usual, because "Love is a thing full of
anxious fear". [14]

Maryann returned for a session a few months later. She was still at home, still as stuck as ever, and more scared.

"I've got to do something," she said, "but I don't know what. I'm either raging at Tom or I'm so depressed I can't stand myself."

To me, raging and depression are pretty much the same emotion, but raging is straighter. Depression is usually a state of repressed feelings where the person's brain is so busily engaged in fantasizing that he or she has no energy left for physical activity. Usually that fantasizing involves anger of some sort—retroflected anger. Like guilt, depression often results when, for example, I don't dare get mad outwardly at someone, so I reflect it off him and back onto myself. It's almost as if that other person is holding a mirror up; when I flash my bean of anger out, it reflects off the mirror and back onto me. There it stays while I quietly, sullenly, sink into a pit of despair. I've found that if I can get in touch with my anger I can let my depression (or my guilt) go. And if I can help another person understand his or her anger, and feel it, the depression that he or she is dealing with will usually lift too.

"What are you feeling now?" I asked Maryann.

"I'm down today," she said. "And I don't understand it. Tom's really been trying to get along. We've had some long talks lately, and he's beginning to understand what I've been feeling."

"Has he agreed to let you go back to work yet?" I asked.

14. Capellanus, p. 190.

178

MORE JEALOUSY

"No," she said, "but he's trying to make it easier for me around the house. He's helping out and taking care of the kids more. But no matter what he does, it's not enough. I don't know what's wrong with me that I can't appreciate it."

"Sounds like Tom's being a good boy lately to keep you off his back," I said.

"Well, he is being good," Maryann agreed. "I can hardly believe it; he's never done so much at home before in all the years we've been married."

"If he's being so good, what does that make you?" I asked.

"I don't understand," she said.

"Think about it," I insisted. "Tom's being so good and trying so hard to keep your marriage together, and you're not even grateful. How can you be so bad to someone who's being good to you?"

"I shouldn't be, I know," she said, "but no matter what he does for me, I can't seem to feel grateful."

"What do you feel when you tell yourself you shouldn't be mad at him and you're wrong for not appreciating him?" I asked.

"Depressed," she said.

"Right," I agreed. "You bury your anger inside, and it turns into depression. You're lucky you haven't thrown knives at yourself."

"Do you know I've been thinking of stuff like that lately?" she said. "Not that I ever would, but I feel so guilty; I'd like to tear my hair out by the roots."

"Of course you do," I said. "You can't get mad at Tom; he's being too good, so who does that leave to be angry at but you? No wonder you're feeling down lately. You're coming down on yourself so hard you can't help but be. And you're going to keep on being depressed if you go on this way, because you're still being controlled."

179

MORE JEALOUSY

"How's that?" she asked.

"Tom's got you right where he wants you," I said. "You're still home; you're not looking for a job. If he can keep throwing you a bone by being such a good boy you'll never go outside the home. He'll lock the door and throw away the key and there you'll sit, tearing out your hair and never knowing why you're doing it."

"I never realized it," she said "You're right. Why that bastard! He's doing it on purpose."

"Maybe not," I said. "Maybe he thinks he's doing it for your best interests. But the truth is whatever he believes, he's controlling you by his goodness."

"Yes, he is," she said. "And don't care if he does think he's sincere. I'm really angry at him. I'd like to tear him apart right now."

"Here," I said, handing her a plastic bat I keep available for clients (and sometimes myself) "Beat the pillow with this; it'll keep you from going bald."

Maryann took out her rage on the beanbag until she was exhausted. Finally she took a deep breath and said, "I feel better. But I know it's only temporary What am I going to do?"

"I don't know," I said. "I'm no very good at giving advice. If I tried, you'd probably just get mad at me because I don't know the answer to your problems—you do even if you can't see it right now. But how about getting yourself a pillow to beat on until you can come up with some options t change your situation?"

"Okay," she said, "I'll do that. sure beats tearing out my hair!"

I know of nothing more contro ling than goodness. Living with a "good" partner can be ten time worse than with a "bad" one. At least if one has a bad partner who is angry, screaming, accusational, bitter, and critical, on can be angry at that person and feel straight about it. But if th partner is good, that very goodness dilutes the anger. How ca

180

MORE JEALOUSY

one get mad at a person who is being so undeniably good? One cannot, of course, unless one is absolutely clear about the dynamics of the relationship. That clarity is difficult to maintain. More often than not we confuse ourselves by repeating our debilitating internal shoulds until we feel so guilty that we take out our anger on ourselves instead of on our good partners. Stuck with ambivalent feelings of anger and guilt, we end up further hooked into passivity. If we believe our Parent tapes enough, we'll escalate our feelings not into explosion, which can be a healthy way of releasing anger, but into incapacitation. We may find ourselves not just turning off and tuning out like Tom, but going nuts! Incapacitation of that sort is actually appropriate for a situation such as Maryann found herself in, for Tom was using crazy-making tactics on her, whether or not he consciously knew it. So if Maryann clung to her feelings of guilt to a great enough degree, she might respond by taking out her anger on herself instead of on him. She might use a knife, acting out on herself instead of him, as she had felt tempted to do. And she might end up in restraints, institutionalized, for being a potential suicide and a menace to herself, while Tom would be his usual passive self, not in the least aware of his contribution to her madness, accepting the condolences of friends and family because he was burdened with such a crazy wife.

Tom was still stuck in the passivity syndrome by being "good," but he had changed his behavior enough to confuse Maryann. He was agitating less by not giving Maryann orders on how to behave. He was overadapting by trying hard to please her. The only way that Maryann could know without a doubt that some manipulation was going on was by checking her feelings. Every time she discounted her own feelings, as was her habit, she felt a little crazier. When she could understand that her feelings were straight and that she needed to pay attention to them, she felt saner. And when I pointed out that Tom was manipulating her by his goodness, she really got in touch with what was happening.

But it was not Tom's fault, any-

181

more than it was Maryann's. Romance is to blame, that romance which tells us to overadapt to our partner's desires, to please our partner, no matter what our own feelings are. As Andreas says, "Let the lover strive to practice gracefully and manfully any act or mannerism which he has noticed is pleasing to his beloved."[15] The lover tries hard to adapt to his partner's expectations, because he believes that's the right way to behave. And the beloved, knowing internally what those feelings are but denying their validity, slowly goes crazy. We have more power of perception than we can comprehend. Our brains are capable of perceiving the realities of those around us regardless of how much they may try to deceive us. No matter what their manipulations are or their crazy-making rationalizations, whether or not they themselves are aware of what they're doing, we can perceive the truth by staying in touch with and giving credence to our feelings. But we confuse ourselves by obeying the rules we've got squirreled away in our heads, the rules that we persist in living by—the rules of romance.

The rules say that love is made stronger by distance and difficulties, and that we should strive to increase these in order to intensify our loves. Two lovers are not encouraged to get to know and understand one another as individuals. On the contrary, they are told to hold themselves off from each other deliberately, in suspicion and mistrust. Then, intellectualizing on the basis of his or her beliefs, the lover rationalizes childhood feelings of abandonment into jealousy of the beloved, trying to find some present-day reason for past but persistent feelings. Suffering the pangs of jealousy, the lovers dream about being together, yet when they finally are their dream bubbles pop. Having relied on their fantasies rather than their feelings, they find each other too abrasive to remain with. In order to recapture the dream, they may have to separate again and increase their distance. "Absence makes the heart grow fonder," we say, as our lover grows more appealing from a distance. But can we truly assert that we are in love with a

15. Ibid., p. 152.

182

MORE JEALOUSY

flesh-and-blood person or only the fabrication of our own imaginings? I'm convinced we've substituted romantic fantasies for love and have made up sayings to corroborate our beliefs.

A jealous love may be romantic, according to the definition of twelfth-century romanticists, but surely that's not the kind of love we seek in our permanent relationships. We seek warm, intimate lovers for our marital partners, or at least we say we do. And love, in a feeling sense, means *not* distancing ourselves from each other. When we fantasize about one another, we numb our bodily feelings and close ourselves off from our loved ones. We intellectualize and, aware only of our jealous fantasies, we lose touch with our feelings and those of our partners. But loving is touching and caring and letting one's feelings flow out to another person. Loving is opening oneself, and the beloved is not the only one to receive the benefit. "The whole world loves a lover," we say, because others around the lover may bask in that warmth.

The rules of romance teach us the opposite of love and openness. They teach us that our partners' striving to be good is right and proper, that our lovers always mean well if they speak to us in the name of love, and that we are bad if we feel anger toward them—ever. The rules teach us that being jealous of our partners is natural, and that we should smother our lovers out of our own fears of loneliness. These rules encourage us to discount our own feelings so that some of us go crazy, and the rest of us go through life burdened with mountains of doubt. Romance tells us to doubt our ability to think rationally, to disparage our feelings, to distrust ourselves. Through doubting, we activate our critical Parent tapes and bring them down not only on our own heads but, quite naturally, on those nearest to us. So another of the rules of romance, even though it's unwritten, teaches us to become judges of our beloved ones, critics of ourselves, and doubters of all.

183

MORE JEALOUSY

8. THE UNWRITTEN RULES: CRITICISM AND GUILT

THESE RULES ARE INTRINSIC PARTS OF
THE ROMANTIC CODE.

The romantic concept that Eleanor of Aquitaine established in the twelfth century was originally developed to control men and women in the name of goodness. Prior to this time, men controlled each other by overt means: by the use of physical force, threats, and displays of hostility. War was a natural extension of the aggressive posturing men used to intimidate other men, as beating was a physical extension of the crude force used to control women. After Eleanor, psychological forces became potent factors in the game of control. Men and women began to change their attitudes about themselves. The control could then be exerted in less demonstrable but clearly effective ways.

Men were to be disciplined by the persuasive powers of love instead of by fear and coersion. Andreas says, "men cannot amount to anything or taste of the fountain of goodness unless they do this under the persuasion of ladies."[1] The ladies were the ones to set up the rules and give the rewards if men obeyed them. Andreas is not as explicit on what would happen if men didn't obey. He says, "the ladies are greatly obligated to be attentive to keeping the hearts of good men set upon doing good deeds and to honor every man according to his deserts."[2] The implication is clear, however. If men do not obey, they will not be honored. They will not be granted the love of their ladies. And without that love they will have no pathway to goodness.

They will, in fact, be punished. Andreas tells us that terrible punishments await those who will not accept the delights of love: ". . . how great is the affliction of those who will not love—to what torments they are subjected, and what glory and honor those have earned who did not close the gates of Love. . . ."[3] Women and men both will suffer torments

1. Capellanus, p. 108.
2. Ibid.
3. Ibid., p. 82.

THE UNWRITTEN RULES

if they willingly withhold their love. Nor will either find that fountain of goodness as have those who have given themselves in love.

The archetypal story "Beauty and the Beast" describes the punishment given men who would not obey the laws of romantic love. What more terrible punishment could a man have than to be turned into a beast; yet, according to the rules of romance, man was already a beast before a woman ennobled him by her love. The classic story turns him outwardly into what he already was inwardly, and warns other men of the punishment that awaits all who act contrary to the force of love. After being appropriately punished for his bestiality, Beast must wait in helplessness and ignominy for a woman to rescue him from himself by the grace of love.

Beast was one man, but all men might suffer the same fate, the story implies, if they do not willingly submit to the dictates of love. Women also must submit or suffer, although archetypal stories of women involve bestiality less than passively awaiting awareness through the kiss of a prince (or being punished for their evil by being turned into witches). As Andreas says, ". . . any woman who wants to have the praise of the world must indulge in love. . . ."[4] So man or woman must submit to fate in the form of Cupid's arrow of love, or be punished.

The punishment was administered by magic only in the fairy tales. In real life, the romantic code provided that it be meted out to errant lovers by their beloved ones. It had an internal force for regulation as well. The psychological beauty of the scheme of romance was that people could, and did, punish themselves if they did not obey the rules of love. If men and women believed they could achieve goodness through love, then they also accepted the idea that badness descended upon them if they disobeyed the code of love. And if they were bad, without hope of achieving goodness, they had a

4. Ibid., p. 172.

188

prior conviction that they would be punished. Lacking an outward jury, they would act as their own judges, assigning sentence as to a criminal in the dock.

We still carry around with us today the internal system of self-regulation that the code of romance established. We judge ourselves on our behavior and set up punishments in accordance with the sins we've committed. We do this by what some call the voice of conscience. Others call it knowing the difference between right and wrong. I call it, almost invariably, guilt. Our internal voices of authorization (conscience) will punish any trangression of the rules of romance by beating us with the whip of guilt. If we act in agreement with our inner voices, we pat ourselves smugly on our psychic backs, no matter how much it hurts to act in accordance with the rules. If we don't obey our internal judges, we mentally berate ourselves for being bad until we reach that state of psychological numbness known as guilt.

We learn to control our behavior so that we'll please our lovers and they'll approve of us and grant us love. We control our thoughts and our feelings so that our conscience—our shoulds—won't whip us for being bad children, as our parents did in childhood. We want approval from the archaic parent figures we carry around inside our heads as well as from our lovers in the flesh. If we feel something other than we think we should, such as anger or resentment, we punish ourselves with our own self-criticism. We activate our critical Parent tapes and freeze ourselves into immobility by the self-doubts that those tapes bring into play. We're caught between the "you should" statements in one part of our brains and the "I want" feelings in the other. We lose our ability to take risks in fear of doing something wrong, so we do nothing. We are suspended in doubt, driven with fear, and innundated by guilt. And when we repress our feelings until we feel nothing, chastised by our "loud voices" into a state of guilt, we set ourselves up for the whole passivity syndrome. We render ourselves incapable of finding any solution to our problems because we can't even see them

THE UNWRITTEN RULES

clearly. We confuse ourselves with guilt because we believe our feelings are wrong, and if only we tried harder we could do whatever it is we think we should.

But our feelings won't go away so easily. Internally we are rebelling against entrapment. We are controlled and we feel it, but we cannot see that our own beliefs have trapped us. After all, romance stipulates that love and love alone will "make" us happy! We have no key to our own doors of happiness; our lovers must open them for us. If we're unhappy, it follows that our lovers have failed to open the doors; our lovers have failed *us*. We have tried to be good. If we are still unhappy, it must naturally be our lovers' fault. If we have expectations such as these, we cannot help but be resentful when our lovers don't bring us that fantasy known as "happiness."

Stuffed with romantic expectations, we are disappointed time after time. But experiencing continual disappointment does not stop us from expecting. We expect goodness and fair play from those around us, fairness from life, and justice from society. When others don't act the way we think they should, we are devastated. We operate on the words "I wish," rather than "this is." Our wish-fulfillment system is ever at odds with the realities of our lives. Yet we go on expecting, believing in the romantic dream that forever colors our separate realities. We never seem to realize that no one—others or ourselves—can possibly meet all of our expectations. Or that even if our wishes are fulfilled for the time being, our satisfaction can't last. Our habit of creating impossible expectations is bound to set up conditions no human being could ever—forever—fulfill.

So, inevitably, we end up believing our lovers are to blame. Since we believe we are not responsible for our own emotions, we criticise our lovers and accuse them of causing our bad feelings. Of course our self-criticism continues to rain down on our own heads as well; once generated, criticism tends to flood out in all directions. We lash out in anger at ourselves and at our lovers in turn. But the anger isn't straight and open; we believe we're wrong for feeling it. So we depress

190

ourselves instead, turning the self-anger into guilt and the anger at our lover into accusations. Unless we recognize the source of our feelings in ourselves, we are set up in advance to pinpoint our lovers as the sole reason for our unhappiness.

Criticism and accusations can thus be seen as integral parts of romantic relationships from the very beginning. We think we trust our lovers, but we don't trust them to be who they are. We trust them only insofar as they live up to our expectations. When they do not, for no one could, we criticize them. Our accusations in the form of "you should have done such and such" or "you should be so and so" naturally follow. Losing trust in our lovers destroys our faith in them. So we open the door permanently to doubt.

When lovers doubt each other they search for signs of betrayal in the other. Fearing hurt, they close themselves off from one another for their own protection. They numb themselves even more against their own feelings and concentrate on their fantasies about what they wish their lovers would be. And they will be certain to find what they most fear in their partners, because they'll create a climate of distrust and negativism. If the doubt wasn't there in the beginning, it will grow quickly, generated by suspicion and fueled by manipulation. Romance tells us to manipulate—in just so many words—in order to increase love. Andreas says, "Love increases, too, if one of the lovers shows that he is angry at the other; for the lover falls at once into a great fear that this feeling which has arisen in his beloved may last forever."[5] He advises his readers to magnify that fear deliberately in order to intensify the love; "It is well if lovers pretend from time to time to be angry at each other for if one lets the other see that he is angry and that something has made him indignant with his loved one, he can find out clearly how faithful she is."[6]

I'm reminded here of Frank and

5. Ibid., p. 153.
6. Ibid., pp. 158–59.

Rita, two lovers who happened to have been married to each other for fifteen years, with the requisite two children, two dogs, two cars in the garage, and a house with a thirty-year mortgage. Outwardly, they were a typical American family living in a large house in a well-groomed suburb. Inwardly, they were explosions waiting to happen. For both Frank and Rita escalated their feelings to the point of violence. They were angry with each other often, and their fights were accentuated by the belligerence each showed when they drank together. They didn't drink together every day; they both worked and sometimes they stopped at a bar together on their way home. They also drank together regularly on weekends and when they had friends over, but much of the time they drank separately.

Frank liked a couple of drinks after work, but even at parties he rarely drank more than three or four. The drinks sedated him, and if he drank too much he would get so sleepy he'd have to go to bed while the party went on without him. Frank insisted he didn't overdo it. He also insisted Rita did. He called her a drunk, and she called him a party-pooper. And the accusations flew. Rita drank less regularly at home than Frank, but when they had a party the drinks seemed to turn her on. The more she had, the wilder she felt and the more she wanted. Rita was usually the last one to quit and the last to go to bed. She liked to drink because the alcohol made her feel high. About once a month she would go to a cocktail lounge with one of her girl friends; one drink led to twelve, and she would invariably close the place down. Sometimes she would call Frank to join them and drive her home; other times she would manage to get home by herself. There were also the nights she stayed at her girl friend's apartment, only Frank did not believe it.

"I know she's out screwing around on me when she doesn't come home like that," he told me during one joint session.

"I am not," Rita said emphatically. "He's never trusted me in our whole married life."

"Tell him that," I said. I hate to

be the middleman (person) in sessions with couples; it's more appropriate for them to direct their anger at each other.

"You've always accused me of screwing around, even when we first got married," Rita told him.

"Well, I love you so much," Frank said. "I hurt inside when you even look at another man."

"When you talk like that you make me want to step out on you," Rita said. "If you've got the name, you might as well play the game."

"And you really play it, don't you?" he said.

"Look, I don't mind you being a little jealous," she said. "It shows you really do love me. But you carry it to the point of being ridiculous. Do you know," she said to me, "he calls me several times a day at my office just to check up on me?"

"I'm not checking on you," Frank said. "I call you because I love you."

"Bull!" Rita said.

"Does this kind of in-fighting go on all the time?" I asked.

"Constantly," Rita said. "We've been doing it for years."

"Yeah," Frank agreed. "It seems like that's all we do anymore."

"Why did you ever get married in the first place?" I asked.

They both had to think about that for a few minutes; they seemed reluctant to remember any attractive qualities about each other. Finally Rita said, "I guess we just fell in love."

There it was again—the irresistible power of love. Both Frank and Rita readily admitted that they had no common interests and that they did not enjoy doing things together. He liked to go camping and fishing and hunting. She liked to go to art museums and movies and dances. Frank and

193

Rita were like so many of the couples I see in therapy; they shared few common interests. In fact, I can't think of any I've worked with who have shared many interests or hobbies. I have sometimes thought that if I could put all the couples I've worked with in a huge bag and shake it up, they would come out better matched, as far as interests go, than when they went in. Some of these people seem to have picked each other for what they didn't share rather than for what they did. Yet they're only following our romantic code, which advises us to marry each other for our differences, not our similarities. "Opposites attract," we are told. How opposite can two people be and still enjoy living together? Maybe that is why I see such couples in therapy. The original romantic love affair may not have been enough to sustain their interest in each other, as opposites, for a lifetime. Frank and Rita shared the one common interest other couples have had when they first met—sex. That was about all they had.

"We stayed in bed for days at a time when we first turned onto each other," Frank said. "We didn't care about doing anything else."

"We used to party a lot too," Rita said, "after we first got married. But then the children came along. We didn't have much time for anything after that, especially each other. Now that we're both working we don't do anything together except fight."

"How do you fight?" I asked. "Just verbally, or do you ever hit each other?"

"He's hit me several times," Rita said. "He gave me a black eye a couple months ago."

"That's because you were trying to kick me in the balls," Frank said. "I was trying to protect myself."

"I don't remember that," Rita said. "You're making that up."

"You were drunk," Frank said. "That was the night I had to haul you out of the bar because you and your girl friend wouldn't leave and the bartender was trying to close."

194

"You're a liar," Rita said.

"She just won't admit she does anything wrong," Frank said to me.

"Neither will he," Rita said.

The complaints sounded very familiar. I often find myself placed in the position of being a judge in sessions with couples. They say, "He's wrong," and "No, she's wrong," and appeal to me to decide who's right. I've become adept at squirming out of that position, for if I make a judgment on who's right, I am in the game. It's called "Courtroom," and is popular with threesomes. Eric Berne outlined the rules in *Games People Play*.[7] The game is actually based on competition such as siblings experience in their rivalry for mommy's attention. If mommy gives one kid approval for being right and the other one punishment for being wrong, she's got a long-term problem on her hands, for the two will be playing the game from then on, even when they grow up and leave home.

Frank and Rita were still playing. They were both trying not to get the upper hand, as some might say, but just the opposite. Each wanted the other to have the upper hand, and to use it in taking care of him or her in a nurturing manner. Each was trying to make the other into the perfect, forgiving parent neither had ever had. Each was seeking the other's benevolent approval. Of course, neither of them was getting what each wanted. Instead, they kept getting more accusations and physical blows from one another. Finally Rita told Frank to get out. He called me for a session.

"I don't know what to do," he said. "I can't live without her. I can't stand the thought of breaking up with her."

"Frank, you've been fighting tooth and nail for years. Both of you know that. Hasn't it ever occurred to you that you might get divorced one of these years?" I asked.

"Oh, sure," he said. "Many

---

7. Eric Berne, *Games People Play* (New York: Ballantine Books, 1964), pp. 96–98.

195

THE UNWRITTEN RULES

times. In fact, I knew before we got married that we weren't any good for each other."

"Why in heaven's name did you ever get married then?" I moaned.

"Oh, Rita threw a snit," he said. "She was ready to get married, she told me. She'd just broken up with this other guy, and she wanted to settle down. She threatened to kill herself if I left her."

"And that was your only reason?" I asked.

"No, not the only one," he said. "We were damn good in bed. We still are, sometimes, when we're not fighting."

"When's that?" I asked.

"Not very often," he said. "But I keep hoping she'll change, and it'll be like it was just after we got married."

"And if she doesn't?" I asked.

"Maybe then I'll be forced to accept divorcing her," he said. "I know one thing. I can't handle her drinking."

"She doesn't drink that much, does she?" I asked.

"Not that often," he said, "but when she does she won't stop. Her father drinks, and he doesn't like me because I won't get drunk with him. He thinks I'm a wimp. And Rita's just like her old man."

"Come on, Frank," I said. "You're coming down too hard on her. It sounds to me like you're jealous because she's having a little fun without you once in a while."

"Yes," he admitted. "I know I'm jealous, but she's a drunk."

I let it go. Frank was sounding like a fanatic, I thought. What's the matter with having a little drink once in a while? Rita said much the same thing when she came in to see me a few days later.

196

"It's just one more thing he's got to criticize me about," she said. "He doesn't like the way I cook, or keep house, or how I dress, or discipline the kids. I can't do anything right as far as he's concerned."

"Doesn't he like anything you do?" I asked.

"Not one thing," Rita said. "He's gotten to be a real drag. Oh, I admit I try to rub it in once in awhile. Like last week, when I had lunch with one of the guys at the office. I like to know that at least somebody appreciates me. I knew it would drive Frank mad, and it did. But he deserves it for being such a bore. The trouble with Frank is he just doesn't know how to have fun."

I had to admit that Frank sounded too critical. And with that I found myself the Courtroom judge. Instead of working with Rita on her feelings, I found myself sympathizing with her. And when Frank would come to see me I could hear myself agreeing with him when he blamed Rita for her erratic behavior. They were blaming each other for their feelings, and I was not helping them.

What I didn't realize then, because I was, frankly, ignorant of the insidious nature of alcoholism, was that *both* Frank *and* Rita had problems with drinking. I should have insisted that they both quit drinking while they were coming to me, or refused to work with them if they would not. I've done that with other clients who told me they had problems with drinking. I insisted that they quit before coming into therapy, and they have. But I confused myself with Frank and Rita by accepting their mutual denial that drinking was their problem.

I was also confused by my own attitude toward drinking. I had bought the romantic fallacy that drinking is a part of the good life—the right table wine makes a meal; a party can't swing without zing, and whiskey provides it; pizza isn't pizza without a beer; a drink before bedtime helps you go to sleep; a drink when you're tense helps you relax. The underlying message to all of these, of course, is that drinking can

197

make you happy. It wasn't long after this that I had several clients in a row who were fighting alcoholism. I started to confront my own addled thinking. And I realized I had my own problem. I had begun to rely on a drink at the end of the day to relax, and looked forward to having drinks at parties and with friends. I wasn't addicted by a long shot, but I was becoming dependent on it in my own mind.

I realize now that alcohol can insidiously addict a person, if not physically at first, then psychologically, before one even knows one is hooked. As Arthur Janov and E. Michael Holden state in *The Primal Man*, "We believe the *Pain-blunting* capacity of alcohol fully accounts for its *widespread* use in our society."[8] Alcohol numbs us out of awareness of our pain and our tension. It feels good going down, like eating too much to fill an emotional emptiness in our bellies. We feel the warmth of taking it in and the numbness blotting out our physical and mental anguish. We are aware only of our euphoria, not the drunken behavior that follows, nor the damage the alcohol does to our livers, hearts, and brains. Neither are we immediately aware of the weight that accumulates around our middles from the liquid calories. The temporary good feelings we get from drinking too much, or overeating, or taking drugs make them so hard to give up—with what can we replace the glow of alcohol or the full feeling of food or the high of drugs but our own tension and emptiness? If alcohol or food or drugs felt bad going down, it would be easier to break our habits!

Even more than that, the use of alcohol (and increasingly, certain drugs like marijuana and cocaine), is advocated by our society as one of the keys to happiness. I am appalled now when I read some magazines to see the amount of space given over to liquor ads. Second only to those are the ads devoted to cigarettes. Both not so subtly sell the good life image by romanticizing these drugs that can "make" us feel good. No wonder we buy the image, for the ads tell us we're happiest

8. Arthur Janov and E. Michael Holden, *Primal Man: The New Consciousness* (New York: Thomas Y. Crowell Co., 1975), p. 181.

198

THE UNWRITTEN RULES

when we drink and smoke—we are more grown-up when we have a cigarette in our hands, sexy when we drink vodka, successful through bourbon, sophisticated drinking scotch. Fifteen years ago I decided to give up the grown-up image, and I quit smoking. After I became aware of the destructive chasm I was falling into with alcohol, I confronted my own romantic images. I decided I didn't need to avoid my pain and my tension any longer. I could survive feeling them, and there were better ways to handle both than having a drink to relax. I did not care about being sexy, successful, and sophisticated anymore (was I truly any of these with a drink in my hand?), or buying the romantic fallacy of happiness that the ads were pushing at me. I decided to change my complacent attitude toward alcohol and would consider it hereafter as my own and our culture's potentially *most* dangerous addictive drug.

About that time Rita dug in her heels. She had been avoiding my increased probing into her drinking habits. She told me she liked to drink, and, of course, she could stop anytime she wanted to. When I kept bringing up the subject she withdrew entirely by refusing to come to therapy sessions at all. Frank came occasionally after that, and I managed to help him stay in touch with his feelings instead of allowing him only to gripe about Rita. I was no longer playing the Courtroom judge. During one session, I shared my awareness about alcohol with him. I told him about my problems with it and my concern about Rita and him. He was way ahead of me.

"I've started realizing that too," he said. "One night—I had moved back in with her—we had a battle royal. She took her ring off and threw it at me. That made me so mad I damn near killed her. I had to take her to the hospital to get stitches in her face where I had thrown her against a wall. Well, that did it. Scared the crap out of me. I decided the next morning to quit drinking."

"Good for you," I said.

"I had to," he said. "I was going downhill fast. I joined Alcoholics Anonymous, and I was really

199

THE UNWRITTEN RULES

surprised to see some people I know there. I'd never have thought they had a problem."

"I know," I said. "Some people have told me that because I'm a therapist I shouldn't have any problems. I tell them that the only dispensation I get is to feel it when it hurts, and maybe do my hurting faster instead of clinging to it for so long. Being a therapist doesn't take away my problems; it just helps me know what I'm feeling about them quicker and hurt more."

"Yeah, I've been doing some hurting since we split," Frank said, "and I don't even have booze anymore to take away the pain. But I'm still here."

"How's Rita doing?" I asked.

"Not as well," he said. "Oh, she won't tell you that. She's been going to a doctor about some female problems of hers, and she talks to him about our problems. But she's still drinking, even more than before. Sometimes she disappears for days at a time, off on some bender. I've had to go get the kids a few times when a neighbor's called me and told me Rita's gone again."

"Hasn't her doctor told her to quit?" I asked.

"No, he's telling her the same things you used to, that one drink won't hurt, that it'll help her relax. Sounds like a lot of people; they think it's a tension reliever. But I'm sure she doesn't tell him how much she's drinking either."

"She could talk to a thousand doctors, but until she makes up her mind that she's got a problem she'll keep on drinking."

"I know," he said. "I can't help feeling guilty about that."

"Why?" I asked in amazement.

"All those years when I was coming down on her for this and that," he sighed. "I know I was too harsh on her, criticizing her for every little thing. Maybe if she had been married to somebody else she wouldn't have felt the urge to drink."

200

"Hey, get off your own back, Frank," I said. "Who're you criticizing now?"

"Me, I know," he said, "but I deserve it."

"Next time I see you I'll give you my cat-o'-nine-tails," I told him. "I don't use it much anymore but you'll keep it in shape."

"I don't need it," he said. "I've got my own."

Some months later, Frank told me they were going through with a divorce. His guilt was still overwhelming him, he said, and he hurt so much inside he could barely get through his days.

"I can't help thinking it was all my fault. Rita is so down and out right now. She lost her job because she was hitting the bottle so much; she's blown all her money, and now she's begging me to come back. I feel so bad for her, and I'm really worried about what the kids are going through, but I can't stay with her. I'm a bastard," he concluded.

"You've tried to go back with her, haven't you?" I asked.

"Yes," he said, "several times. It's always the same. She tries to be good and stay off the booze for a few days, and then she gets pissed off at me and starts drinking again. I don't know what to do."

"What do you feel when you're with her?" I asked.

"Guilty," he responded quickly. "Guilty as sin. The harder she tries to be good, the guiltier I feel and the harder I come down on myself. Then when she starts drinking I go crazy. I'm afraid I'm going to hit her again. So I leave and we both cool down, and then it starts all over again."

"What's your guilt about, Frank?" I asked.

"I'm really confused about that," he said. "I'm aching with guilt inside; every day's an agony. Rita's so great when she's sober; she's so good for me. I should be more

201

THE UNWRITTEN RULES

tolerant. But when she drinks and starts to yell at me, I turn into a beast. I don't even know myself. What's the matter with me?"

"Sounds like you're feeling torn apart," I suggested.

"That's just what it feels like," he said.

"That's the problem in dealing with someone who's addicted—the inconsistency. One minute she acts one way, and the next she's totally different," I said. "How come you're taking it out on yourself?"

"Who else should I be?" he asked.

"It's okay to be angry at Rita, even if she's being good," I said.

"Oh," he said, as if he hadn't thought of that before. "Oh!"

"It's much more appropriate to be mad at Rita than getting mad at yourself and then feeling guilty." I said.

"You're right," he said. "Damn, I am angry; I'm so angry I'd like to wring her neck." I gave him a pillow to wring and after he'd about destroyed it, twisting and punching, he gave a deep sigh and said, "I feel better now. I never realized how tough it is to live with someone who's trying so hard to be good."

"I know," I said. "Are you feeling sorry for Rita still?"

"I guess so," he said, "but less now. She's always seemed so helpless. I know she can support herself; she's very good at her job when she stays off the booze, but I've always felt she needed me to take care of her. There are times I'd have liked to lean on her, but it seemed like I was the one who always had to be strong."

"Don't you get mad sometimes, taking care of her?" I asked.

"Do I!" he said. "You bet I do.

202

THE UNWRITTEN RULES

That's what's been scaring me about myself. I didn't used to be a woman-beater before Rita. Now my temper gets out of control, and it's all I can do to keep my hands off her."

"Why do you keep putting yourself in that position?" I asked.

"I've asked myself that too," he said. "I guess it's because I can't stand her sounding so hurt when she calls me. And then, of course, I'm worried about what will happen to my kids."

"Right, the kids are a real problem. If this goes on, you may have to get custody in order to protect them. But you're going to have to stop taking care of Rita. Her only hope for growth is if you let go of her," I told him.

"I don't understand," he said.

"Look, you've told her about Alcoholics Anonymous, haven't you?" I asked.

"Sure, but she doesn't think she's got a problem," he replied.

"Well, until she admits that she does, there's nothing you can do," I said. "So quit rescuing."

"You mean don't go back when she calls?" he asked.

"That's right, don't go back, and don't give her any extra money, the way you have been," I said. "All you've been doing is supporting her dependency, both on you and on alcohol."

"That's going to be tough," he said.

"It's going to be tougher on both of you if you don't," I said.

"I hate to admit it, but I think you're right," he said. "I'll try it, but I know I'll feel guiltier than ever."

"Stay with your anger; it's a lot more real than your guilt," I said. "Just don't take it out physically on Rita."

203

THE UNWRITTEN RULES

"Okay," he said. "I'll go out and chop wood everytime I'd like to bash her in the head."

"Yeah," I said. "Have a warm winter."

Frank was beginning to find channels for his negative feelings. When he could confidently change his behavior, he discovered solutions to his problem, unlike Rita who was stuck in her behavior patterns. The two of them had been stuck in the passivity syndrome for years, unable to find a way out. Their behavior had predictably gone from the do-nothing stage to violence and back again. They stayed stuck because of their continual discounting. Rita discounted her ability to handle problems other than by taking a drink. She discounted Frank's need to be taken care of once in a while, viewing him always in the role of a stern parent. Frank discounted his feelings by coming down on himself with his internal shoulds. He also discounted Rita's ability to cope, even though he acknowledged that she had done very well before he met her. Furthermore, although they had both worked on feelings in therapy, they had discounted one important capability each of them had—their abilities to think.

I have said before that awareness is the key to change, the first step to realizing what the problem is. Awareness may come creeping over one slowly through the years, or it may come in a blinding flash of light—Ahah! That's it! That's what's been bothering me and what I've been feeling all this time! Awareness is the goal of therapy, helping people to get in touch with their past so they can discover how they've used previous experiences to create their present lives. Awareness, of inestimable value, allows us to grow. Awareness, a creative, internal process, gets us in touch with ourselves.

We can do two other things for ourselves in the process of growth that may even precede awareness. We can recognize our feelings, and we can permit ourselves to think. Recognizing our feelings means paying atten-

204

tion to our bodies and allowing our feelings to be inside without discounting them. When we tell ourselves we shouldn't feel this or that, whatever it is we are, our feelings obediently disappear. We doubt our feelings; we don't accept ourselves; we tell ourselves that we shouldn't exist. Conversely, when we recognize our feelings, we permit ourselves to be. We accept ourselves as we are in this world. We give ourselves a place in the universe.

When we also allow ourselves to think, we give ourselves permission to seek options based on our own needs rather than on what our internal voices tell us we should do. We all have options available to us in any situation, but when we're stuck in the passivity syndrome we may be unable to see any at all. We stay stuck by being unwilling to own up to our feelings and to risk thinking. Although our entire society says we should blame our partners for our circumstances, we don't have to do so. We can risk thinking for ourselves and making decisions based on our own thoughts and feelings. And when we begin to see our options, we will stop wasting our energy on fantasizing and see ways out of our problem situation.

Frank found several options that could alleviate his problem with Rita. At my suggestion, he spent some time brainstorming solutions and writing them down, no matter how far-fetched they seemed. He read me his list once, and I agreed that some of them were pretty far out. His list read:

1. *Kill her!*
2. *Beat her to a pulp!*
3. *Commit her to an asylum!*
4. *Tell her to stop begging me to come back.*
5. *Ask some friends from A.A. to call on her.*
6. *Stop giving her extra money.*
7. *Work out some kind of joint custody to protect the kids.*
8. *Move out of state.*
9. *Disconnect my phone.*
10. *Start dating other girls.*
11. *Find some new interests, or do old ones more—fish, hunt.*

205

THE UNWRITTEN RULES

12. *Take a vacation to someplace new.*
13. *Join a club for divorced parents.*
14. *Quit feeling guilty!*

Although some of his options were reflections of his anger and would have landed him in jail, others were viable, and he acted on them. He began to date more and found a whole new world of attractive women friends. He worked out joint custody with Rita's lawyer so that he would take the children for weekends and vacations, including part of the summer; this eased the pressure on Rita. He asked one of his friends from A.A. to call on her, and, with her permission, the friend stopped by. By this time Rita had recognized that she had a drinking problem, and although she did not commit herself to join A.A., she was willing to listen. She cut down on her drinking thereafter, and started to look for a job. Rita was doing her own growing.

Frank and Rita are now divorced and seem to have gotten over the worst of their hurting. They're managing to work out a relationship in which they can at least talk to each other without feeling animosity. Each is starting to date other people; they realize now that they could never live together again as a married couple. Frank has seen how destructively he behaved in protecting Rita to the point of discounting her as a human being. He's resolved never to get into that type of relationship again. He has said that if he ever catches himself feeling sorry enough for a woman again to want to solve all of her problems, he's going to run. He had real hangups for some time about Rita's going out with other men. He knew he was being irrational; he was dating other women at the time himself. But he said he couldn't help feeling that Rita shouldn't date, that somehow she was no good if she went out with other men, particularly if she had a sexual relationship with them. Frank and I had a session to work on his jealousy, and once more discovered his early feelings of abandonment at the bottom of it. Once he realized where they originated, and what part his childhood feelings toward his parents had to do with his present feelings toward Rita, he was able to let most of his jealousy go.

206

THE UNWRITTEN RULES

Frank has resolved to give up his image as the strong rescuer and protector of women. He's throwing his romantic stereotype out the window and allowing himself to feel whatever he is at the moment. He won't find it easy going, I know. He'll have to put up with people like Rita's father calling him a wimp for not being a "real man" who can drink everybody else under the table. If he tells a woman she can handle her own problems, he may be told he is callous by women who would prefer to have a man write their meal ticket instead of earning it themselves. If he expresses his feelings around other men, he may be accused of being weak, for men are not supposed to have feelings of helplessness or sadness or insecurity.

But he will feel less controlled. For the romantic stereotypes that we carry around in our own minds trap us into passivity as much or more than our partners do. If we didn't already hold that internal stereotype, our partners could not control us, no matter how hard they tried. We trap ourselves. We put on our own bit and reins by conforming to the romantic images that we've been trained in since childhood. Then we seek our partners, even unknowingly, to pull the reins this way and that, criticizing them all the while for pulling too harshly, or pulling at all. But it is our own problem. All we have to do to get them to quit pulling is to take off the bridle, reject the romantic stereotypes we've been living by, blast apart our own belief systems, *think!* We have other options that we can find to change our lifestyles, options that will enable us to free ourselves up to be who we really are—to be!

First, we need to examine our stereotyped images and see if they hold up in real life. Must we really be protective and strong and unfeeling if we are men? Must we really be fragile and helpless and compliant if we are women? Do we really have to be who we believe we *should* be? If we can discover the boundaries of our internal images, we can decide to discard them. Some have. Some have discovered how destructive their romantic conceptions of themselves are. Some have taken off their self-imposed bridles by allowing themselves to feel *and* to think.

207

THE UNWRITTEN RULES

9. THE STEREOTYPES OF ROMANCE: LOVERS AND MARITAL PARTNERS

WE ARE TRAINED TO ACT OUT OUR
ROLES.

I n speaking of the stereotypes of romance I'm being redundant, because the two, in my mind, are synonymous. Stereotype is defined in my dictionary as, "a fixed or conventional notion or conception, as of a person, group, idea, etc., held by a number of people and allowing for no individuality."[1] A definition of romance states, "an exaggeration or fabrication that has no real substance."[2] What's the difference? A romantic image is a fixed notion that allows for no individuality, and a stereotype is a fabrication that has no real substance. The two are alike and interchangeable. Both are concepts that have been accepted in our collective minds as truths, when in fact they are fantasies. Because of our long and pervasive training in romance, we fashion our self-images out of these fabrications and pattern our behavior after these conventional notions.

The stereotypes have changed somewhat over the centuries. In the beginning, romantic love was restricted to that which existed between lover and lady; husbands and wives weren't supposed to experience that kind of love. Andreas says, ". . . if the parties concerned marry, love is violently put to flight, as is clearly shown by the teaching of certain lovers."[3] He reasons:

> . . . *everybody knows that love can have no place between husband and wife. They may be bound to each other by a great and immoderate affection, but their feeling cannot take the place of love, because it cannot fit under the true definition of love. For what is love but an inordinate desire to receive passionately a furtive and hidden embrace? But what embrace between husband*

1. *Webster's New World Dictionary of the American Language*, ed.-in-chief, David B. Guralink, Second College Ed. (Cleveland, Ohio: World Pub. Co., 1976), p. 1397.
2. Ibid., p. 1234.
3. Capellanus, p. 156.

211

*and wife can be furtive, I ask you, since they may
be said to belong to each other and may satisfy all
of each other's desires without fear that anybody
will object?* [4]

The concept of romantic love was originally formulated as an ideal enhanced by the very furtiveness of its nature and by its impossibility. If men and women were given societal sanction to live together in the state of marriage, that very approval made love impossible. The relationship between married people was therefore defined as something quite different than that between lovers.

Another factor that made love impossible within the approved state of marriage was, as Andreas tells us:

*But there is another reason why husband and wife
cannot love each other and that is that the very
substance of love, without which true love cannot
exist–I mean jealousy–is in such a case very
much frowned upon and they should avoid it like
the pestilence; but lovers should always welcome
it as the mother and the nurse of love.* [5]

The feeling that husband and wife had for each other, Andreas explains, is affection, not love, an affection based on a secure relationship. That kind of security cannot be known in love relationships distinguished by its opposite—insecurity. Romantic love, in twelfth-century terminology, has dissatisfaction at its core, and the constant anxiety that comes of the negativism generated by jealousy and suspicion.

The state of love, as defined by Andreas, is a compelling, overwhelming feeling, intensified by its "natural" companion, jealousy, into a driving passion. This kind

4. Ibid., p. 100.
5. Ibid., p. 101.

212

THE STEREOTYPES OF ROMANCE

of passion is not only improper in a marital relationship, but viewed as sinful. He says:

> *For whatever solaces married people extend to each other beyond what are inspired by the desire for offspring or the payment of the marriage debt, cannot be free from sin, and the punishment is always greater when the use of a holy thing is perverted by misuse than if we practice the ordinary abuses. It is a more serious offence in a wife than in another woman, for the too ardent lover, as we are taught by the apostolic law, is considered an adulterer with his own wife.*[6]

Over the centuries these concepts have changed somewhat. Romantic love has retained the elements of jealousy and furtiveness, along with the compulsive element, the obsession that tells people they're really in love. But it has come to have another goal than the inevitable sadness romantic lovers used to find at the end of their journey. In the Middle Ages, enobling love was an ideal that could sustain lovers for a lifetime but offered no contentment. Romantic love was what the Grail lovers sought; finding it, however, offered no surcease. They had to continue loving hopelessly because they could never cement their love through marriage. If they remained lovers they were condemned to a life apart. The very separateness of love was its sustaining quality. Coming together in marriage spelled the death of love.

Today in the United States we expect that the romantic love, which we believe to be the only kind, will run straight from first blinding meeting to the altar, and then proceed undiluted to twin graves. Our goal in romantic love is marriage. Hardly a lover enters into an affair without considering his or her beloved as a possible choice for a marital partner. Certainly many of us have flings, telling ourselves that we do not want to get married, that we're just having fun for

6. Ibid., p. 103.

213

today with no thought of eventual commitment. But our culture conspires against us. In the back of our minds is our nationally accepted dictum that love leads to marriage, and if our present lover is not our permanent choice, then the next may be.

I have found, through working with many, many couples, however, that we are not without a sense of sin in our common conception of romantic love. In redefining the goal of love from hopeless but ennobling estrangement to an approved state of marital happiness, many of us seem to retain a queasy uncertainty. Before we marry, we can expose our feelings in the passion of romantic love, living for ourselves and our loved ones in total absorption with the moment. After marrying, we seem to pull back, to encase ourselves in some primeval conception of propriety. We cover our nakedness with our mantles of dogma and control, closing ourselves off from intimacy. We wrap ourselves in the cocoon of our particular or collective stereotypes and become proper married couples.

In my work as a therapist, I don't often see couples who agree on their marital stereotypes. If two people have similar ideas about marriage, they'll have no squabble. Believing in philosophic harmony that the wedding day spells an end to the courtship fling, they will settle down in sobriety to the business of marriage and child-raising. No, the couples who've come to me for help with marital problems have had differing ideas about love. Usually one partner has accepted the idea of marriage as a yoke, with harnessed partners pulling their weight patiently, ploddingly, on to the eventual—and still yoked—end. That partner tends to have a sense of vague sinfulness at the thought of continuing the passionate romance of premarital days. The other person still wants the wild highs and excitement of courtship. Discovering that the passion has disappeared forever does not seem to help the dissatisfied partner accept the seriousness of marriage. That person still insists that the dutiful one return to his or her former romantic and fun-loving self and when that doesn't happen, the dissatisfied one screams loudly and unceasingly.

214

THE STEREOTYPES OF ROMANCE

Consider the case of Shirley and John S. To look at them you would think they had it all together. I always marvel at the discrepancy between a person's appearance and the problems underneath. Some people who appear to be serene and composed on the surface carry around the most horrendous problems internally. Shirley and John were like that. Both in their early thirties, they made a handsome-looking team. Shirley could have been a model, and John looked like the answer to any girl's dream. They were both intelligent, talented people; they should have been pleasant company for each other. They had worked together to establish John in his own business; they had an expensive home, all the material things money could buy, and three children between them. Shirley had two by a former marriage, and they had had one boy since marrying five years before. They took annual vacations to Hawaii, Las Vegas, or San Francisco; they went out to dinner and movies often. Seemingly they had no worries in the world. But they weren't happy together. Shirley was particularly vocal.

In an initial meeting with them she blurted out, "John swears that he loves me, but he doesn't show it anymore. I'm on the verge of leaving him, but he says he doesn't want me to break up the home. I don't really want to leave. But he won't give me anything."

"What do you want?" I asked.

"Anything, anything at all," she sighed. "He won't give me gifts, he won't give me help around the house. Mainly, he won't give me time. He's so busy working I hardly see him at all."

"You don't realize what I'm going through in the business right now," John said patiently. "I've tried to explain it, but you don't seem to want to understand."

"Baloney," Shirley said. "You're not acting any different now than you ever have. After we got married it was the house; when we finished the house it was getting the business started—you were gone every weekend.

215

THE STEREOTYPES OF ROMANCE

You say it's the business now, but it was the business then, too. The truth is you just don't want to spend time with me. When you are home all you do is sit in front of the television and watch some game. You say you love the kids so much, especially our son, but you won't even spend time with him."

"Shirley, I don't know what you want," John said. "You've got everything in the world; we take vacations together every year; we go places together."

"Yeah, we go places together but you're never there. Even when you're there you're never there," Shirley said.

"I don't understand what you want from me," John said.

"I want to feel loved," she said firmly.

"Oh, brother," John groaned in exasperation.

I knew what Shirley meant by John's never being "there." I've complained before about being so "there-there" as a therapist. When people have commented about how tiring it must be to hear others' problems every day, I've told them I rarely try to solve problems; I give others the credit for being able to find their own solutions. But I do get tired of having to be doubly there: there in body when I get crisis calls at night and on weekends, there in spirit when I give someone my full attention. (I find that the longer I'm a therapist the less *full* attention I give someone *all* the time. My ears tend to go to sleep on trivia but perk up when I hear important words.) Anyway, what I heard Shirley saying was that she wanted some full attention, some "there" attention, from John. And John not only would not give it to her, he really could not. He had no conception of giving another person total attention in the sense that Shirley wanted it. What she wanted was empathy, his attention on her as a person. What she got was his looking *at* her but not perceiving her, listening *to* her but not understanding her. John spent his time doing verbal acrobatics in his left brain. He could not per-

216

ceive people other than through his intellect, so he had no awareness of their feelings. Nor was he in touch with his own. When he felt anxious or tense, he usually hastened to do something, anything—he went to his office or worked at some project, and if there was nothing else to do he sat watching television and drinking beer. And whatever feeling he had had went away for the time being. He did get a lot of headaches, however, and no doctor had ever been able to tell him why.

Shirley described feeling nonexistent, almost invisible, when she was with John. She felt discounted through his inattention and somehow disappeared in the process. She described herself feeling as if she were an observer of their interactions, not a participant. She was right. John was so involved in his own thought process and the fantasies in his own mind, her presence couldn't penetrate. No matter what Shirley did or felt, she rarely got through to John. Once in a great while, Shirley's anger broke through his barriers and John raged back. Ordinarily, though, he kept his feelings under strict control.

He had not been that way when they were courting. During that time he shared his feelings openly with Shirley. He showed tenderness, excitement, apprehension; he even cried. He focused his full attention on her and seemed to perceive her feelings. But as soon as they were married, he went back to his old habit of intellectualizing. Back in his habitual shell, he snapped himself shut tighter than a clam. Shirley was safe, Shirley was securely fixed in the role of a housewife. Whatever she did after that would have to be filtered through John's preconceived fantasy of what he thought a wife should be. No wonder Shirley felt invisible. To John, she was.

But she didn't put up with the situation passively as many women do. Shirley could express her anger at the top of her lungs. But the more she raged, the more John would retreat into his cold rationality, using words to try to reason with what he considered was a screaming bitch. Of course he was right; Shirley admitted that all too readily. She couldn't

217

control her emotions as John could; she said he didn't seem to have any. To her he was like granite, a statue who would not give. Even when she was sick, or tired, and would have loved a hug, a back rub, or the offer of a cup of tea, John looked through her as if she weren't there, or walked out, leaving her to her misery.

John complained that Shirley was either screaming at him or the kids or was so depressed she wouldn't get out of bed. The more emotional Shirley became, the crazier John thought she was. He even suggested once that she go into an institution. Shirley responded to that idea with vulgarities. The louder she got, characteristically, the more John retreated into himself. He stayed away from home even more, and when he was there he buried his nose in the paper or watched television, speaking only when he was spoken to. He wanted above all to have peace and contentment, and didn't understand why he couldn't have it. He thought of himself as a peaceable man, but the calmer he acted the more violent Shirley seemed to get.

I suspected that the rage and repressed resentments the two were experiencing were affecting them in all areas of their life together. When partners have the problems that Shirley and John had, they cannot avoid having their feelings spill over into that most basic of marital arenas.

"How's sex?" I asked. I view sex as a form of communication; if a couple is having problems talking, I assume they're having troubles in the bedroom as well. Much of the time I have to bring up the subject, because the two I'm with will not, no matter how much they're concerned with it. Shirley and John, like so many others to whom I've mentioned the word, looked uncomfortable.

"Rotten," Shirley said.

"John?" I asked. He shrugged his shoulders.

"For me, it's okay," he said. "But Shirley's always bitching."

"What do you mean when you say that it's rotten?" I asked Shirley.

218

THE STEREOTYPES OF ROMANCE

"Well, I'd like it more than once a month, but John always has some excuse. I'm climbing the walls, and he calls me oversexed. I don't think that's fair. To me, it's just one more thing he doesn't want to give me."

"Maybe you're not oversexed, but that's all you think of," John said. "You can't get it through your head that there's more to life than love and sex."

"Like what?" Shirley squared off for battle.

"Did you ever have good sex?" I broke in.

"Yes, we did before we got married," Shirley said. "John was a fantastic lover. I wouldn't have married him if he hadn't been. I'd been through a bad marriage; I'd known a lot of men. I didn't want to get hooked up with someone again in a lousy sexual relationship. But the minute we got married, he changed. He turned off, and he hasn't turned on since. It just isn't fair."

"Oh, I haven't changed that much," John said. "But nowadays I can't give Shirley the time I used to. We didn't have anything to do before we got married except be with each other. It was a lot different before we got saddled with responsibilities."

"That isn't true, John. I had two kids before we got married, and we both dealt with that okay," Shirley said. "It was marriage that changed you, not the responsibilities."

"All right, so it changed me," John said. "Before we got married I had some energy; now I'm tired all the time."

"Yeah, too tired for sex," Shirley agreed.

"Have you ever thought that each of you has a different pace?" I asked. "If you want sex more than John, why don't you initiate it, Shirley?"

"I used to do that once in a while," she said, "but John doesn't like it. So I quit."

219

THE STEREOTYPES OF ROMANCE

"What's the matter with Shirley asking for sex, John?" I asked.

John squirmed. I asked him again. Finally he said with obvious irritation, "It doesn't seem right if she starts it."

"What?" I couldn't believe my ears. Here in the United States, in the liberated, free-swinging seventies, I was hearing a young man expressing old-fashioned, Victorian ideas. Since then I've learned not to be surprised. I've heard such ideas from many people. Usually, they're expressed by women. We haven't yet let go the antiquated ideas about sexual purity that have come down to us through the centuries. Even in this so-called enlightened age, many women put aside their identities as sexual beings when they marry. They shelve their conception of themselves (if indeed they ever had it!) as women free to swing with any man of their choosing, as well as to enjoy sex as exciting, wholesome fun. They become images of propriety and respectability—housewives and mothers. Even if the woman doesn't change into a piece of ornamental artwork, she may put her man's needs before her own. If she isn't sexually satisfied she may, like many of her sisters, pretend that she is. To keep up the masquerade and prevent a hassle, she'll fake it.

The sexy bombshell has no place within the repertoire of the properly married woman. I know of some women who passively wait for their men to undress them, believing that they should not even do that for themselves. The rest of their sexual performance must show equal inactivity! And there are those who, terrified of displaying any portion of themselves other than what naturally sticks out of neckline, armhole, and skirt, keep the central part tightly hidden under wraps. When bedtime comes, these modern-day mummies undress in the closet or the dark. For them, not only the sexual act itself but even their bodies have taken on the aura of sin.

Women have long been aware of the taint of sin pertaining to anything sexual, including their bodies. Nancy Friday asserts that the only identity many of us

220

THE STEREOTYPES OF ROMANCE

have been taught is that of a "nice girl, not really sexual at all."
She says of one woman:

> *She still wanted to be nice, to obey mother's rules,*
> *to be loved for not entering sexuality. We want to*
> *be women. We want to remain daughters too. In*
> *this split we live.*[7]

Men have also been taught the regulations about "niceness" in
our sexual mores. The double standard is one that we as a nation
have accepted as a part of our culture. We have by no means left it
behind as we come out of the dark ages of sexual prohibitions.
Men may say they like women who exhibit sexual openness, but
more often than not they will shrink from committing themselves
to a woman who "puts out." I've heard many women clients
complain that men they've gone with have been out for "just one
thing," and when they get it, the men have disappeared, never to
call again. Friday corroborates this, interviewing sex therapists
for their opinion:

> *"A man will relate the kind of experience you just*
> *mentioned. 'What kind of woman is it,' he asks,*
> *'who carries her diaphragm around in her purse*
> *just in case?' He's half embarrassed but he means*
> *it, and the other men nod sympathetically. 'We*
> *don't ask that she be a virgin,' they explain,*
> *'but. . . .' "*[8]

In John's case, the double standard was almost nonexistent. He
had one standard for both himself and his wife—sex was bad.
True, he had seemed to enjoy it before marriage, but that period
was brief and not part of his ordinary reality. After marriage, he
went back to what he had been before—a good boy. He expected

7. Friday, p. 300.
8. Ibid., pp. 311–12.

221

THE STEREOTYPES OF ROMANCE

Shirley to be what he felt himself to be, and when she exhibited sexual desire first he showed his disapproval by not responding or by feigning some excuse for his lack of interest. The truth is, John's preconceived image of a wife didn't include Shirley's being a sexual being, other than for procreation. He had strong beliefs about how a wife should act. He believed that women should be "ladies," and that a wife should be the finest lady of them all. He believed that a woman should run the home, which was why he rarely offered to help around the house. He regarded the kitchen as woman's domain, so the thought of cooking dinner or doing the dishes simply never occurred to him. He would not change a diaper or feed a baby; even the minor disciplinary problems with the children were, he believed, his wife's concern. He did come in on the major problems; he got very upset when she threatened the children instead of spanking them. He thought they were going to grow up undisciplined because she wasn't strict enough.

John expected Shirley to be aggressive in what he considered were her areas—the home and children. So he did not object when she yelled at him for tracking across her clean floor. That, he felt, was her right. What he could not understand was her complaining about sex. John believed that sex was man's prerogative, woman's duty. He used sex to relieve his tensions when he had no other alternative. The idea that sex could be fun was foreign to him, as was any thought of taking the time to give Shirley pleasure. He was simply not concerned about whether or not she enjoyed it. He made no attempt to warm her up before intercourse, either with loving words or physical caresses. Shirley complained bitterly that she could remember many times when they'd been fighting all day, then John would want sex while she was still fuming. He couldn't understand why she wouldn't want to get close to him. And, she said, he didn't believe in sexual foreplay. All he did was climb on, reach his climax in a few minutes, then climb off. If she climaxed at all, it had to be before he did because afterward, he would quickly fall asleep. And Shirley was left with her internal rage. Lately, she said, she had felt nothing except irritation and discomfort during sex.

222

I felt like an ant measuring the mountain I had to tunnel through. Confronting John's beliefs and Shirley's rage seemed like an insurmountable task. But I'm a stubborn ant. I started out by giving them an assignment; I asked them to get *The Joy of Sex* by Alex Comfort and to read it together during the week before our next session. Somehow, I had to penetrate John's stubborn belief system and confront some of his archaic ideas. But Shirley had her own problem with beliefs. She shared some of these with me at our next meeting, to which John didn't come because of what he said were work conflicts.

"I guess I've never felt good about initiating sex either," she said. "I've always felt a little guilty, like I shouldn't be doing that. Besides, I shouldn't have to. He should know what I want."

"What do you mean?" I asked.

"Well, I think that if two people are in love they should each know what the other wants and give it without having to be asked. If you have to ask," she said, "it isn't the same. In fact, it means the other person doesn't really love you."

"Wow, that's a heavy," I said. "What do you do if you want something and he doesn't give it to you?"

"Then I don't get it," Shirley said.

"Do you have the idea that a woman is supposed to wait until a man does what she wants, instead of doing it for herself?" I asked.

"That's right," she said.

"Let me check how that applies to your problem with sex. If you're frustrated with John sexually, do you ever masturbate?"

"Oh, no," she said.

"Why not?" I asked. "Men masturbate."

"That's different," she said.

THE STEREOTYPES OF ROMANCE

"I've tried it but I feel so foolish. Besides, I know John is really uptight about it. He caught me doing it once and he wouldn't speak to me the rest of the week."

"If he feels threatened, that's his problem," I said. "Why shouldn't you take care of your needs if you feel frustrated? You don't have to wait for him to do it for you. All you get from that attitude is more anger."

"I don't know," she said. "I'll have to think about it."

"Look, Shirley," I said. "I think you're as hung up on romantic stereotypes as John is. You probably even think you have an orgasm only through intercourse."

"What other way is there?" she said.

Shirley sounded the way I did fifteen years ago. I struggled through five years of a marriage kicking myself because I felt nothing during intercourse. All the books I could find on female sexual response at that time told me that unless I could achieve vaginal orgasm through intercourse I was "unfeminine," actually "aggressive and masculine." Believing I was basically, unalterably flawed, I gave up and settled for calling myself frigid, even though I knew I was not frigid before I got married. Not until I read *Human Sexual Response* did I understand that vaginal and clitoral orgasms are not separate; both organs react together to create the experience of orgasm. As Masters and Johnson explain, the clitoris is the female sex organ that "is totally limited in physiologic function to initiating or elevating levels of sexual tension."[9] I explained this to Shirley, emphasizing that she was not alone in feeling frustrated after John's rapid, self-centered lovemaking. Other women whose partners wanted nothing more than quick relief experienced no arousal of sexual tension either. Since they were not "turned on" in the first place, they could never reach orgasm.

"No wonder I feel angry," she said. "I think John assumes I should climax just because he does."

9. William H. Masters and Virginia E. Johnson, *Human Sexual Response* (Boston: Little, Brown & Co., 1966), p. 45.

224

"Then you'll have to tell him about your needs and insist he do what you want for a change," I said.

"I don't know if I can do that," she said.

"It's up to you. You can keep on being angry at him for not reading your mind and giving you what you want, or you can take responsibility for yourself and start telling him about your needs," I said. "Another idea you probably have that's false is that you have to reach orgasm together."

"I've always thought people did," she said.

"It's nearly an impossible goal. People respond to stimuli differently, and they have different paces. So why not anticipate that you'll achieve orgasm at different times rather than expecting to be together? Wouldn't you feel a lot better about sex if you could reach a climax before John does?"

"Sure, but he's so quick that I don't know how I could manage it," she said.

"If you give up the idea that you've got to wait for intercourse to achieve orgasm, you will realize there are other ways. Convince John to give you some pleasure first. Quit taking care of him. And be specific. Ask for exactly what you want," I told her.

"It sounds pretty unromantic," she said.

"It is. Romance has taught women to cater to men's needs and disregard their own," I replied. "Romance teaches us to fake it."

"Well, I haven't faked orgasms because of romance," Shirley said, "or love."

"What, then?" I asked.

"I fake it when it's too uncomfortable and I want him to stop. Sometimes even two minutes is too much," she said.

"You sound sad," I said.

225

THE STEREOTYPES OF ROMANCE

"I am," she said. "I hate myself when I do that, but there are times when I can't stand John. Even when he tries to do what I want, when he tries to give me what I've been screaming about for months, I'm repelled. I want it over and done with. So I pretend to come and he does come, then he rolls off and I cry myself to sleep. I feel sad just thinking about it."

"Why in the world have you let this go on for so long?" I asked incredulously.

Shirley sobbed, "I really love John, and I want to stay married to him. I don't want another divorce, and I know he loves me. But I can't stand this much longer."

"Then be firm with him. You've got to insist that he take the time with you this week to at least do your homework," I said. "Make sure he sticks to his part of the bargain. I don't want to see either of you again until you read the book that I assigned you last week—together!"

"I'll do it," Shirley said with emphasis.

Although the main problem area between Shirley and John seemed to be sex, it was actually only one aspect of their troubled relationship. But it was there that their problems became apparent. As with so many of us, the culmination of their barriers to communication surfaced and became visible in the bedroom. Their problems were compounded, if not started in the first place, by the stereotypes they lived by. Both Shirley and John had changed after they got married. Despite Shirley's assertion that she had insisted on a free sexual relationship, she, like John, had become an embodiment of the image she held in her head—a proper wife. Each of them had left behind their images of self-identity they had held before marriage and encased themselves instead in the armor of marital propriety. Their mutual sense of sinfulness did not apply to the sexual area alone; they felt guilty for retaining their identities as individual beings as well. After marriage, their "we"

THE STEREOTYPES OF ROMANCE

status took over, and they expected to act as a team from then on. They both deliberately, and in accordance with their conceptualized stereotypes, put their freedom as separate beings behind them.

Shirley accepted her role as keeper of the home and children with willingness at first. She wanted another baby almost as much as John did, but for different reasons. If she hadn't proposed having another child, it was because she knew the work involved in raising an infant. But when he suggested they have a baby, she acquiesced, believing that having a child would help their relationship. She also believed that she should be the one to stay home and take care of the children and the management of the house. She never thought of going out to work; she knew John would provide.

And John did. He saw himself as the family's breadwinner and chief decision-maker. John put himself in charge of all the territory, not only that of his business but also the home. He balanced the checkbook, paid the bills, and made the decisions on all major purchases. When Shirley wanted money, he gave her a monthly allowance. If she overspent, he angrily accused her of being a spendthrift; she often rebelled by going on a shopping spree just to get even. Shirley was enraged at the control John exercised over her in the financial area. She told him about her feelings at our next joint meeting.

"You act like I'm a child and you're giving me my allowance because I've been good. I have to earn it, and if I don't you won't give it to me. How do you think that makes me feel?"

"You haven't complained much," John said.

"Maybe not enough," Shirley said, "but I've told you about it before, and you've never done anything. You seem to think that if you don't do or say anything the whole thing will go away. Well, it won't. Another thing I'm mad about is my money. You've promised it to me, but you've never given it to me."

227

"What money?" I asked.

"When we got married," Shirley explained, "I had ten thousand dollars in the bank from the settlement on my divorce. John told me he'd invest it for me, so I gave it to him. He invested it, all right, in his name. And every time I ask him about it he tells me, yes, he'll return it, tomorrow he'll give it back to me, but he never has."

"You keep harping about your money," John said. "That's yours, and everything I make is ours. I invested that money in a good stock; what's the difference whose name it's in? I thought that what we have between us we share."

"That was all I had," Shirley said. "You've got everything—you get the paychecks; you buy the cars and the house and the furniture. Whatever I want, I have to get from you. I want something of my own. I want my money."

Neither could understand the other's reasoning on the whole issue of money. John could not comprehend Shirley's anger at being controlled, but he didn't want to give up one bit of his control. Shirley wanted control over what she considered hers, but she did not want to assume more control herself; she wanted John to give it to her. She expected John to bring in a good salary without being obligated to earn any herself. They had both accepted their stereotypes—the man as provider and manager of the family income, and the woman as homemaker and home manager. They both assumed that John would be the logical organizer of the whole financial area, because women aren't supposed to be smart when it comes to money. Shirley had willingly handed her money over to John to invest it for her since she assumed she had no capability to do it for herself (nor did he).

Even more subtle was her deep conviction that she should be passive in the financial as well as the sexual areas. Somehow the two were inextricably intertwined. She felt that if she assumed more control of money, either by investing or earning it, she would be giving up her femininity.

228

THE STEREOTYPES OF ROMANCE

She would, she believed, be aggressive and therefore masculinized. So she resisted having anything to do with money other than receiving it from John, almost as a sexual favor. While she complained about John's not allowing her to have control, it was more her own subtle conviction that prevented her from assuming that control. Perhaps that was an added reason she was so embittered about John's lack of sexual aggressiveness; she believed down deep that since she had granted him control over her, he should use it to give her happiness.

Many of Shirley's resentments were double-edged in this way. She resented John for controlling her, but she had allowed that control, even set herself up for it in the beginning. And when she complained he, in effect, conspired with her, agreeing to do what she wanted, but he never intended to carry through. They had what seemed to be a secret contract between them—to keep him in control, and to let her blame him for it. Shirley even blamed John for impregnating her, although she loved their son. She believed that again John had made the decision, and she'd only gone along with his program.

"I wasn't ready," she said bitterly. "You decided you wanted a baby, and you pressured me until I gave in. That's the way it always is with you. Once you decide, you don't quit until you get what you want." She turned to me. "I can't hold out against him."

Shirley felt helpless and blamed John for "making" her that way, but couldn't see her own complicity. Holding the image of a delicate "lady" in her mind, she acted out that role until she was indeed helpless and incompetent. Her training had convinced her that she could not do things for herself, could not even think; therefore she didn't. Her parents told her she would grow up to be a lady and a mother; both seemed to exclude decisive action. Her teachers influenced her to take art, languages, and home economics; naturally, she stayed away from math, physics, or chemistry, because she was afraid she couldn't pass them. She didn't go to college because she expected to get married; she did when she was eighteen. She was an excellent

229

THE STEREOTYPES OF ROMANCE

housekeeper and hostess. She could cook, bake, sew, and take care of babies, but she had no skills to support herself in the working world. Although she was angry about John's control, she didn't believe she had the ability to support herself. She gave him control as much as he assumed it, but she resented him all the way.

John, too, had been trained for his role. His parents expected him to begin supporting himself, other than giving him food and shelter, when he was thirteen. He got a paper route. From that he went on to other jobs, gaining skills with each one, until he felt capable of managing his own business. He was competent at his office and in dealing with his employees, but he felt awkward around his own home. His mother had assumed control of the home and kitchen, and he expected Shirley to do the same. If Shirley didn't have dinner ready for him when he got home he went hungry; he hadn't ever prepared meals, so he wouldn't try. He knew little about babies and felt uncomfortable around them, so he wouldn't even offer to help take care of his son. He was perplexed by Shirley's moods, believing she should be able to control herself better, like him. His role as a competent, tough, driving business administrator left him totally unequipped to deal with emotions and simple problems in the home.

Both Shirley and John were trapped by their romantic conceptions of the roles a husband and wife should play. They felt controlled by each other and by their togetherness. They believed that they should do things together: go on vacations together, eat together, and share their checking account. They had great difficulty understanding that they didn't have to be and do things together all the time, that there was room in their marriage for separateness and expressions of individuality. They had trouble giving up their conception of themselves as a married team, yoked in the same harness—together.

But give it up they did, slowly, and with a good deal of screaming on all sides, me along with them. The three of us fought our way through many sessions,

230

battling through their romantic concepts one by one. Gradually, their relationship began to improve. Shirley threw out her image as a passive participant who had to have things done for her. She began to work on her own sense of competence in some far-out ways. She took a class in auto repair, and soon became better versed in maintaining a car than John. She joined a karate class and no longer felt afraid to leave the house alone at night. As her karate chops improved, so did her self-confidence. She started her own checking account and decided to take a course in investments, because John finally put ten thousand dollars in her name. As her sense of self-esteem rose, her resentments decreased. She began to initiate sex with John when he was not too tired, and if he was she would alleviate her own sexual tension by masturbating. She became less frustrated as she started to take care of her own needs, and a great deal happier with John and the children. She also found her own body turning on more during sex as she assumed more control of her life. Her previous bodily numbness disappeared as her resentments drained away one by one.

John, too, made changes in his behavior and his belief system. As Shirley's disposition improved, he no longer stayed at work as late or on weekends, nor did he walk out the door when she was depressed or angry. He made sincere attempts to hear her feelings, and if her voice rose a few decibels he didn't feel compelled to withdraw; he stayed and listened to her. He also planned outings with the children while Shirley went to her classes, and he spent time with them every weekend. He began enjoying his children more than he ever had before. He even tried his hand at making dinner for them, finding out that he could cook, steaks, pizzas, and salads being his specialities.

As he began to understand that there was more to good sex than intercourse, his lovemaking improved. John took more time with Shirley and listened as she made suggestions about what she liked or didn't like. He started feeling more turned on with her and began to initiate sex more often. He realized that his unspoken resentments had weighed

231

him down too; when he had felt angry at Shirley in the past, he simply turned over and went to sleep. As his resentment evaporated in his new found communication with Shirley, he discovered he wasn't as tired anymore!

John and Shirley changed very slowly from romanticists to realists. They still enjoy romantic outings, trips, and evenings out. But they use their time together to communicate their feelings to each other. They are beginning to view each other and themselves as individuals and not as stereotypes. They realize their human potential for being whoever they want to be; neither has to be passive or active, intellectual or emotional, helpless or competent. Neither has to be controlled. They have learned that they can respond to each other as people, not as a stereotypic man or woman but as individuals, retaining their self-identities within their marriage. They have found that they can discard their romanticized images and be themselves while still functioning effectively as husband and wife.

I don't know whether John and Shirley are going to make it to their golden anniversary, or even to their tenth. They have so many pressures on them that their grandparents did not; we all do. Divorce is far easier today than it was even ten years ago. We no longer have automatic stigmas attached to us if our marriages fail, so the societal pressure to stay married, regardless of the immensity of the problem, is far less. But John and Shirley have a better chance to stay together now than they did while they still clung to their romantic stereotypes. They have the opportunity now to be marital partners and still maintain their identities as individual beings.

Not too many people have that chance. I see unhappy people every time I'm in a crowd, people who are blind and deaf to each other, encased in their shells and barricaded from their partners, yet trapped in sterile relationships by their romanticized images of each other and of themselves. Many of them are desperate and would change if they only knew how to. Others will not recognize their loneliness; they

232

don't want to experience the pain of changing so, encased within their lonely shells, they suffer in silence.

Some who come to me for therapy say they want to work on their relationships. Many books and articles today stipulate that you must "work on" your marriage to make it good. But how can you work on a feeling? Sometimes the harder you try to work on your relationship, the worse it gets. You're working hard to make yourself feel different, when perhaps the way you feel right now *is* your actual feeling. I believe we get to the heart of the problem fast by becoming aware of our feelings and those of our partners, not by "working on" the problem, but just by accepting the feeling and recognizing it for what it is. And this is what we may need therapists for—to help us become aware. With that awareness, that knowledge of what the feeling is about and where it has originated, we can learn to communicate intimately, without barriers between us.

We don't ordinarily speak to each other with intimacy. We use safe, nonpersonal phrases, never intruding into the other's personal space: "It's rainy out today." "The dog needs food." "How did your day go?" "Junior got into a fight at school." "What do you want for dinner?" We rarely ask each other what he or she is feeling; many of us don't want to know. "What are you feeling right now? You look depressed." "You sound tired, are you having a tough day?" "You seem angry, are you?" We may not want to hear the answer if we ask, because an outburst of feeling is uncomfortable; it's more peaceable (although ultimately alienating) to let it ride and hope it will all go away. We rarely share our own feelings: "I'm lonely." "I'm hurting today and I don't know why." "I'd like a hug," "I'm felling blue." "I like you."

We *need* to intrude, to chip away at walls—ours and our partners. We *need* to break down barriers to gut-level communication. We *need* to throw away our objectivity and dig for feelings, even if it's uncomfortable and if it hurts. Of course it will hurt. If you ask someone for feelings you may get

233

them—anger, rage, spite, sadness, pain. You may find your own, and that's not fun either. But your feelings are real, moods are real. I hear some people saying, "I'm a moody person," deprecating themselves. I used to say that about myself. I've changed that to, "I'm a feeling person." You can change the words, too. Because you are a feeling person, as I am. If you don't know why you're feeling what you are, that does not change the fact that you're feeling something real and appropriate to what's going on inside—or outside—you. It may take time—days, months, even years—for you to figure out *why* you're feeling *what* you're feeling, but give yourself that grace nonetheless; permit yourself to experience your feelings.

John and Shirley did—slowly, painfully—and each permission they gave each other and themselves made the next easier. John stopped thinking Shirley was crazy to be moody or angry, and she did too. As he permitted her to express her feelings he found it easier to become aware of his own. Shirley no longer escalated her anger to rage as she was able to verbalize it to John. She began to feel more competent as she permitted herself to think, and blamed John less as she took over control of her own life. They both got out of the passivity syndrome as they gradually cut the bonds of their symbiosis. They found that conversing was easier and more interesting as they stopped talking impersonally to each other. When they began probing, seeing, hearing each other's feelings, they experienced sharing and intimacy. They became less lonely, angry, and frustrated as they opened themselves to each other. They began to see each other as persons without the masks of their stereotypes to cover their features.

The stereotypes of romance have affected every facet of our lives. They've told us how to behave, think, and feel. They've told us how to love and to be loved. If we don't act out our stereotypes, we believe we are wrong. If we don't cover our feelings with our stereotyped masks, our partners think we're crazy. So we cover up even more, and we try harder to be what we have been taught to be.

234

THE STEREOTYPES OF ROMANCE

We try to be good wives, serene mothers, and, always, ladies. We try to be virile lovers, strong fathers, and good husbands. We try to fit the image to our features, and if we hurt by doing so we disparage our own feelings in favor of the mask. But lovers and marital partners aren't the only ones afflicted, with our romantic notions. Children are, too, and parents. Mothers in particular conform to romantic stereotypes in America, and the consequences of that romanticization have been terrible.

235

THE STEREOTYPES OF ROMANCE

10. PARENTS

MOTHERS IN PARTICULAR, BUT FATHERS
TOO, CONFORM TO STEREOTYPES.

From the beginning, romance has been invested with an aura of spirituality. The literature and songs that evolved from the romantic tradition glorified an ideal kind of love through which men and women could experience heaven on earth. The hellish part was integral to the original concept, but nobody emphasized that. Early troubadours and lyricists praised only love's enobling qualities. They sang of the power of love to lift man out of his baser ways and transform him into a virtuous person. Romantic love was the pathway to goodness, and woman, as its agent, was sanctified.

The glorification of woman was enhanced by her identification with the Virgin Mary. Women were to be honored as agents of love on earth as the Virgin was glorified by her saintly love in heaven. The discrepancy between the sexual purity of the Virgin Mary and the adulterous relationships that romance advocated apparently bothered no one at first. Women began to view themselves as earthly models of the Virgin while still engaging in love affairs, platonic or otherwise, whether single or, more frequently, bonded in marriage to their warrior husbands. That attitude took some time to change, but change it did. The liberal view that the twelfth-century woman had of adulterous love affairs changed as later women modeled themselves ever more carefully on the Virgin. Man's attitude and behavior didn't change as much; man still permitted himself to "sow his wild oats," as a part of his "nature." But feminine behavior was increasingly characterized by traits attributed to the Virgin—humility, passivity, serenity, and chastity. Even though women engaged in sexual activities within marriage, many conceived without sexual pleasure, remaining virginal in their idealized attitude about themselves, if not in actuality.

Another reason for their abstinence from sexual lust was a curious dichotomy that arose in the fourteenth century. The separation of woman into two halves had begun in earlier centuries—the Virgin-Mother superimposed

239

upon the image of the lady at one extreme, with Eve, the sin-inspiring seductress of the Garden of Eden at the other. In those years, it was believed that evil was done by male sorcerers and devils. But with the advent of the Renaissance and concomitant changes in the intellectual, economic, and social orders, the equilibrium of the Church was seriously upset. Casting about for an explanation for the changes, the hierarchy of the Church hit upon a new race of malefactors on earth, woman as seductresses. Suddenly, everything that went wrong—famine, disease, storms, and deformed children—was the fault of women who were blamed in a form heretofore blameless on earth, the witch. Clergymen also discovered that the witches' evil deeds "were the work of Satan, carried out by his new hordes of female vassals"[1] and were dominated by sexual matters. It is not surprising, therefore, that sexuality in any aspect took on the aura of sinful-ness, and women began to put on asexual demeanors to avoid all threat of the burning stake.

In time sexual lust, although still tainted with evil, was not regarded as singular cause for the rack and pinion. If lust was indulged in, it was most likely outside of marriage, but the "forbidden activities" assigned to the curse of a witch gave way in later centuries to those men enjoyed with the cooperation of the prostitute. The accepted form of romantic love, meanwhile, was ever more closely aligned with Christian love. So intertwined were they in the minds of western people that they seemed to be one and the same. It wasn't until C. S. Lewis discussed the two that we had opportunity to grasp the difference between them. M.C. D'Arcy says:

> *To those who had been brought up in Victorian days, the truth came as a shock; they had had . . .*
> *their imaginations so soaked in images of romance that they had subconsciously identified Christian and romantic love. Now they had to*

1. Hunt, p. 192.

learn that while Christianity extolled marriage
and constant fidelity, the troubadours gave not a
thought to marriage, but sang of a fair lady and of
love outside the marriage bond. [2]

But few people changed their concepts because of Lewis's revelations. When his book was published in 1939, specialist circles resounded with the news while the general public was unaffected. Most people did not read his exposé; if they did, they certainly didn't use it to alter their attitudes about their own relationships. Most probably regarded it the same way as one woman who told me, "I thought romance always was as it is today. I never knew it had a beginning. And if I had known it did, and it began as adultery, I'd have just rejected the whole idea!"

By the time Lewis's book brought to light the factual origins of our romantic tradition, we had solidified our beliefs, accepting romance in our culture as a customary prelude to marriage. The spirituality inherent in our romantic relationships had long been accepted as fact, as attested to by the many lyrics praising stardust, moonlight, visions of goodness, and angels. Lover's hearts were netted as easily as salmon, their fantasies winging them through the wildly exciting first encounters to that inevitable destination of the altar. Moreover, romance became interwoven with our other relationships. That between parents and children, particularly between mother and child, was especially devastating, invested as it was with romantic undertones.

This romanticization was more evident in the last century than it is now. I believe we are letting go of some of these concepts today; otherwise I wouldn't be able to verbalize the destructiveness of these myths, nor would others who are increasingly demanding an end to our ambiguous romantic attitudes. But yesterday? Yesterday we were inextricably harnessed with our beliefs. The etiquette books of the nineteenth

2. D'Arcy, p. 34.

century, steeped in romanticism, poured off the presses in an unending stream. From about 1830 through 1860, etiquette books appeared at a rate of more than three a year. The books not only gave rules on how one should act in society but referred to manners in a moralistic sense. One woman writer (most of the writers were women) said, "Not only is the violation of good manners inexcusable . . . it is sinful." She continued, "Politeness is . . . a religious duty and should be part of religious training." Other writers enlarged on the religiosity of etiquette, imbuing it with a "sacred terror" that echoed the romantic precepts of the twelfth century, but with a subtle difference: The sacredness granted woman as the earthly representation of the Virgin was enhanced by her becoming that which we still celebrate today in poem, song, and national holiday—Mother.

Catharine Beecher (whose sister, Harriet Beecher Stowe, added her own chapter to history with *Uncle Tom's Cabin*) wrote *The American Women's Home* and gave household drudgery an air of professionalism, labeling it "domestic science." She put into words an image of motherhood that was to be held up as a model of virtue for Americans for years to come: "Woman is . . . the guardian of the nursery, the companion of childhood, and the constant model of imitation. It is her hand that first stamps impressions on the immortal spirit, that must remain forever."[3] Woman was not only the spiritual counselor of childhood but, in Miss Beecher's opinion, also the veritable backbone of a nation. And through her words echo the strains of the philosophy of Eleanor of Aquitaine seven centuries before: "For a nation to be virtuous and religious, the females of that nation must be deeply imbued with these principles: for just as the wives and mothers sink or rise in the scale of virtue, intelligence and piety, the husbands and sons will rise or fall."[4]

Wife and mother became, in the nineteenth century, more than virtuous or pious. Mother in par-

3. Barbara M. Cross, ed., *The Educated Woman in America* (New York: Teachers College Press, 1965), p. 67.

4. Cross, p. 71.

ticular came to be equated with her otherworldly image, the Virgin Mary. The mother on earth, at least in her image, became as saintly as Mary, whom we worship as the Mother of God. No longer was it just woman, as in Eleanor's time, who was granted that healing quality of goodness; no longer was it only the love of a woman that could salve man's wounds and uplift his spiritual self, absolving his sins in the process—in the nineteenth century it was a woman made sacred by the fact of her giving birth—mother. The outcome of such propagandizing was that mother became a symbol of all that was good in life—all love, virtue, and purity. Carl Bode says, "The wife as mother became the favorite sentimental symbol in the family circle. . . . Print after print shows her surrounded by her children, in a veritable atmosphere of love."[5]

The belief that mothers are sacred simply because they have borne a child is a little alien to us today in its immensity. Yet we haven't entirely left it behind. Generations permeated by such a myth don't let it go easily. Any change in such traditional mythology is more likely to occur between generations than within a generation, and even then it's hard to drop. When we associate disbelief with sinfulness, we're more likely to cling to our orthodoxy longer, from the sheer terror of being penalized. And when it's mother who's brandishing the switch, the penalties involved are most likely nearer than some distant purgatory. The penalties are meted out at first hand, making life plain hell, by a righteous, avenging mother.

Even today we believe to some extent that women are glorified just because they become mothers. A friend told me of her irritation with this belief, saying, "When I got pregnant everyone said, 'Isn't it wonderful you're going to have a child. You're so fortunate!' It would have been a lot more realistic if they had shared their experiences with me and told me what to expect after the baby came. But maybe if

5. Carl Bode, *The Anatomy of American Popular Culture: 1840–1861* (Berkeley: University of California Press, 1959), p. 272.

PARENTS

they'd told me the real part of it I wouldn't have wanted to have a child at all!"

The stereotype of sainthood has been hard for mothers to bear. After the baby is born, a woman is supposed to be transformed into a perfect, all-loving creature. As if by magic she becomes not whatever self she was before conception, but madonnalike, serene and overflowing with maternal compassion. The fable is far from reality. Marriage is a hard enough turning point. Before we wed, we are supposed to be virginally ignorant about sex—although that idea is becoming outmoded, and it's about time! After we marry, we have society's blessing to propagate. We're supposed to turn into sexually knowledgeable people overnight, released from our former inhibitions by the sonorous pronouncement of the clergy. Silenced then are all the parental no-nos and the prohibitions about touching our or our partners' bodies. Suddenly sexuality is lauded, sex is available for the taking, and roles of virtuous abstinence we had to assume in premarital days are now reversed. I do not meet many people who take this change in stride. I see a good many in therapy, particularly women, who suffer because they can't immediately mutate into fantastic sexual partners. They were never given permission to be sexual before they got married; how then can they gain permission from their own minds to turn on instantly afterwards?

The problem of motherhood is different in its stereotype but not in its expected spontaneity. After the pregnancy has been confirmed, one is supposed to glow. Personally, I never figured out how to glow when I feel nauseated by my unaccustomed womb companion and the suddenly oppressive odors surrounding me. But no matter what the reality of the situation is—how tough the pregnancy, how worrisome the finances, how wanted the child—the comment is the same: "Isn't it wonderful, you're going to have a baby!" No matter what the mother-to-be feels, what fears, qualms, or apprehensions she has; all else is suddenly subordinate to the event to come. And after the baby is born, the flowers, the cards, the calls from

244

long-absent relatives proclaim the event and herald the mother as the accomplisher of the greatest deed in the world—giving birth.

The hoopla is soon over, and the new mother is stuck with the care of an insatiable infant whose constant demands leave her fatigued and enervated. She's also stuck with the romantic image foistered on her by our "isn't it wonderful" society—that within the space of a few hours of labor she's supposed to have turned from a woman accustomed to dealing only with the needs of herself and her husband into a maternal, nurturing figure devoted to caring exclusively for a small, helpless human being. Because she's had a baby she's a mother and knows, again as if by magic, all about taking care of that child. It's "mother instinct," we are told. I ask, "What instinct?" Believe me, or ask anyone else who's had a baby, one does not gain instant knowledge or have instant maternal instinct or instant anything else by giving birth. One learns, just as one learns anything, by experience and through time. And in our learning, being human, we make mistakes. I remember one delightful woman in a class of mine years ago who said, "Back in Massachusetts we have a saying. 'The first child, like the first pancake, should be thrown out!'"

Unlike pancakes, we don't chuck out a firstborn; we let them grow, and they teach us to be parents. By the time the second child comes along, we've relaxed a bit in our child-raising techniques. There's no question about throwing out the second! We've learned, mainly through trial and error, to become reasonably knowledgeable parents and caretakers of our children. We have learned about the realities of quieting screaming infants and washing diapers and cleaning up spilled milk and cookie crumbs. We've become used to slowing our pace to theirs and meeting their needs before we meet our own. We've gotten to know how high the fever should be before we worry, and how to patch a skinned knee, and what strange and different meanings various words have to the mind of a child: circus, school, bath, vegetable, toys, Santa Claus, candy, egg, Easter egg. But even if

245
PARENTS

we know all the details and take care of our children as well as we can, we're still tormented by the thought that we are not good enough mothers.

Our romantic tradition teaches us that we should be perfect. Mothers are sainted, mothers are blessed with maternal instinct, mothers are automatically perfect because they are mothers. If we respond to our little tyrant with feelings of anger or resentment or irritation, it means we're not the good mothers society says we're supposed to be. So we bury our feelings of rage that are not supposed to be there but nevertheless persist in occuring, and guiltily tell ourselves we're bad mothers. Of course, not all of us pay attention to the image. Some of us manage to ignore it entirely; others attend to i lightly and with a sense of humor. One woman told me recently "Good mother? Of course I'm a good mother. I don't do a damn thing, but I worry!" Most of us, however, take the image seriously and try to model ourselves on it, *no matter what we feel* And when we castigate ourselves for being "bad," we depress ourselves rather than exposing our unacceptable anger.

Our children corroborate our self-guilt. Our little creations, whom we in our premotherhood days envisioned as our angels on earth, will not fail to lay it on us They may not do so intentionally. Maybe our baby screams in discomfort or sickness; our older child has emotional or school problems; our teenagers get in trouble with the law, or involved with drugs. Our thoughts are the same: "What have I done wrong? It's my fault he (or she) is turning out this way. If I had been a good mother my child would be acting differently." In our minds, we're always to blame because we haven't been the perfect mothers society and our parents have told us we should be.

Our children will also accuse us deliberately. My little girl does when I won't buy her the toy she wants, or give her candy, or take her where she insists on going She says, "You're not a good mother." I am not hung up on the image so I can reply easily, without a stab of guilt, "I know I'm not, and I'm still not going to buy you candy." Many of my client

246

still cling to that image of perfection, however. I doubt if they would respond to such a blatant accusation from their kids either, but they punish themselves with their own accusations. They knock themselves out to do for and take care of their children as they believe they should, but they can never do enough to satisfy their indomitable internal commander. And when their children express negative feelings, as normal little feeling people do, the mothers stuck with the "good" image are devastated by guilt. "What have I done to deserve this?" they ask themselves with anguish. And the answer comes back from their own minds, "Everything!"

Such mothers may live their entire lives for their children, giving up their own dreams and plans in order that their children may have all their needs met (although it may be questionable as to whose needs they are—the mother's or the child's.) They may sacrifice their own desires, scrimping and saving to make sure their kids have what they themselves did not. Their children will have the music and dancing lessons, the clothes and the toys that they missed out on in their own youth. Their children will go to college and be popular and have all the opportunities that they, the mothers, missed. It is no easy task for these mothers; sacrificing one's own needs hurts. They do it because they believe they should, and everyone around them will hear of their martyrdom. Yet they believe they will get their rewards when their children grow up.

These mothers hope that their children will conform to their expectations; they expect to savor their children's lives vicariously, to make up for all their sacrifices. These mothers believe that their children will appreciate all that was done for them, and will one day express that gratitude profusely. That day rarely comes. The children grow up and go their own way, rarely acknowledging their mothers' sacrifices. Even if they know, they don't spend much time on appreciation. They do not recognize the obligation their mothers believe they are owed. The children are ungrateful, unperceiving, and unaware. They leave, and when they're gone, the

247

PARENTS

mothers are, even if still married, essentially alone. The children never call or visit enough, and the mothers are angry. They are not only angry at their children, but also at themselves. They realize that they have sacrificed all their lives, only to be left alone in the end. And the realization that they've given up their own dreams for an eventual empty nest hits them hard. Where is the romantic promise of child-raising if the end result is loneliness?

Of course some fathers are stuck with the "good" label too, and struggle in guilt and despair to give their kids what they, the fathers, think they should. They call themselves bad when they don't meet what they interpret as their children's needs. They may feel a terrible responsibility toward their offspring, terrible for their own insides. Not being permitted by our society to be as teary and depressed as women, fathers will more likely cover up their feelings with stoicism, alcohol, or drugs, finally resorting to sharp commands and spankings to shape their recalcitrant charges into line, or walking out and away from the whole problem. If they stick around, they may work their whole lives at jobs they hate, believing they should be good providers, because quitting to do what they really wanted to would be called, by their own definition, bad.

Fathers are not perceived by our society as saintly, however, simply because they've succeeded in impregnating a woman. A man may feel that he has proven his manhood by having visible signs of his potency, but nowhere does it say he gets a halo for doing so. Nor does he have to suffer the weight of that halo for the rest of his life in order to sustain the image. Fathers are allowed to make more mistakes with their children, to display more anger, to show less "paternal instinct." (Is there such a term that equals "maternal instinct" in impact?). Fathers are permitted to be away the majority of the time at work (and at play) without being labeled bad fathers. Not mothers! Whether they want to or not, mothers are stuck with being good, and if they exhibit a noncaring or a detached attitude toward their offspring they are automatically bad mothers.

The "good" label is, as it always has been, a part of the romantic nonsense we believe in. The

image of the Virgin that was used as model for the lady of the twelfth century is with us still, although today we call her mother. Mothers don't need to attain fame exactly as did the Virgin Mary, however. Who of us has the supernatural ability to conceive our children miraculously, without the help of a male partner? But we don't have to follow the example of our heavenly model in every respect in order to cloak ourselves in her image. We have the romantic conception to verify our innate virginity, even if we're sexual beings who've given birth the ordinary way. Mothers teach their daughters the same beliefs about their purity as they themselves have been taught. So continue the destructive beliefs, down through the generations. Nancy Friday says:

> *Mothers raise their daughters as fools because*
> *they believe in the divinity of innocence. . . . Our*
> *mothers keep us pure and dumb, knowing that*
> *even if sex is our future, it will also be our doom.*[6]

Mothers also keep themselves sexually innocent by equating their femininity with motherhood. Women may never allow themselves to experience sexual feelings of any kind with a man, certainly not orgasm, but may surrender themselves totally in a kind of sexual release to their children, being emotionally open with them, perhaps even permitting themselves to experience the pleasurable sexual feelings that nursing a child brings. They may surrender themselves entirely—their lives, their time, their attachment—to their children yet hold themselves back from their men.

Eric Berne talks of the game "Rapo" in *Games People Play* as an existential position of "I am blameless."[7] Rapo is a game played by women to subtly or not-so-subtly take out their unpermitted anger on men. By proving that "men are no damn good," and that "all men want is sex," the Rapo player justifies her anger against men and blames them at

6. Friday, p. 286.
7. Berne, p. 129.

249

PARENTS

the same time for causing it. She righteously reestablishes her virginal state of purity each time she accuses a man of being "dirty," and becomes once more her mommy's good, nonsexual girl. She becomes even angrier when the men who don't want to play the game accuse her in return of being a tease. And she is a tease; some Rapo players hold themselves back physically, others even more subtly withhold themselves emotionally. Whichever degree of Rapo she plays, her anger is ever apparent, just under the surface, ready to flash out at any moment and blame men for making her angry, vindictive—and sexual.

The Rapo player is not entirely at fault for taking out her subtle, indirect anger on men. Our society encourages her. In fact, I would call the game of Rapo central to our society, taught to us by our parents and parent figures, deeply believed in and approved of by all of us because it has always been an essential and integral part of romance. The lady that the troubadours coveted may have given herself to her lover on occasion, but the purest, most perfect love was that which was long-lasting, intense, and *un*consummated. This kind of love was purer because of the immutable distance between the lovers and was made more intense by the lady's unapproachable beauty. Andreas says:

> *It is the pure love which binds together the hearts*
> *of two lovers with every feeling of delight. This*
> *kind consists in the contemplation of the mind*
> *and the affection of the heart; it goes as far as the*
> *kiss and the embrace and the modest contact with*
> *the nude lover, omitting the final solace, for that*
> *is not permitted to those who wish to love purely.*
> *This is the kind that anyone who is intent upon*
> *love ought to embrace with all his might, for this*
> *love goes on increasing without end . . . and the*
> *more of it one has the more one wants.* [8]

8. Capellanus, p. 122.

250

PARENTS

I know of some people who have been so infatuated in their youth that they clutch the memory of that fantasy person to their hearts, no matter how old they get or how realistically lovable a partner they have in the present. Others fight continually when they are with their lovers but think obsessively and in glowing pictures about the beloved when apart. Still others feel (and give) no warmth or physical affection to their mates, saving their caresses for their extramarital partners, yet they wouldn't consider divorce. And all of them, men and women alike, justify their behavior by falling back on and quoting endlessly our ancient and long-accepted code of romance.

Our entire society *seems* pointed toward sexuality but it isn't, anymore than was the original conception of romantic love. We practice seduction in our dress, our use of cosmetics, our mannerisms. But we don't really mean it. The sexuality advertised in magazines, droned on records, and dripped off the television screen is no more than a veneer, a come-on, a promise that we all know can't realistically be fulfilled. This superficial sexuality is a cheap imitation of the depth of feeling that two open, aware human beings can have for each other. Yet this blatant display of sexuality—the tease, the playgirl (or boy), the magazine model, the suavely attired stranger—is only following the guidelines established long ago in the name of romance. It's the promise we're after, not the real thing. When we get into an actual sexual relationship, many of us don't know how to handle it.

Even though I get angry at the superficiality of our particular version of sexuality in the United States, I'm not above my own game of Rapo. I've caught glimmers of hidden feelings at times, marveling that I've never been aware of their existence before. I remember doing an exercise with a male partner at a workshop a few years ago. The leader instructed us to act flirtatiously toward each other. I did so, feeling awkward, clumsy, unfeminine, and mean. I was surprised enough at my awkward feelings, but mean? Where did that come from, I wondered in amazement? Yet there it was, and whether it

251

PARENTS

had more to do with my mother or myself I honestly couldn't say. At the time I thought it must have had to do with my perception of my mother—what I had picked up of her feelings toward men when I was a kid. Surely it couldn't have been me! Today I'm not so sure. Since then I've gone to bed, feeling angry with my husband, and, quickly pretending to be asleep, have heard the spiteful words drifting through my mind, "Ha, serves you right!" The accusation implicit in those words tells me that somewhere along the line I've accepted a "blameless" attitude, so that even as I scorn Rapo, I sometimes indulge my own feelings of persecution by playing the game.

Feelings, particularly sexual feelings, are not acknowledged openly in our society. If we have them, we don't talk about it. If others have them, we don't think about it. How many of us have been amazed to realize that our parents "did it;" we know it must be fact because of our birth, yet the thought seems preposterous—surely they don't feel those feelings (let alone do those things) too! To distract our minds from the overwhelming fact of sex, and to preserve our naiveté, we confuse the term with romance. One woman points out in *My Mother/My Self:*

> *I used to get a tremendous amount of sexual feelings through watching them make love in the movies. . . . I had no idea that I was reacting not romantically to the people on the screen but sexually.*[9]

We don't dare admit to ourselves that our romantic fantasies are actually sexual feelings. Our nostalgic yearnings are commonly acknowledged to be normal parts of the maturation process, fantasies we are supposed to have, innocent nonsense that we will, given time, outgrow. We're not supposed to have the sexual feelings, just the fantasies. How differently mothers might feel

9. Friday, p. 246.

252

PARENTS

about the crushes their teenage daughters have on rock stars if they used the term "emergent sexuality" instead of "romantic fantasies." How differently girls might feel about themselves if they admitted that their excitement, pink cheecks, and shrill cries were caused not by the singer's lyrics, but by the sexual feelings within their own bodies.

It's not nice, in our society, to talk about sexuality in reference to adolescent (or other) crushes. It's much more acceptable to disguise our sexual excitement under the cloak of romance. It's much less dangerous to talk about hearts and flowers than bodily feelings. We view feelings of any kind with general disdain and abhorrence. We seem to think it's bad enough that people have feelings, let alone express and act on those emotions. The minute someone verbalizes an unacceptable feeling in some circles, others will rescue, distract, ignore, or belittle the speaker. "We don't talk about that here," they infer or say outright. If this is so, how can we separate the mental fantasies of what we have been taught to believe from the bodily feelings we know but refuse to acknowledge? How, for that matter, can we expect to know what our feelings mean when our entire society tells us, "Don't feel?" I remember when I was twenty and going steady, having the experience of petting heavily with my boyfriend one night. The next morning I woke up shaking and I thought, "Why am I shaking from cold when it's the middle of summer?" Sexually retarded as I was, I had no way of knowing that my shakes were due to normal tension generated by lack of sexual release, and not from the weather.

We are confused about our bodies, ignorant of our feelings, and cheated out of our sexuality by our romantic beliefs. We also project our own fears of sex onto those around us. If mothers pray for their daughters' "innocence," they are less afraid for their daughters than for their own tightly controlled selves. Fearing sexuality themselves, they are terrified that their daughters will betray them by acting out their unacknowledged fantasies. But the mothers' deepest terror may have little to do with sexuality. They may say it does; they may

253

swear they fear for their daughters, and even admit under duress that their real fear of sex is for themselves. But they have another, even more compelling, fear than that. They're afraid, each and every one, that if their daughters act out sexually, they will be labeled bad mothers. So the fact that their daughters have sex with their boyfriends, or get pregnant, or marry because they "have to" has less importance to these mothers in the long run than having the "sins" of their offspring found out. "What will the neighbors think?" they moan to their daughters in anguish, not, "How do *you* feel about it?"

Mothers, and fathers too, in our society, have the full cooperation of the legal system in maintaining control over their daughters' sexual behavior. Their sons's sexual experimentation worries them less than their daughters'. If their sons display sexual precocity during their teenage years, "Boys will be boys." If the daughters exhibit similar behavior, however, a great hue and cry goes up over their loss of sexual purity. Far from the lenient attitude toward their sons, the stern treatment given their daughters is governed by the belief, "She's bad and should be punished." And punishment, quite often, is meted out by the watchful eye of the law—the court. One recent study of teenage sexual offenders indicates that seventy-seven percent of girls in reformatories in 1978 were serving time for status offenses, in which sex often was a crime. The authors state:

> *Parents are more likely to push daughters into the arms of the law than sons because "parents fear their daughters' sexual misbehavior and may brand as delinquents girls who exercise the sexual rights that traditionally have been reserved for boys,". . . . "Ungovernable" is the charge minors in New York State are most likely to face, a charge that "in the case of females may be translated as being promiscuous."*[10]

10. Cammy Wilson and Henry Harris, "Making Sex a Crime," *Human Behavior* (February 1979), p. 44.

254

Such charges need not be proven for punishment to be administered by the enforcing agencies. The authors contend that "even just the suspicion of sexual intercourse is often all juvenile authorities need to arrest and ultimately convict an unmarried girl, as if she were guilty of shoplifting, assault, or robbery."[11] We are not as far removed from the era of having to wear a scarlet "A" emblazoned on our chests as we'd like to think!

Parents don't get off lightly while the sins of their daughters (or their sons) are being purged by the authorities. Parents suffer because they believe that the admission of their children's guilt signifies their own failure in raising them. They were not good enough; they did the best they could and still they fell short of being perfect mothers and fathers; they suffer their own guilt for being bad. Even while they are beating their children or using emotional abuse to try to discipline their charges into perfect behavior, they criticize themselves for not being good enough parents. The more these parents do for their children, believing that they should do it for the children's sake, the more they suffer when their children act as normal little self-concerned, mistake-making, experimenting people do.

Because their worlds are usually more involved with their children, mothers particularly suffer. They may do very well at first, feeling needed to care for and nurture their small, helpless infants. Their relationships with their husbands may be unfulfilling and sexually dissatisfying, but they are nonetheless content. The baby who responds to them as the focal point of existence fills them with love. They feel important because of being so needed, accepted in the community by the fact of their motherhood, and somehow justified. They have fulfilled their role and have displayed their goodness. The worth of their existence has been indisputably proven by that role of universal mother.

Then the child grows older and gets to be a rebellious two year old. He or she learns that wonderful word "no," and uses it at every opportunity! Whatever

11. Ibid., p. 43.

mommy wants, the child does not. The rebelliousness of the child is a natural part of the maturation process, which will continue throughout the rest of his or her life, until that day when the healthy decision is reached that mommy is no longer necessary for survival. Healthy for the child, but not for the good mother. This mother, still dependent on the child for her self-esteem and feelings of worth, won't tolerate any exhibition of separateness—any thought, opinion, feeling, or action that shows independence on the part of the child. When the child rebels against her wishes, this mother feels bereft, no longer important and even betrayed. The child should not say "no" to her, she says, because "mother knows best." So the mother who believes implicitly in her own goodness and infallibility will do her best to make the child obey, to conform to what she, the mother, wants, and to become, in time, a miniature representation of herself.

Of course father figures in here too. Men who have been raised by authoritarian fathers or mothers themselves will not tolerate rebelliousness in their children, anymore than their own parents did. Such fathers respond to their child's "no" as a bull might to the matador's red cape. "Hey, toro," the child might as well taunt, for the fight is on. These fathers, imbued as they are with the righteousness of the romantic conception, often use mother as their excuse to make the child "mind." "Don't you sass your mother," they say in all seriousness, not wanting to admit that it's their own anger welling up when the child shows any sign of rebelliousness, particularly when the child utters the unforgivable word, "no." "You respect her," they say, "and mind."

"Mind" is ambiguous enough to me; to a child it may be incomprehensible. I had a conversation with my little girl about it not long ago.

"What does minding mean, mommy?" she asked me.

I had to think about it. Finally I said, "It means doing something you don't want to do when

mommy or daddy tells you to do it." I thought my explanation satisfied her. She said, "Oh," seemingly content with it.

Then, after a long pause she said, "What else am I allergic to?"

"What do you mean?" I said.

"You're not allergic to anything that I know of."

"Yes I am," she responded. "Daddy told me I'm allergic to minding."

Another child was confused by a word continually told to him by his parents. In a workshop, one participant told the group about her cousin's confusion:

"When he was small, his parents would tell him to 'be good.' 'be nice,' and 'behave,' " she said. "He used to say that he could figure out what 'good' and 'nice' meant, but no matter how hard he tried he just couldn't understand what 'have' meant. So he assumed that he must be a bad boy; he didn't know how to be 'have'."

Fathers who won't tolerate rebelliousness in their children will not allow them to have "allergies" such as not minding. They insist that the child "behave." These fathers feel not only angered, but put upon, when their children do not conform to the expected behavior. They may take the child's natural tendency to rebel as a personal affront, viewing their children not as tiny people in their own right, but as extensions of themselves. These fathers have a strong sense of righteous indignation in their authoritarianism. They've put in their years working for the family, years they could have used for themselves. They've spent their youth at the shop or the office, on the assembly line or at the factory. And what do they get for it? Ingratitude. The least their children could do, think such fathers, is to feel grateful.

Of course the children do not. The children may love, even like, their parents, but what child feels grateful for what the parents do? A child regards whatever the parents do or give as his or her right. Any gratitude the child feels may come years later, in retrospect. And any debt the child

257

PARENTS

owes the parents will rightly be paid to his or her own children. But the parents who believe in their own goodness demand payment. Many children are forced to pay by conforming to their parents' expectations of what they should be and how they should feel. They pay by assuming the same goodness that their parents have been taught to assume, and end up adopting a similar set of principles. They pay by learning to be good for the sake of their families and harnessing themselves for the rest of their lives to the popular stereotype of what a good mother or a good father should be. They grow up to be parents themselves, still yoked to their internal images of goodness.

There's no way out for children, as there is no way out for parents. If they believe in that image of goodness, any expression of negative feelings, let alone acting out on those feelings, automatically brands them as bad. The only way they can deal with their negative feelings at all is to disown them, to say that someone else caused them and to deny all responsibility for having had them. So they accuse other people, usually other members of their family, for making them angry or irritated or bitchy or out-of-sorts. "You make me mad when you don't behave," says the father. "You hurt me when you're bad," says the mother. "You made me cry," says the child. Each one is stuck in his or her helplessness, powerless to change self or situation because they have all bought the belief that they should be good, and if they are angry or depressed or unhappy—if they have any feelings other than the approved "happy" ones—it means they aren't good anymore.

They are all locked into blaming everyone else for their bad feelings and their inadequacies, and there is nothing left for them to do with their lives other than defend themselves against what they consider to be their failings. They cannot change because they have not taken responsibility for their feelings, thoughts, or actions in any way. Having given away their power to the people around them, they dance as mechanically as puppets, because they believe everyone else is making them feel, think, and do. Even though they feel helpless

258

and hopeless and entrapped, still they try to be good, to uphold the family name, to live up to the expectations of others around them—no matter how much it hurts. Is it any wonder we suffer so much pain in our lifetimes? And see around us so many wasted lives?

Women waste their lives, even more than men, because of our culturally accepted belief system. Men expect to go out and make a living, and by and large they do. Ask a little boy what he wants to do when he grows up and he will tell you, "I want to be a fireman," or a policeman, or an astronaut, or some other occupation that promises glorious adventure. Ask a little girl and she may say, "I want to be a mommy and have babies." (Happily, many little girls are being taught today that they can, if they want to, be doctors and engineers, police officers and executives.) Women expect to fall in love and get married and raise children. Even if they want to work, or are forced to because of circumstances, they still look toward love and marriage for their self-fulfillment. When they do not get what they have been taught to expect from their husbands and children—happiness—they feel victimized and embittered. All through their young lives they were told that if they were good they would one day find their true love, and they would be happy. When they find instead discord and upset with their husbands, fatigue and frustration with their children—children who leave the nest as soon as they can—these women are likely to feel victimized. After all, they think, they've been good, they've done the best they could; they should be rewarded. Instead they find loneliness, even despair. One therapist says of such women:

When a woman perceives that she has been neglected or abandoned by her husband or her grown children or others, she may keep herself as miserable as possible in order to punish those who in her view are responsible for her bereft condition. If she is to choose to make a good life for herself she would have to give up the "right" to

259

PARENTS

punish. At the back of her mind she may feel that if she were to prosper and enjoy life, she would reveal to the rejecting persons that she didn't need them so much after all, so whatever they "did" to her wasn't so bad either. That's a hard position for some "victims" to take, particularly those who derive much of their potency from their moral superiority. [12].

Their "moral superiority" gives them a sense of righteousness; they believe that even if their families are against them, they have the backing of the greatest power of all. "At least, they reason, God and right are on their side, and this reasoning helps give them the illusion of strength and control."[13]

God, right, and the authorization of romance are on the side of the victimized woman—because she has borne a child; she is a mother. Therefore, she believes, her man and children owe her—their time, their efforts, their very lives. Many of these women try their best to tie their men down, and to prevent their children from leaving. This type of mother does her best to control her children with guilt and prevent them, emotionally if not in actuality, from ever leaving her. I remember one client of mine, a woman in her thirties, who had been married twice, had a child of her own, had worked at several jobs, and lived in many different parts of the world. She left me after a session one day and stayed overnight with a friend. Her mother called me that night.

"Where is my daughter?" she demanded.

"She's not here," I said, feeling instant irritation. I fight phantom parents in my clients' heads (plus my own) so much that I can get in touch very quickly with my anger at parents.

12. Elizabeth Friar Williams, *Notes of a Feminist Therapist* (New York: Prager Pub. 1976), p. 92.

13. Ibid.

260

PARENTS

"Where did she go?" the mother insisted.

"I don't know," I said sulkily.

"I'm really worried about her," the mother went on. "She never calls to let me know where she is; she's always upsetting me that way. I just don't know what to think about her."

Well, I knew what to think. From such a brief conversation with her mother I could understand more of my client's problems than before. The symbiotic hook the mother put out was enormous—but entirely justified in her view. Her daughter, no matter how old she got, should always inform her, the mother, of her whereabouts. If she did not, the daughter was a bad girl, and the mother felt victimized, though righteous in her wrath.

Through my own quickly activated childhood anger, still stubbornly apparent despite my years of letting it go, I could see this mother's hurt. She really believed her daughter owed her allegiance—and as a consequence of her firmly held belief, she felt hurt when her daughter in ignorance or, more likely, spite, didn't call.

"I'm sorry," I told her. "She didn't tell me where she was going, but I'm sure she's all right."

"Well, I'll just have to wait until she decides to call, if she ever does," the mother said in a depressed tone of voice. My client phoned to apologize the next day, after talking to her mother.

"I suppose I should have called her," she said, "but I didn't even decide to go to my friend's until after I'd left your place. Then I just forgot. But she really lays on the guilt; you'd think I'd committed a major crime. She acts like I'm still a little kid."

"Yes, I heard that," I said. "She sounded like she was really angry at a little kid and didn't know what to do about it. Is she depressed a lot?"

"Depressed?" my client said. "She wrote the book on depression!"

261

PARENTS

I had no doubt her mother suffered. Such a load of helpless anger, such a strong victim position, could lead to nothing else. She was not alone in her chronic state of depression. Women who limit themselves through conditioned dependency suffer that anguished sense of incapacitation as a common problem. Trained as they are to be passive, patient, and superficially "nice," they can't see any other options than to wait for what others give them. Women have no greater inborn ability to depress themselves than men do, but they have a greater tendency to do so because of their feminine stereotype. If they follow its dictates long enough, that image serves to undermine any normal capabilities they might have. The dependency construed to be central to femininity creates a sense of helplessness in women which renders them incapable of responding to a problem situation assertively. One author studying the problem of women and depression states:

> . . . *in times of interpersonal drought—when sources of emotional supply are unusually low, or not there—the "normally feminine, normally dependent" woman may experience her inner world as emptied of what is good and meaningful to her. The props of her self-regard, if they've been held in place primarily by feedback from the environment, may simply begin to crumble and fall down. Under the circumstances, a woman may become far too harsh in her assessment of herself and of her worth and usefulness as a human being. She may feel helpless about her life circumstances, and hopelessly ineffectual in terms of her capacity for mastering or changing them. She may, in a word, become depressed.*[14]

Depression is a problem of staggering proportions among women today, not because women are more apt to seek medical aid, not

14. Maggie Scarf, "The More Sorrowful Sex," *Psychology Today* (April 1979), p. 52.

because they're more likely to be labeled "depressive" by doctors, but because their dependence on others for any sense of self-esteem creates in them a conditioned helplessness. According to statistics compiled at the Depression Section of the National Institutes of Mental Health, at least one in every five Americans shows moderate depressive symptomatology, which figures out to be about forty million people, two-thirds of whom are women.[15]

Despite the genuine national concern over this problem and the attempts of the medical establishment to treat the symptoms, depression is a valid way of responding to helplessness. For an enormous group of women, no doubt larger than the above figures suggest, depression is an appropriate response to an intolerable situation. What else can one do, feeling routinely helpless, than sink into intermittent, if not chronic, depression? Making some move, even seeing options, may be not only difficult but impossible when one feels powerless. One could certainly express the anger that underlies most depressions, but it's not nice for a woman to get mad! So the dutiful wife, the good mother who has done her best for her man and her children, yet does not get what she thinks she deserves, has no other recourse than to be depressed. And the doctor or social worker who tries to cure her may not realize that depression may be her only sane way of responding to a situation in which she feels totally trapped and unable to make any move to change her situation.

The trap is marriage—not a marriage of two free adults in which each feels able to gain satisfaction out of his or her life, but a marriage based on the romantic principles of the fragile wife and the protective husband. This type of marriage encourages a woman to play a submissive role, to disparage her abilities, and to seek vicarious identity through her man and children. Such a condition of restriction and self-limitation may be the source of her depression as well. E.F. Williams observes:

15. Ibid., p. 90.

263

Ironically, we teach little girls that marriage is the best thing that can happen to them when they fall in love, when in reality it may be the worst . . . recent sociological research indicates that contemporary marriage, although it is good for men, may well contribute to women's physical and emotional disabilities. [16]

Women may also be exhibiting symptoms of depression because of their discontent with old roles. Our stereotypes are changing, but not fast enough. We know our roles are not as circumscribed as were those of our grandmothers, but what can we as individual women do about it? Women who are already trapped by the actualities of small children, financial worries, and husbands who hold them (and themselves) to traditional roles, women who are unskilled and overage for entry positions in the job market may have little to fall back on except their depression. Such women may feel as if they're drowning in sight of an island—they know it's there but they can't reach it fast enough to save themselves. They're still at sea and sinking fast, and many don't realize that their own attitudes are the weights that keep pulling them under.

The old code of romance is cracking. Women are no longer viewed exclusively as fragile, dependent creatures by their more enlightened male counterparts. Men are beginning to understand that the old beliefs have kept them enslaved as much as women. They are realizing that when they keep women dependent on them, they add to the weight of their own burden. They are beginning to see that their load is not all that necessary; that women will not break if they have to work, or crumble if someone expresses anger directly, or melt if they go out in the rain. Men are realizing that women are not only women, but human beings, just like men.

Men are demanding equal rights as well, recognizing that their position has been as unequal as

16. Williams, p. 30.

women's, although in different ways. One organization called "Free Men" is calling for an end to the oppressiveness of the old concepts. They want to free themselves from conditioned competitiveness, overreliance on jobs for identity, a mistrust of feelings, especially withholding expressions of anger from women, and the inclination to turn wives into permission-giving mother figures. They want to be out from under the pressure to marry early and to father children in order to prove their manhood and worthiness as protectors; they want to stop worrying about what women think of them and liberate themselves.[17] Even the legal profession is recognizing the change in roles of men and women. Men are being awarded alimony in some cases, contradicting the age-old concept that men protect and support women. And judges are increasingly awarding divorced fathers custody of the children because of their recognition that mothers aren't necessarily the only nurturing parent by virtue of motherhood alone.

We are beginning to realize as a society that motherhood is *not* sacred, that mothers are *not* saints, and that mothers—and fathers—are *not* right just because they happen to be parents. That realization, tough as it may be to accept, lets all of us off the hook. We no longer have to be good and seek the approval of whichever parent figure we're dealing with—whether we're four or forty-four. We don't have to be right; we don't have to be perfect in any way. All we have to be is what we already are—people. Some are big, some are little; some wear pink booties in infancy, some blue (there are fortunately other ways to distinguish between sexes), but all of us have a common bond—we're people. And when we let go of that constricting code of romance we can allow ourselves to do that which we do anyway, whether or not we chastise ourselves in the process, to learn by the mistakes we make. We learn by our failures, and when we no longer hold to the ideal of perfection, we can allow ourselves to be the imperfect creatures that we are. Then we can make mistakes without endlessly castigating our-

17. "Free Men tired of taking blame for oppression of women, leader says." *Seattle Times* (October 22, 1978, sec. K), p. 8.

selves for being "wrong;" we can express anger or hurt or unhappiness without being labeled "crazy" or "weak;" we can experience all our feelings—even sexual feelings—without being called bad by others or ourselves. We no longer have to romanticize ourselves out of our existence and destroy our relationships because of our belief in some imperative yet impossible "goodness."

Some of us won't want to let go of that image of goodness. It's easier to hang on dogmatically, insisting that of course mothers are pure and fathers are right. That's what we've been taught; that's the belief we've been raised with, and, besides, it's always been that way. To change means that we create stress in our bodies and within our relationships. Change hurts. We'd rather put up with what we know than risk the unknown of something new. And it's easier to manipulate others with the old ways. It's easier to control, as it has always been easier. In particular, it's easier to control our children.

PARENTS

11. CHILDREN

ROMANTIC STEREOTYPES AFFECT
CHILDREN MOST DESTRUCTIVELY OF
ALL.

Today in our twentieth-century society, eight centuries after romance was established, we still live by its principles. Originally formulated to refine and discipline the young charges of Eleanor of Aquitaine, the rules of romance were deliberately designed to *control* behavior, so that lovers would learn to act in a manner approved by the ladies of the court. Goodness was established as the criterion of control, and woman set up as its model, judge, and enforcer. Man was expected to be good for the sake of goodness; if he was not, or if woman did not uphold her image, each suffered the built-in scourge of romance—guilt. It was, and is yet, that *control* of romance internalized in our minds which drives us back into conformity—the whip of guilt.

These rules by which we still regulate our behavior tell us to control ourselves in the name of romance (or love, as we mistakenly call it.) We carefully monitor our feelings according to whichever image, masculine or feminine, we adhere to; we keep our lovers in line by our expectations of them. And we control our children by the same means, expecting them to be good so that they will match (or more likely, outdo) our own state of goodness. We control their behavior as we were controlled in our own years of childhood by overt means or by subtle, ingrained messages. No matter how aware we think we are, our messages affect us adversely if we were at all controlled—corrupted—by goodness in our youth.

I remember one day when my little girl was screaming out her rage at me. I felt fairly centered until the thought ran through my mind, "After all I've done for you and this is how you treat me." I sank into instant depression. Luckily, I didn't say it. If I had, I think I would have bitten off my tongue. What a guilt trip I almost laid on her, and I didn't know that thought was lurking in my mind! Yet there it was, full blown, ready to surface when I least expected it. Another of those sneaky hidden messages I've kept in my brain, like a dormant

269

CHILDREN

virus all these years. My awareness of that sentence and it
probable origins (my own Parent tapes) released me from my
depression. I was awe-struck once more that I could retain such a
message intact for all the years since my childhood. I don'
remember hearing it when I was small, but it must have come
from somewhere. Such is the subtlety and staying power of
parent messages. I can only wonder what's coming up next. A
least I'm able to keep my mouth shut, knowing that such a
message would not be a pearl dropping out!

What if I had verbalized tha
sentence, and did so repeatedly, innundating my daughter with
guilt? The good mother image in my own mind would say, "I've
tried to be so good for you, and you're so bad to treat me thi
way." My child would react in some way to this message, mos
likely feeling bad and guilty—for the rest of her life. I would fee
depressed, believing she had victimized me with her badness
And I would make sure she could not escape my goodness becaus
I would be cementing that symbiotic bond, tying her to me wit
cables of guilt, making sure that she would create her own ver
sion of the good mother syndrome in her head for the devastatio
of her own children. And of course they would be devastated i
some way, because living with such goodness is crazy-making

I don't wonder that so many o
us actually go crazy and suffer neuroses, if not psychoses, ou
whole lives long. We are actually responding very appropriatel
to our environment. How can one live with the superficial pre
tence of goodness and *not* go nuts to some degree? We know, o
are told, that our good mother is doing her best. We know w
should be grateful for all she's doing, but the more she tells u
how good she is the worse we feel. We believe we have no right t
be angry but we are, and we're not sure why. The angrier we ge
the guiltier we feel. She makes it clear to us that we're bad fc
being angry. We believe we should love and respect her becaus
she is our mother—and when we hate her instead, as all childre
occasionally must in the course of any normal relationship, w
feel like the bad children we've convinced ourselves we are.

270

CHILDREN

As children, we are always wrong. Good mothers can't be wrong. Even if they say they are, we know they can't be, because they're our mothers. Most will not admit they're wrong, ever. Good mothers have been taught that mothers are always right, and they pass this belief down through the generations. I can still hear my mother's voice over the phone, and feel the stab of fear inside of me, even in my supposedly grownup forties: "Don't lie to me, I'm your mother!" It didn't matter that I hadn't lied; what mattered was that she was right by virtue of the fact that she was my mother. I felt wrong even though I wasn't wrong.

There is no way out for children of good mothers. Who can feel free of sin, getting angry at the Virgin Mary? It is inevitable that children feel bad, or wrong, or even crazy if they get mad at their mothers, who have the weight of the ages to back up their intrinsic maternal goodness. If the children don't return the love offered them in all its flowing abundance, they must be bad. Even if the love isn't all that abundant, they must still be bad because mothers are graced with that special aura of virtue and can't be at fault. If the children are unhappy, it could not be because mother isn't taking care of them so that they feel nurtured and secure; it must be because they are basically, unalterably bad. So the children are stuck with feeling guilty for having negative feelings at all, with self-recrimination in the face of so much goodness, and with being angry for the rest of their lives because they weren't permitted to be angry with mom when it counted—in childhood.

Good mothers do more than prevent their children from ever expressing anger, whether in small degree (such as irritation) or large (hate). Good mothers—some unconsciously, some quite deliberately—load their children down with guilt by acting out the martyr role. The role is entirely in keeping with their saintly image and their victim position. They are, indeed, martyred by our ingratitude, our rebelliousness, our noncompliance. And we, their torturers, can't help but know it; know it as a constant pain inside of us—we caused, and keep

271

CHILDREN

causing, their suffering. We are the stakes to which they are tied; we are the faggots circling their feet. We are the spark that lights the flame of their martyrdom; we are the fire that consumes them. Is it any wonder we feel guilty? We, so our good mothers tell us, will be the death of them yet!

Once when I was a small child I saw a woman disciplining her son. She gave him a ruler and held out her hands to him, palms up. "You were a bad boy," she told him. "Now hit my hands with this ruler, like you've already hurt me by being so bad." Even then I thought there was something sick about her method. Now I know there was—and it was the inflicting of guilt on her son. She instilled more guilt with each blow of the ruler, until her son would be molded into emotional compliance, ensuring that he would do her bidding, and even when she was dead and gone that he would be haunted by ghosts of guilt whispering in his inner ear, "You're bad; you hurt your mother!"

We—you and I—like that boy, struggle against our badness and our inner certitude of guilt for our whole lives. We are shackled with defending ourselves against our self-guilt by blaming someone else, captives forever to the relentless grind for approval. We're off on an impossible quest because we'll never find it. We persistently seek total acceptance, someone to say, "You're okay no matter what you do." Few will ever say that, because there are few people who can accept the reality of anyone else as an imperfect human being without imposing romantic expectations on that person. Even if we find another person who accepts us unconditionally, we're likely to impose expectations on ourselves. We'll set our own Parent tapes in motion, calling ourselves bad, or wrong, criticizing ourselves into nonexistence. We'll belittle ourselves for making mistakes, even if no one else does it for us. We learned to do that in childhood, to please our parents, and we continue to do it as adults. We learned to receive, and to give ourselves, conditional acceptance.

Romance is a conditional reward

system. The implied reward is, "I will love you if you're good." And if you're bad? Or wrong? Or disobedient? The love is yanked away. If our parents didn't yank it away when we were small, we learned to do it for ourselves. "Bad girl," or "naughty boy," we said to ourselves, imitating the tones of our mother's or father's voice. When we grow up and do (or think or feel) something wrong, our lovers don't have to punish us for being bad. We'll do it ourselves. Our neat and effective internal whip of guilt will chastise us, robbing us of any sense of self-approval. We learn, by being conditionally accepted and rewarded, to be good in order to be loved. We learn to seek approval.

I call it "sucking approval" in my own mind because it feels like sucking, seeking, begging, pleading, whining—please, please, please, tell me I'm good and that you love me, mommy! I feel very little and helpless when I suck approval from someone. The other person might respond appropriately by sticking a bottle of milk in my mouth; I feel that infantile! And when I suck approval from someone else, I don't have to take responsibility for feeling or acting on my own. I can stay small and helpless, and if the other person does not give me what I want I can always blame him or her. "Tell me what I should do to be good (or right or perfect)." If the other person does tell me what to do, and of course is wrong because only I know, internally, what my needs are, then I zap him or her, "It's all your fault." Neat system. Works every time.

I can understand intellectually that one who persists in seeking approval is expressing an unwillingness to grow up. I know that not all of us are ready or even able to grow up, no matter how old we may be chronologically. If we haven't worked through our early growth stages adequately, we are blocked internally from further growth. We are unable to take responsibility for ourselves because we are still unconsciously seeking some nonexistent nurturing parent to fulfill our needs. So it's useless to criticize someone for unconsciously (or even consciously) begging approval from others. I cannot blame people for their unmet needs, although I admit that it's hard to

273

CHILDREN

live with someone who's continually seeking reassurance. I know too well my own limitations in growing up. I do not blame myself I have learned to forgive myself my own feelings of littleness. I do blame the system, our romantic tradition that encourages us to cling to our symbiotic ties and to seek the approval of our parents, our lovers, our friends in order to be "good." We should be helped instead to recognize our separateness and to take the risk of feeling alone in order to grow up. If we must believe, according to our romantic code, that we should be good to please our sainted mothers, we will never be able to grow up. We can't afford to, because to grow up and let go of our needs for approval means that we would have to reject our entire value system in regard to ourselves as human beings—good or bad, right or wrong, sane or crazy. We would have to accept ourselves as we are without any moralistic evalua tion of how we should be—and our whole culture is based on our romantic shoulds, our common expectation that we strive for virtue and perfection. Success is what some call it. Ashley Mon tagu writes:

> *The impersonal child-rearing practices which*
> *have long been the mode in the United States . . .*
> *will produce individuals who are able to lead*
> *lonely, isolated lives in the crowded urban world*
> *with its materialistic values and its addiction to*
> *things . . . perhaps a higher degree of closeness*
> *within the family, commencing with the primary*
> *mother-child tactile tie would help Americans to*
> *feel somewhat more anchored in the family, while*
> *an acceptance of the importance of emotional*
> *tactile needs beyond childhood might help them to*
> *withstand the impersonal pressures of our*
> *times. . . .*[1]

1. Ashley Montagu, *Touching: The Human Significance of the Skin* (New York: Colum bia University Press, 1971), p. 287.

274
CHILDREN

Montagu compares other cultures and their tactile, uncritical acceptance of their young to ours, condemning our methods of molding our children relentlessly to our standards. He says, "The contemporary American family constitutes only too often an institution for the systematic production of mental illness in each of its members, as a consequence of its concentration on making each of them a 'success'."[2]

We, as parents, don't deliberately want to destroy our children. Quite the opposite, we want them to be happy, successful, and fulfilled. We want so desperately for them to succeed in their lives (since we often believe we have not succeeded in our own) that we try to make them feel certain ways, make them feel, think, and act the way we believe they should. Why? Because we believe that we have learned what is right for them by virtue of our added years. We will not let them just grow at their own pace and in their own time; we will not let them express their own individuality. We constantly tell and show them what is good for them, according to our own beliefs. We constantly try to make them perfect.

Even if a child has been raised with little physical or verbal abuse, that person can suffer from the expectations of his or her parents. One woman told me, "My parents always praised me for being so good, and for getting such good grades in school. I can't ever remember getting spanked or screamed at like some of my friends. But I felt uneasy all the time. I remember wondering what they would think if I didn't get good grades, or if I didn't act right. I never dared find out. I guess I was afraid that they'd stop loving me if I didn't live up to their expectations."

If a child has suffered abuse during childhood he or she will find it that much harder to let go of parental expectations in later years. Knowing only abuse, the child may seek out situations in which he or she continues to be abused in the name of love. I remember one client who had been

2. Ibid.

275

CHILDREN

continually beaten by her alcoholic father when she was a child, as well as verbally castigated by her embittered yet passive mother. After she grew up and left home, she visited her parents as little as possible and talked about them less. But she refused to connect her present behavior to her past. She clung to a boyfriend who treated her with as much contempt and physical abuse as had her parents. "Why," I asked her, "do you keep going back to him, even after he's hit you and sworn at you and told you to get lost?"

"Because I need him," she said. "I can't live without him."

I had no doubt she felt that she needed him. Her existence as a child had depended on recognition from her parents. If the recognition came in the form of beatings and abuse, still it was recognition of a sort; it proved she was alive, and it was the only "love" she knew. Because of her parents' mistreatment of her she had long ago decided, "I'm to blame; I'm no good. I don't deserve to be loved." So she picked a man who gave her these messages and continued to reinforce her childish self-image, which she retained intact even though she was twenty-five years old. And she would hang onto him—or someone just like him—until she had explored her childhood feelings, and had dug out and rejected her parents' standards of goodness from her mind.

"You're no good," parents say to their children in an attempt to mold them into goodness. "Okay," the children decide inwardly, "If mommy and daddy say I'm no good, that's what I am." So the self-image becomes solidified, and the child begins the lifelong round of searching for people and situations to prove that the parents were right and that the way to get love is to keep on finding others to recognize that basic badness in a continual recapitulation of the parental comment. Or the child forever strives to be good, to be perfect, in order to win the approval of parent figures and thus hold on, even tenuously, to conditional love.

So a child can win some rewards and gain some praise for accomplishments—doing good work in

276

CHILDREN

school, being active in sports, behaving or acting right, being a good church member, gaining societal approval for deeds or status—but how many children or, for that matter, adults can get unconditional praise just for being? How many of us are told verbally or nonverbally, "I love you just because you are!" Not many, yet unconditional acceptance and love are what we all need, and crave, and try incessantly to find. Total acceptance gives us the inner security we need to attempt and accomplish anything we want in this world; without it, we feel like failures no matter how much we actually succeed in doing. We need acceptance not only for the right things we do and the good ways in which we behave, but for our blunders, our failures, and our negative feelings. But we don't usually get hugs and pats on the head for what we do wrong—it simply isn't accepted in our society to be less than perfect.

Rationally, we may know that no one can be perfect, that it's humanly impossible to be all good, all right, all wise. Still we drive ourselves to try for that goal—believing that if we err we not only make a mistake, we sin. How could it be otherwise? If sacredness is what we're dealing with in our sainted mothers, then any negative feeling toward her (such as hate, irritation, or anger), any harmful fantasy (such as we wish she'd go jump in the lake, we wish lightning would strike her), any inappropriate or perhaps *very* appropriate action (like sticking out tongues or making faces) would be not only wrong but sinful. One client told me, "I can't tell my mother I'm angry with her, even in Gestalt work when she's not actually sitting here in this chair. I can't hurt her feelings. Besides, it seems like it would be a cardinal sin."

Of course we regard any wrongdoing on our part as sinful. If our pure mothers have given up their lives for us, have sacrificed themselves on the altar of sex just to have us, and—as many of them tell us endlessly—have given up their lives to raise us, then if we aren't good, we have sinned. And we must spend the rest of our lives doing penance for that sinfulness.

277

CHILDREN

The taint of sin that hangs ove
us all as errant and willful children applies especially to our bodil
parts known as genitals and those feelings, secret and unmer
tionable, known as sexual. Again, this fits with our built-in cor
cept of romance. Our mothers' purity convinces us when we ar
very small that we can never be all good and that therefore w
must be bad children for being interested in such things as toucl
ing our forbidden parts, exploring others' through nasty game
such as "Doctor," having overwhelming and barely conceale
interest in tits, weenies, panties, bottoms, pee-pee, poo-poo, ar
all the rest of the kid names that pertain to anything sexual c
excretory.

With such early and continu
reminders, often on our tender posteriors, from our virtuou
mothers, our hard-working fathers, and our enforcing societ
watchdogs—the teachers, ministers, police, even go
ernment—who believe they must keep their collective ey
on the public and private morality of just about everyone, is it ar
wonder that we have a lifelong, abiding prurient interest
anything that titillates our early childhood no-nos? It is entire
appropriate, albeit ironic, that a country in which the romant
vision of the sacredness of love and the saintliness of women h
been so carefully preserved should have such a thriving trade
pornographic films, magazines, and books, and so much exploit
tion of sexuality in advertising—even though there is real
nothing realistically sexual about any of it. Even as adults, v
remain less mature sexual beings than perpetual kids, indulgir
ourselves in one of the strongest prohibitions of childhood-
voyeuristic peeking.

And we can't talk about it wi
anyone, although finally, as we come out of the dark ages of ot
romantic nonsense, we begin to let go of our hangups. Still, eve
as we enter the eighties, most of us can't discuss these ideas wi
our parents—or even with each other—rationally. We car
admit that we are people who like sex, that we're thrilled I
sexual feelings, that we're interested in people who turn us o

278

that we cherish our and others' bodies, and that we like to look at, feel, and pleasure those bodies. These admissions are still bad, perverted, and nasty to any of our parents or parent figures who are still hung up on the image of sacredness. Who among us could admit to a sainted mother any of the above, and have her understanding? More likely she would suddenly go deaf on us, but not before she had labeled us, verbally or nonverbally, as bad children, and indicated with hostility that she disapproved.

I remember once in Europe, when I was waiting in line for the women's toilet, a woman in front of me, seeing no line at all in front of the men's room, threw up her hands, said the German equivalent of, "Ach, they're both the same," and went to use the men's. I followed her, marveling at my idiocy in not thinking of it first. But how could I? I have been trained to be ashamed at any display of my natural curiosity regarding men's and women's biological functions, and I've been embarassed if I happened to stray into a public men's room (which I've done), even though I have lived with men for years and shared bathrooms with them at home. Europeans are much more accepting of their bodies than we are. The woman who used the men's room did so not because she was curious; she was not. She knew all about the differences between the sexes, and accepted them. She simply followed a rational course of action without any shoulds to prevent her using a facility when she needed it. She used the men's room to pee, not to peek!

Another example of European acceptance of biological functions comes to my mind. I heard of a topless bikini bather who had been arrested on a French beach and hauled into court on a charge of indecently exposing her breasts. The French judge wasted few words in hearing the case. "Mammary glands," he snorted, and dismissed the charge. This might happen here in America among the enlightened few, but it would be rare. Here we are still seeing the turmoil that ensues when a woman worker tries to breastfeed her baby at work, even though she discreetly hides herself away in a separate room. We will not be open about our sexuality, even when it comes to such a

279

natural function as breastfeeding an infant. We must pretend that the entire subject doesn't exist in our daily lives. The closest we get to talking about sex openly in many circles is the sex joke, and we have thousands. So we titter and we peek, and we sneak into X-rated movies, and we ogle naked men and women in ever more explicit magazines. But when it comes to sharing feelings, or being honest about our own sexual practices, we feign ignorance. Mommy said that wasn't nice, so let's not talk about it and then maybe nobody will know what we think, and feel, and do in the privacy of our own bedrooms.

The child abuser, or the spouse of a person who has sexually abused a child, maintains that attitude of concealment. "Let's not let the neighbors find out, and we'll pretend it didn't happen." They know it's a sin, and they'll be penalized if the knowledge ever slips out, so they keep it quiet—even if the abuse continues. I've had several clients whose mothers knew that the father, or the grandfather, or the uncle was molesting the child sexually, and did nothing to expose the man for fear someone else might find out!

These abusive people are not innately evil. They have their own growth hangups. They do not want to destroy their children. They're reacting against their own prohibitions of goodness. They know they are being bad, but they act out their desires anyway, rebelliously, taking out on their own children their anger at their own sainted mothers and righteous fathers. These people may suffer overwhelming guilt because of their actions, but the guilt doesn't stop them. They are still compelled to act out their fantasies; they have been set up to rebel because of the very criteria of goodness.

We all rebel against that goodness in some way because we need to separate from our parents in the normal course of growing up. Many of us seek separateness indirectly. Woman complain that their men won't spend time with them, that their husbands spend their time with other men—at bars, sports events, work. They complain that their men won't communicate with them. But how can men feel comfortable

280

with their women when the men associate femininity with goodness, when they transfer their childhood fear of doing wrong—sinning—from their sainted mothers onto their good wives? I've heard experts discussing men who have problems establishing their masculinity. One commonly accepted reason for their problem has been said to be the absence of their fathers from home, fathers who were commonly absent at their jobs when the boys were small. Having little or no access to their fathers within the home, the boys were overwhelmed, the experts say, by the sheer daily presence of their mothers. I certainly believe that role modeling is important and that sons need their fathers' companionship, just as daughters do. But the main reason boys are overwhelmed by their mothers' constant presence, in my opinion, is that she expects them to be good.

The problem, in our society, is not caused by the normal growth struggles sons and daughters have in separating from their mothers and fathers—the problem is caused by goodness. We fight our parents because they do not accept our basic human need to make mistakes, and we chastise ourselves for that same basic failing for the rest of our lives. We label ourselves, or accept the labels of others, and feel wrong. We call ourselves failures, or incompetents, or crazies. We think that if only we are good enough we'll find acceptance and approval. So we try, and try, and try, and still we can't achieve the perfect goodness that will bring us the approval we crave. Our problem is not only individual, but national. We believe that if only we are good enough we will find goodness in return. So we seek, we suck approval from others, and we react over and over again in wide-eyed astonishment when we get slapped instead of kissed. Our approval seeking, on a national level, is called "a policy of appeasement;" on an individual level, it is nonassertiveness. But getting slapped doesn't stop us from trying. It is all we know.

I remember talking to my dad one time shortly before he died. I was studying Transactional Analysis at the time and had read that we often put the main parent messages of our lives into one phrase—our epitaph. So I

281

CHILDREN

asked dad, half-kidding and not knowing that he would soon be gone, what he would want as his epitaph. He responded quickly, without thinking about it, "I tried." I feel so sad when I write this. He did try. He tried so hard all his life—to be good, to succeed, to be loved. He tried to be a good guy and people loved him, but never enough. He tried to succeed, and he did—in other people's eyes, but never his own. He tried to be nice, and hold in his anger, and rarely got mad at anyone except himself. And he suffered for fifteen years from the worst kind of rheumatoid arthritis, his hands and knees and spine so misshapen that toward the end he could no longer raise himself in bed, and still his aching, gnarled joints screamed out, "I tried."

We all try. We all want desperately to please our parents. We all try so hard to be good. We learn to say "please" when we ask for a cookie, "thank you" when we get it, and "excuse me" when we belch out our satisfaction. We learn to be polite because our parents want us to be accepted by our larger society, so we let go of our childish urges to eat spaghetti with our fingers and to sit upside down in chairs. We learn good manners, and the better mannered we are, the higher many of us rise in society. I've met a lot of good, well-mannered people in my workshops for business and government, especially government—people who've learned to be good guys and adapt, be polite and never talk back and don't buck the system. They have entered their jobs with enthusiasm, creativity, and perception; then slowly, through the years, they've dribbled away their fire by going along with the program in order to keep their jobs—because they've been good. In a recent workshop, one man asked me if I held the same belief as so many others, that government workers are lazy and taking advantage of the taxpayer.

"People are people," I responded, "whether they're in government jobs or any other. I've met some government workers who've gotten so frustrated trying to be creative that they've stopped and decided to just ride it out until they retire. 'Don't make waves,' they say. And I've met some who've tried making waves and have gotten reprimanded for it."

282

We are all caught in the same perfectionistic, conformist syndrome. We are very much alike no matter what field we're in, what job we work at. We have been taught to be good and to adapt to authority figures—our parents and those that later take their place. And when we conform totally through trying to please those childhood gods, we give up our feelings, our desires, our very identities. We give up, and from then on it's "Don't make waves," and "I tried."

We have been taught not only to be polite but to be considerate. Granted, we all need a little training in manners and consideration; we're uncomfortable around someone who is totally unaware of others, totally self-centered and unmindful of proprieties. But millions of us have been drowned in consideration. We've been taught to be considerate to the exclusion of ourselves. The pleasers of the world, those who discount their own feelings and their own needs, are all so considerate: "After you, my dear." "No, after you." And so we dance to the same tune, adapting our steps to another's, not wanting to risk saying, "Me first," because of our long, centuries-long training in self-abnegating consideration.

People brought up in other cultures, who've been allowed to be children in their childhood— to be rebellious, recalcitrant, curious, perceptive, and maladaptive—have no problem saying, "Me first." They have no qualms about pushing their way to the head of the line or grabbing all the territory, the monies of the world, that they can get. They haven't been raised to hand over their earthly goods early in order to win approval. They have not been trained to please regardless of their own desires, and taught that they are sinful if they aren't good. But we have been. We have been so rigorously trained in goodness that we no longer know who we really are. We have no individual identities—only those identities established for us by our parent figures. As individuals we don't exist in this world. We exist only in the eyes of others, only if we conform to their expectations, and only if we get their approval. If they reject us, we cease to be.

I have spoken endlessly about

283

CHILDREN

the inability of one person to make another person feel, and many people have argued with me on this point. I realize that the issue boils down to a semantic quibble—can you make someone angry, or does he or she truly originate that feeling? I know that people respond to situations and other people with certain feelings, and sometimes it seems that one can make another feel something simply by knowing which button to push, knowing how the other ordinarily reacts, and providing the proper stimulus. But I like to stress that we are unable to make another person feel a certain emotion for this reason: If we believe someone else has the ability to make us feel something, we have no sense of power in changing our own feelings and our situations. We must succumb to feeling persecuted because we believe everyone else has the power to make us feel, to cause us to act the way we do, and we have none.

So that we won't continue to believe in our own emotional impotence, I believe it's important to understand that we are responsible for our own feelings. In the case of children, the responsibility is not quite as clear. Can a parent make a child feel? Or is that child responsible for his or her own feelings in the same way an adult is? Even little children have a wide choice of feelings available to them. But a parent can mold a child; a parent can instill beliefs by repetition and the pain of spankings or abuse; a parent can even hypnotize a child.

Before we reach that stage of life known as adulthood, we are all easily hypnotized. Ronald Laing talks about "attributions," which, he says, help a child create a self-image that may persist for a lifetime:

> *We are told such and such is the case. One is, say,
> told one is a good or bad boy or girl. . . . An
> attribution, as I am using the term, may be
> kinetic, tactile, olfactory, visual. Such an
> attribution is equivalent to an instruction to be
> obeyed "implicitly." So, if I hypnotize you, I do
> not say, "I order you to feel cold." I indicate it is
> cold. You immediately feel cold. . . . Hypnosis*

284

CHILDREN

may be an experimental model of a naturally occurring phenomenon in many families.[3]

In a sense, parents are hypnotizing their children everytime they tell them not only what they should be but are. A parent might say, "Mary is so pretty, she'll never have to work for a living." If Mary believes that, she may grow up to rely on her prettiness, and her intellectual incompetence. Or, "Jim is so clumsy he trips over his own feet." If Jim adapts to that one, guess who's a hazard on the dance floor! Or, "You're so lazy you'll never get anywhere in life!" If the child buys that curse, for that's what it is, he or she will accept failure as a constant companion.

We are hypnotized by such attributions and by the images we accept, the roles we decide to act out. We stumble thereafter through our lives like zombies, not having the freedom from our childhood curses to think, feel, and do what we as individuals really want to. We don't even know who we are. We know our zombielike selves, but is that shell of adaptivity really us? One unhappily married man told me, "I've been depressed for so long I don't know who I am anymore. My kids (they were teenagers) have never seen the real me." My hunch was that *he* had never seen the real him either. He had adapted for so long—since childhood—to his shoulds, that he had no idea of how to act, how to feel, how to think, other than how he was supposed to. He had, ever since he could remember, tried hard to be good and to please, and he had belittled himself in the process.

Our self-belittlement is so much a part of us we find it hard to extricate the reality of us from our zombielike shells. We start to belittle ourselves so early in life that by the time we grow up it's a habit, ingrained into us like supernumerary teeth, hidden but waiting to erupt into verbalized Parent tapes and critical messages. By then we accept and trust no one, not ourselves, not anyone around us. Distrust,

3. Ronald D. Laing, *The Politics of the Family and Other Essays* (New York: Random House, Pantheon Books, 1969), pp. 78–79.

285

CHILDREN

doubt, criticism, repressed feelings, depression, and a habitual state of negativism become our only known reality, pervading our world and spreading out to all those around us. Yet through all our doubts and downers we retain one ray of hope that drives us on—hope that somewhere, with someone, we'll find the total acceptance we yearn for, and that will change our self-belittlement into self-praise. We hope that someone will appear and magically change us from depressed and deadened zombies into revitalized human beings. We hope that someone, somewhere, will make us happy.

We usually find that magical someone and discover as a corollary, fascination. And fascination, as I've explained, only serves as a further vehicle for our self-deprecation. Even the fascination that we direct toward our lovers in adulthood has a symbiotic tie back to our parents. When we were small, we saw certain qualities in our parents that we admired. But if we felt unaccepted and controlled by them, those positive qualities had a backlash. If we believed our mothers were beautiful, we felt ugly in comparison; if we thought our fathers were competent, we felt untalented; if we believed our parents were poised and socially adept, we felt awkward, inadequate, and dumb. The better we believed they were and the more we admired them, if we felt unloved, the worse we felt about ourselves in comparison.

We transfer our archaic belief in our parents' magnificence to our lovers after we grow up, if our symbiotic bond is still intact. We even seek our lovers who have positive qualities similar to those of our parents, and continue to belittle ourselves in comparison. I realize that when I was younger I sought out men who were adept at conversations because, as a child, I had admired that trait in my mother. I felt fascinated but dumb in comparison to her, as I felt dumb in later years with my men friends. As we are awed into immobility by our parents, our fascination with lovers reinforces our zombielike state of deadness. We are still being hypnotized, although willngly, out of our essential selves by our obsessive concern with another person. And when the fascination ends, as it must, when he romantic vision fades and the stark, sepia tones of reality take away the magic, we go back to depression, self-disparagement, and hope.

The hope is the last to go. The romantic promise of happiness that has been luring us on, ever since we began our quest, is fueled and sustained by hope. The hope is the hardest to let go of, the most difficult to understand. Hope is the hook that keeps us tied to our parents, our lovers—and keeps us divorced from ourselves. In order to grow up and cast off our uncomfortable, thorn-studded cloaks woven through with romantic dreams, we must let go of our hopes. I had a client some time ago, a young girl who was having problems with her boyfriend.

"How do you want him to act that's different?" I asked her.

"I want him to spend more time with me. I want him to do things I like to do. I want him to love me," she answered.

"Doesn't he now?" I asked.

"He says he does, but I don't feel loved," she said. "I want to feel loved."

It came out, during our session, that she had never felt loved by her parents. They had done their best, but, like so many of us, their own emotional hangups prevented them from adequately nurturing their daughter. Their great and real love for her was obscured by their own problems; while they believed they were giving her a torrent of love, she felt only a trickle. So she kept on trying to find love after she grew up. We talked about her feelings toward her parents and her boyfriend. She said she understood why her parents did what they did when she was young and, although she couldn't quite bring herself to forgive them entirely, she could empathize.

"But what," she sighed, "should

287

I do now? I know all about why my parents acted the way they did, and what effect it had on me, but that doesn't help me feel better. What can I do right now to change the way I feel?"

"Quit," I responded. "Quit trying to find love, quit trying to make your boyfriend love you, quit hoping. If it works, it works. If it doesn't, nothing you can do will make any difference. So quit."

"That hurts," she said, and started to cry. After a short time, she nodded. "I see it now. I see that my wanting love so much was driving my boyfriend away, and my hoping that he would give me all the love I've always wanted was just bringing me disappointment. And it was my wanting so much and my hoping that was making me so unhappy. I guess if I quit trying so hard to find it, I won't hurt so much. And if I never find the love I want, I won't die. I haven't yet, and I won't now."

"You're right," I agreed. "You won't die. And if you stop chasing after love and stand still for a while, it will find you."

Our hope and our wanting, our trying desperately to find love, keeps us in the circle of our discontent. After we want, then try hard to find love, and fail, our hope brings us full circle once more and sets us up for another resounding defeat. But when we let go of our hope we find not the emptiness we fear, not the death we fantasize in dread, but the fulfillment of our beings. Sheldon Kopp has said, "The only meaning in our lives is what we each bring to them. Killing the Buddha on the road means destroying the hope that anything outside of ourselves can be our master."[4]

So we let go of romance, and empty promises, and the hope of perfection and supreme goodness in ourselves or anybody else. We let go of our romantic dream and we find the meaning to our lives—*our* minds, *our* feelings, and *our* selves.

4. Sheldon B. Kopp, *If You Meet the Buddha on the Road, Kill Him!: The Pilgrimage of the Psychotherapy Patient.* (New York: Bantam Books, 1976), p. 188.

288

CHILDREN

CONCLUSION

The courtly love system promulgated by Eleanor of Aquitaine revolutionalized the philosophy of people of twelfth-century Europe, ennabling them to reach for heights previously unknown. Prior to that time, men regarded women as possessions, exciting or tedious as their mood suggested, but objects nonetheless. After Eleanor and her contemporaries vanished in the mists of time, men held radically different images of women. Woman, in theory, had become the Grail for which man quested, the one who would calm his discontent and uplift his spirit. Men were excited by the idea of love as the path to salvation, and with woman, the agent of love, as their inspiration.

For that reason alone, the romantic code should be praised, not villified. In the beginning, romance inspired men, and women too, to improve their manners, their general behavior, and to attempt greater self-actualization. Other attributes of romance were equally commendable. For the first time in history, ideal emotional relationships between men and women (and many real life ones too) had at their core the emotions of tenderness and gentleness. The code stressed fidelity of one man to one woman, also a novel idea, with respect and admiration on each side important to a mutually satisfying relationship. Even more than that, as Hunt points out, "It was courtly love through which erotic or semierotic emotions began to be wedded to moral achievement."[1] Throughout history, no matter what the changes have been in its interpretation, romantic love—which incorporated these elements—has continued to have immense appeal to the western world.

1. Hunt, p. 171.

Not so the eastern half of the world. As C.S. Lewis says, "Even our code of etiquette, with its rule that women always have precedence, is a legacy from courtly love, and is felt to be far from natural in modern Japan or India."[2] Despite great familiarity with western ways, people of other parts of the world still hold a most unromantic view of love. The top record in Japan, as of September 1979, is a song in which a "husband and master" tells his bride-to-be to "keep quiet and follow behind me."[3] Such a musical statement could hardly claim popularity in the United States, with our long training in the romantic concept of women first. Objectionable enough is the thought of a woman's following behind a man, but keeping quiet for his sake. Not likely! Of course, some women have kept quiet, believing that such behavior will keep the peace in their relationships with their particular men, but most women would not, having the certain conviction it is their right to be deferred to by men—their own especially but all men in general.

Without our romantic heritage, women of the western world might still be following behind their men too. Western men might also have missed the special qualities romance instilled in them: a sense of themselves as individuals, of their uniqueness as sensory beings, of their capacity to seek perfection and moral integrity through love without needing the intercession of some higher nobleman. Romance also gave men and women another dimension to life, a level of fantasy that could incorporate human desire into divine aspiration. What would artistic achievement have been without our long involvement with romance—our poetry, literature, music, and dance? Certainly romance added depth and latitude to our culture and we, throughout the centuries, would have been impoverished by its absence.

I recognize these attributes of our romantic tradition and hold a deep appreciation for these positive contributions to our culture. I know that on some level of

2. Lewis, pp. 3–4.
3. *Seattle Times* (September 23, 1979, sec. A), p. 19.

290

CONCLUSION

ny inner being I will always be touched by the tender and beautiful things of life, and I will respond to romantic inspiration. I know that I will cherish the creative side of romance, as I do now, that I can be lifted out of my doldrums by its powerful stimulation. Yet I have an equally firm belief that the negative aspects of our romantic tradition drag me, all of us, down into depression and despair. I believe we need to magnify these faults of our romantic belief system to understand their effect on our present-day relationships. Many people today are beginning to realize that our romantic beliefs put our relationships in jeopardy. We must realize more than that; we must see clearly that our romantic beliefs *prevent* the establishment of warm, open relationships with each other and *destroy* any acceptance of one another that we may have. We must see that our romantic beliefs are in direct opposition to open relationships, that romance demands manipulation and conniving and control. So while my examination of our romantic origins may seem narrow, I believe we must emphasize the negative in order to clarify our behavior and change our treatment of one another.

When we base our relationships on our romantic fantasies we abdicate, giving our power to our partners. Helpless then, we wait for them to bestow on us the mantle of grace. If we don't get it we may keep right on anticipating, in misery and resentment, criticizing our partners for not giving us what we expect. We want to be taken care of, as the perfect parents we hold in our minds (but none of us had) should have done but didn't. Romance encourages our continual search for these nonexistent parents, transmuting our ideal mommys or daddys into our lovers, who are then supposed to provide us with happiness. If they don't, says our romantic code, it can't be our fault—we have no power—therefore, it must be our lovers'.

We're caught in a double bind when we fall in love. We're taught that our romantic fantasy of love is the real thing, which means that we love our own mental creation, not an actual person. We're also told that we should doubt, distrust, and be suspicious of that person. We try hard to be good, as we tried for our parents, but the very goal of goodness

291
CONCLUSION

ensures that we perceive ourselves at times, if not generally, as bad. So we fluctuate back and forth, trying hard, floating on self-made clouds of fantasy about some ideal love, picking out flaws in our partners because they don't match our ideals, then whipping ourselves with guilt for doubting at all.

When we marry on the strength of our romantic attachments, we wed ourselves to our misery. We marry because of nonsensical romantic reasons, but since everybody else is doing it too we don't question our beliefs. We marry because we're terrified of losing our lovers, convinced that the ceremony will cement him or her to us and prevent our ever having to experience the threat of loneliness. We marry because we think we owe something to that person for loving our undeserving selves, so we pay that debt with certificate and ring—and pay, and pay, and pay! We marry because we're afraid that our lovers will crumble into nothingness if we tell them what we really feel, or show our emotions, or run. So we rescue them from themselves by marrying them, we protect them from our inadmissible anger by trying hard to please them, and we live with our hostile facade of niceness for the rest of our lives or until one of us breaks down in the process. Meanwhile we tell ourselves that our partners have so many good qualities, we should be ashamed of ourselves for being so critical, that we should stop complaining and settle down and just be happy with what we've got.

We believe that if we break up and divorce, that we will have failed. Many people are pondering today the fate of the American family. Many are wondering if our increasing rate of divorce means the demise of the family. I don't share their worries. I do not believe that the family, or marriage, is in trouble because of the high divorce rate. Divorce is one of the healthiest signs I see of people who realize they are unhappily mated and are willing to go through the stress of breaking up their homes. Provided that the divorced person does not seek out a person similar to the last partner and enter into another heavy

CONCLUSION

symbiotic relationship, divorce can be beneficial. Far from destroying the family, it can provide a constructive alternative to ongoing misery. If I can name one factor that is the root and cause of our problem, it is not divorce at all but our high *marriage* rate, marriages that are entered into hastily, based on mutual fantasies, with each partner living by and believing in archaic, unrealistic concepts of romance.

We need to separate romance from marriage and love from romance, not confuse ourselves by worrying about divorce. We need to realize that marriage is *not* the be-all and end-all that our present-day code of romance tells us it is. Love is *not* the sole reason for our existence in this world. Happiness is *not* a permanent state of being. Romance itself is an impossible dream. At times, the dream is fun and we can ride the bubble of our romantic fling as far as it goes, hoarding another memory for our rocking-chair days. We can let ourselves be carried away, along with the panting, submissive heroines of romantic novels or imagine ourselves the handsome, stalwart heroes. But when the bubble bursts—as bubbles do—and we crash back down to solid earth, we need to be aware that it was only a dream, and see it go without regret. It was only our romantic fabrication, not the real world, only a bubble after all.

Marriage is no fabrication but an all-too-constant business of living with another person under the same roof and in the same bed (although not always), sharing the same time-space continuum with another person. Marriage can be fun or a drag: enjoyable to a swinging twosome, life at hard labor to a dutiful pair. Yet it can be worthwhile *without* romance, a comfortable, open, caring relationship in which two people center their lives around each other, finding meaningful work, interesting play, and satisfying loving in an interdependent—as opposed to dependent or independent—way. Marriage *can* be a creative partnership *without* romance.

With romance we're stuck with the pretense we've played out for centuries, burdened with false

293

expectations, phony images, and predetermined roles. Our relationships are doomed before they start by these impossible ingredients. *With* romance we expect too much of each other, more than any living human can give or be. We expect our own ideals to clothe themselves in flesh and blood, exactly as we picture them in our minds. We expect our fantasies to walk in the shapes of our lovers, our children, and our parents. No child can be that ideally behaved, no lover faultless. No parent can be that perfect mother or father the child carries in his or her mind. Our emotions, our moods, changing as the tide and mercurial as the weather, ensure that whoever expects another person to live up to some inflexible standard of behavior will be disappointed.

I have found even in my own life that the more expectations I've had of someone, the greater my disappointment. Conversely, the more I can accept a person as he or she is, the better *I* feel. (The other person may care less; my disappointment hurts my belly, not his!) I have discovered, since I divorced, that I *like* the men I was married to previously. I can afford to like them now because I see them as people; I have no expectations of them. I saw my parents in a new way too when I learned to accept them, "faults" and all. (After all, what were faults in my eyes may have been virtues to others.) When I stop expecting others to live up to *my* standards and satisfy *my* demands I feel more amiable toward them, and certainly more at peace with myself. The less I expect of anyone, the more I am apt to feel affectionate and trusting toward that person.

I, for one, no longer need the upset that results from my preconceived expectations. I don't need my romantic fantasies to keep me alternating between irrational hopes and debilitating despair. None of us, men or women, need our restrictive romantic code today. We do not need a set of outdated and meaningless rules that do no more than confuse our minds, destroy our relationships, and cause us life-long misery. The romantic code has served its purpose; now we need to let it recede back into the mists of time from which it came. We need to let ourselves exist as we are, as we feel and

294

link in this world. When we stop relying on romantic concepts, we can stop seeking approval from parent figures; we can stop justifying our actions and trying to prove how good we are. We can accept ourselves as we are and seek our own options, based on our own feelings and rationality. We can turn off those internal voices of authorization we have listened to all our lives, disregard our built-in shoulds, and begin to establish what is right for ourselves. We can examine the messages we got from our parents and our society and, based on our own decisions of personal integrity, decide which to keep and which to discard. We can start becoming truly conscious and, without romance, be freed.

295
CONCLUSION

BIBLIOGRAPHY

BERNE ERIC, *Games People Play*. New York: Ballantine Books, 1964.

BLOCH, MARC. *Feudal Society: The Growth of Ties of Dependence*. Translated by L. A. Manyon, vol. 1. Chicago: University of Chicago Press, 1961.

BODE, CARL. *The Anatomy of American Popular Culture: 1840–1861*. Berkeley: University of California Press, 1959.

BROOKS, POLLY SCHAYER, and WALLWORTH, NANCY Z. *The World of Walls: The Middle Ages in Western Europe*. Philadelphia: J. B. Lippincott Co., 1966.

BUCHSBAUM, MONTE S. "Tuning in on Hempispheric Dialogue." *Psychology Today*, January 1979, p. 100.

BUTCHER, S. H., trans. *Aristotle's Theory of Poetry and Fine Art*, Introduction by John Gassner. New York: Dover Pub., 1951.

CAPELLANUS, ANDREAS. *The Art of Courtly Love*. Introduction and translation by John Jay Parry. New York: W. W. Norton & Co., 1941.

COMFORT, ALEX. *The Joy of Sex*. New York: Simon & Schuster, A Fireside Book, 1972.

CROSS, BARBARA M., ed. *The Educated Woman in America*. New York: Teachers College Press, 1965.

D'ARCY, M. C. *The Mind and Heart of Love: Lion and Unicorn. A Study in Eros and Agape*. New York: World Pub. Co., 1962.

DURANT, WILL. *The Story of Civilization: The Age of Faith: A History of Medieval Civilization—Christian, Islamic, and*

Judaic—from Constantine to Dante: A.D. 325–1300, part IV. New York: Simon & Schuster, 1950.

FISHER, DONALD D. *I Know You Hurt, But There's Nothing to Bandage*. Beaverton, Ore.: Touchstone Press, 1978.

FRENCH, MARILYN. *The Women's Room*. New York: Jove Pub., 1977.

FRIDAY, NANCY. *My Mother, My Self: The Daughter's Search for Identity*. New York: Dell Pub. Co., 1978.

GAYLIN, WILLARD. *Feelings: Our Vital Signs*. New York: Harper & Row, Pub., 1979.

GOLEMAN, DANIEL. "Special Abilities of the Sexes: Do They Begin in the Brain?" *Psychology Today*, November 1978, p. 48.

HALL, EDWARD T. *The Silent Language*. New York: Doubleday & Co., Anchor Books, 1973.

HEER, FRIEDRICH. *The Medieval World*. New York: New American Library, 1961.

HUMPHRIES, ROLFE, trans. *Ovid: The Art of Love*. Bloomington, Ill.: Indiana University Press, 1957.

HUNT, MORTON M. *The Natural History of Love*. New York: Minerva Press, 1959.

JANOV, ARTHUR. *The Anatomy of Mental Illness: The Scientific Basis of Primal Therapy*. New York: Berkley Pub. Corp., 1971.

JANOV, ARTHUR, and HOLDEN, E. MICHAEL. *Primal Man: The New Consciousness*. New York: Thomas Y. Crowell Co., 1975.

JAYNES, JULIAN. *The Origin of Consciousness in the Breakdown of the Bicameral Mind*. Boston: Houghton Mifflin Co., 1976.

KEEN, SAM. "The Lost Voices of the Gods: Reflections on the Dawn of Consciousness." *Psychology Today*, November 1977, p. 58.

KELLY, AMY. *Eleanor of Aquitaine and the Four Kings*. New York: Random House, 1950.

KELLY, KATHY. "A Radical Sex Manual." Unpublished Paper, 1972.

297

BIBLIOGRAPHY

KITTO, H. D. *The Greeks*. New York: Penguin Books, 1969.

KOPP, SHELDON B. *If You Meet The Buddha on the Road, Kill Him! The Pilgrimage of Psychotherapy Patients*. New York: Bantam Books, 1976.

KRUTCH, JOSEPH WOOD. *A Krutch Omnibus*. New York: William Morrow & Co., 1970.

LAING, RONALD D. *The Politics of the Family and Other Essays*. New York: Random House, Pantheon Books, 1969.

LEWIS, C. S. *The Allegory of Love, A Study in Medieval Tradition*. New York: Oxford University Press, 1958.

LOOMIS, ROGER SHERMAN, intro. and trans. *The Romance of Tristam and Ysolt by Thomas of Britain*. New York: Columbia Univesrity Press, 1951.

LOUDIN, JO. *Act Yourself: Stop Playing Roles and Unmask Your True Feelings*. Englewood Cliffs, N.J.: Prentice-Hall, Inc., 1979.

LOUDIN, JO(ANNE MARIE). "The Changing Role of the Comic Woman in American Drama from 1900 to 1940." Unpublished Dissertation, University of Washington, 1974.

LOVEJOY, ARTHUR O. *The Great Chain of Being: A Study of the History of an Idea*. New York: Harper & Row, Pub., 1936.

LYNES, RUSSELL. *The Domesticated Americans*. New York: Harper & Row, Pub., 1963.

MASTERS, WILLIAM H., and JOHNSON, VIRGINIA E. *Human Sexual Response*. Boston: Little, Brown & Co., 1966.

MAY, ROLLO. *Power and Innocence: A Search for the Sources of Violence*. New York: Dell Pub. Co., 1972.

MISSILDINE, W. HUGH. *Your Inner Child of the Past*. New York: Simon & Schuster, 1963.

MONTAGU, ASHLEY. *Touching: The Human Significance of the Skin*. New York: Columbia University Press, 1971.

PIRSIG, ROBERT M. *Zen and the Art of Motorcycle Maintenance: An Inquiry into Values*. New York: Bantam Books, 1974.

POWER, EILEEN. "The Position of Women." In *The Legacy of the*

298

Middle Ages, edited by G. C. Crump and E. F. Jacob. London: Oxford University Press, 1927.

ROSS, SIR DAVID, trans. *The Works of Aristotle*, vol. IX. London: Oxford University Press, 1966.

SCARF, MAGGIE. "The More Sorrowful Sex." *Psychology Today*, April 1979, p. 45.

SCHIFF, JACQUI LEE. *The Cathexis Reader*. New York: Harper & Row, Pub., 1975.

SCHLESINGER, ARTHUR M. *Learning How To Behave: A Historical Study of American Etiquette Books*. New York: MacMillan Co., 1946.

SHAIN, MERLE. *Some Men Are More Perfect Than Others*. New York: Bantam Books, 1973.

TAYLOR, HENRY OSBORN. *The Mediaeval Mind: A History of the Development of Thought and Emotion in the Middle Ages*, vol. 1. Cambridge: Harvard University Press, 1959.

WATTS, ALAN. *The Wisdom of Insecurity*. New York: Random House, Vintage Books, 1951.

WILLIAMS, ELIZABETH FRIAR. *Notes of a Feminist Therapist*. New York: Prager Pub., 1976.

WILSON, CAMMY, and HARRIS, HENRY. "Making Sex a Crime." *Human Behavior*, February 1979, p. 43.

WOOD, CHARLES T. *The Age of Chivalry: Manners and Morals 1000–1450*. New York: Universe Books, 1970.

INDEX

303

INDEX